HEALTHY SOUTH INDIAN COOKING

Hippocrene is NUMBER ONE in International Cookbooks

Africa and Oceania
Best of Regional African Cooking
Egyptian Cooking
Good Food from Australia
Traditional South African Cookery
Taste of Eritrea

Asia and Near East
The Best of Taiwanese Cuisine
Imperial Mongolian Cooking
The Joy of Chinese Cooking
Healthy South Indian Cooking
The Indian Spice Kitchen
Best of Goan Cooking
Best of Kashmiri Cooking
Afghan Food and Cookery
The Art of Persian Cooking
The Art of Turkish Cooking
The Art of Uzbek Cooking

Mediterranean
Best of Greek Cuisine
Taste of Malta
A Spanish Family Cookbook
Tastes of North Africa

Western Europe
Art of Dutch Cooking
Best of Austrian Cuisine
A Belgian Cookbook
Cooking in the French Fashion (bilingual)
Celtic Cookbook
Cuisines of Portuguese Encounters
English Royal Cookbook
The Swiss Cookbook
Traditional Recipes from Old England
The Art of Irish Cooking
Feasting Galore Irish-Style
Traditional Food from Scotland
Traditional Food from Wales
The Scottish-Irish Pub and Hearth Cookbook
A Treasury of Italian Cuisine (bilingual)

Scandinavia
Best of Scandinavian Cooking
The Best of Finnish Cooking
The Best of Smorgasbord Cooking
Good Food from Sweden

Central Europe
All Along the Rhine
All Along the Danube
Best of Albanian Cooking
Best of Croatian Cooking
Bavarian Cooking
Traditional Bulgarian Cooking
The Best of Czech Cooking
The Best of Slovak Cooking
The Art of Hungarian Cooking
Hungarian Cookbook
Art of Lithuanian Cooking
Polish Heritage Cookery
The Best of Polish Cooking
Old Warsaw Cookbook
Old Polish Traditions
Treasury of Polish Cuisine (bilingual)
Poland's Gourmet Cuisine
Taste of Romania
Taste of Latvia

Eastern Europe
The Best of Russian Cooking
Traditional Russian Cuisine (bilingual)
The Best of Ukrainian Cuisine

Americas
Argentina Cooks
Cooking the Caribbean Way
Mayan Cooking
The Honey Cookbook
The Art of Brazilian Cookery
The Art of South American Cookery
Old Havana Cookbook (bilingual)

HEALTHY SOUTH INDIAN COOKING

ALAMELU VAIRAVAN AND PATRICIA MARQUARDT

HIPPOCRENE BOOKS
NEW YORK

For information, address:
HIPPOCRENE BOOKS, INC.
171 Madison Avenue
New York, NY 10016
www.hippocrenebooks.com

ISBN 0-7818-0867-7

Photography by K. Vairavan.
Book and jacket design by Acme Klong Design, Inc.

Cataloging-in-Publication Data available from the Library of Congress.

Printed in the United States of America.

This book is dedicated to the cherished memories of
Aiyah RM.Kasiviswanathan Chettiar
Ayal Valliammai Achi
William Marquardt
and
Appachi AV.M. Palaniappa Chettiar,
for their love and inspiration.

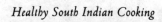

TABLE OF CONTENTS

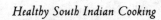

ACKNOWLEDGEMENTS

We would like to express our deep appreciation to Alamelu's husband Dr. K.Vairavan (KV), for his continuous encouragement and guidance throughout the writing of this book. KV's involvement in our cookbook project goes far beyond the photographs he took for this volume. Despite his extremely busy professional life, he even tested some of the recipes himself, suggested revisions, and truly provided the inspiration that kept the project progressing when outside demands intruded on the authors' time and energy. It is no exaggeration to say that KV is the muse who sparked our creativity!

Expressions of gratitude are also in order for Valli Vairavan, Ashok Vairavan, Umayal Palaniappan, PL. Lakshmi, and Visalakshi Alagappan for their unfailing support and encouragement. Alamelu would particularly like to express gratitude to her first culinary teacher, Nedungudi Natesan, who is now a widely known chef in Chettinad, South India. He has continued to provide useful suggestions to her during her many trips to India.

The authors also express appreciation to Susan Dunn (Suzie), who provided the nutritional analysis for the recipes included in this book. A Registered Dietitian, Suzie is herself a knowledgeable and an enthusiastic cook of South Indian food. Her enterprising attitude and practical contributions were invaluable. Suzie's husband Jeff, who provided computer support for the nutritional analysis, has also been helpful.

Numerous other friends and associates also contributed suggestions that were valuable to us in writing this new book. Specifically, we would like to acknowledge Dr. Charles Kahn, Heather Kahn, Gabrielle Haskell, Beth Dietz, Muthiah Nachiappan, Meena Nachiappan, Kannamma Vairavan, Abirami Ramanathan, Grace Anthony Doss, and Pat Bailey. Other friends who were helpful during this project are Carolyn Nemiroff, Maya Sikdar, Dr. Jim Shey, Dr. Leonard Levine, and Jason Bacon.

The authors are grateful for the comments from members of the Whitefish Bay North Shore Junior Women's Club who prepared many of the recipes from their first cookbook (*Art of South Indian Cooking*) and offered helpful suggestions for clarity and improvement. Thanks are also due to participants in Alamelu's numerous cooking classes at the Milwaukee Jewish Community Center, OutPost Natural Foods, Orlanu Therapies, and Bayview Community Center. Receiving the overwhelmingly enthusiastic responses of these participants was an exhilarating experience and a source of inspiration for us. Mention must also be made of several Milwaukee area hospitals that promoted our recipes as models of a healthful diet through their community education programs. We should not forget to acknowledge the countless E-mail messages and telephone calls received from people we had never met with comments and questions related to our first book. These encouraging contacts were very helpful and resulted in improved presentations of many recipes.

Finally, it has been a great pleasure to work with our cookbook editor, Carol Chitnis-Gress, who provided extraordinary warmth, support, and guidance. We could not have expected greater support from an editor. Every contact we had with Carol was not only pleasant but also encouraging. Our acknowledgements would not be complete without mentioning George Blagowidow, the publisher of Hippocrene Books, New York, whose confidence and vision have brought this new cookbook to light!

COMMON PREFACE

When we set out to write our first cookbook, *Art of South Indian Cooking*, we wanted to write an easy-to-follow guide on South Indian cuisine that would be accessible to modern day cooks. In this new book we have aspired to far more. We expanded the explanations of our recipes, refined the previous recipes, and added numerous new ones. We have also added new features, including nutritional analysis and photographs of spices and dishes. An important aspect of this new book is that it reflects the suggestions and comments we received from many people who tried our recipes in the past three years.

We believe that this book will be useful to those who are unfamiliar with Indian cooking as well as to those who have experience in it. The cooking techniques presented here reflect authentic methods from South India. While most of the dishes presented are classic South Indian dishes, we have also included innovative additions influenced by our experience with western cuisine. Many of our recipes have their roots in the rich cooking traditions of Tamil Nadu and, in particular, its Chettinad region. Most of these foods, however, can be found in the various regions of South India.

It is our hope that the reader will find in this book a guide to discovering the joy of South Indian cuisine and cooking. But, first things first. Here is a guide to this book. We continue this preface in the following sections with our own individual notes on this collaborative work. In a subsequent section on South India, we give a glimpse of this extremely interesting part of India with a focus on its cuisine. Next is an introduction to the nutritional aspects of South Indian food. Following that introduction we have included useful sections on spices, dals, and other ingredients; a glossary of South Indian dishes; and general cooking tips primarily aimed at those who have little knowledge of South Indian cooking. Those who are eager to try these recipes may read these preliminary sections selectively and go on directly to the main recipe section, which is grouped into various categories. You will find the category of the vegetable dishes to be the largest in this book, since vegetables are predominant in the South Indian diet. South Indian vegetarian cuisine is unmatched for its variety of vegetables and methods of cooking and its exquisite taste. As a result, don't be surprised if the South Indian recipes actually result in a much greater enjoyment of vegetables by you, your family, and your friends.

Finally the reader may find the last two sections to be especially useful. One section offers sample menus to guide those who wish to plan complete South Indian meals. The other section will help those wishing to integrate South Indian dishes into traditional western meals. Explore and enjoy!

Alamelu Vairavan and Patricia Marquardt

PREFACE
by Alamelu Vairavan

The Chettinad region of Tamil Nadu, South India is where I was born and raised. I grew up in a large household with a professional cook and regularly shared in an abundance of delicious foods. Although I knew nothing about cooking itself, I did greatly enjoy good food. After my marriage in 1967, I accompanied my husband to the United States as a young bride. While my husband was finishing his doctoral studies at the University of Notre Dame, I was in New York, learning how to cook from professional Chettinad chef Nedungudi Natesan under a most disciplined but enjoyable regime, imposed by my aunt Visalakshi Alagappan in her home. Necessity, as they say, is the mother of invention. Following my cooking lessons and orientation to American life in New York, I joined my husband at Notre Dame.

To my surprise, I found immediate joy in cooking. I am people-oriented and love to entertain. My husband and I have entertained numerous friends and family from all over the world. Frequently, when friends dine with us, they indicate how much they enjoy the food. Many have even asked me for the recipes. These compliments not only gave me joy but inspired me greatly. I also gave numerous cooking demonstrations in the community, participated in block party contributions for neighbors and friends, and conducted cooking classes. All these activities greatly encouraged my interest in cooking.

As my interest grew, I discovered that there were very few books on South Indian cooking written in English. This fact, plus repeated requests for recipes from friends and my own growing interest in cooking, led me to write a South Indian cookbook. Another motivating factor was my desire to pass on my recipes to our children and to the generations to come.

My co-author, my dearest friend and neighbor Dr. Patricia Marquardt, and I set out on the exciting adventure of writing our first cookbook. I was thrilled to have Pat observe my cooking, ask questions, request precise measurements of the ingredients, and help write the recipes in an organized manner. My dear husband KV, Pat's late husband Bill, and my children Valli and Ashok provided the ongoing inspiration that kept the project alive despite many lengthy interruptions. Our collaboration, which began with a vision of a good South Indian cookbook accessible to today's cooks, culminated in our first publication, *Art of South Indian Cooking*.

The goodwill that surrounded that book from the beginning has truly been a blessing. After the manuscript was accepted for publication, I was invited to appear on a national television show to demonstrate some of the recipes from the book. The program we taped aired numerous times over the past three years and was favorably received by the viewers. I was also encouraged by the positive articles about the cookbook that appeared in newspapers and magazines. An article in the *Milwaukee Journal* (October 29, 1997), entitled "Aromas, Friendship and Cookbook," for example, captured the true essence of the friendship that led to the cookbook. *India Today*, an international magazine, stated "the comprehensive cookbook even has the recipe for Madras coffee minus the baking soda!" This was a reference to a hilarious event when, as a young bride, I had served my husband coffee with baking soda, mistaking it for sugar.

A major blessing of the numerous book signing events was the opportunity to meet new people who discovered an enthusiasm for South Indian food and to strengthen bonds with established friends. I must mention, in particular, the late Min Klieger, a dear friend in her eighties who had resided for a time at the Seven Oaks nursing home where I still work. On a blustery winter Wisconsin evening, Min traveled alone by bus to attend our book signing event at a local bookstore. Throughout our presentations and subsequent interactions with the audience that evening, Min stood happily in the room radiating admiration and love. Min's presence at the bookstore inspired me immensely. Another memorable book signing event was held at the Barnes and Noble bookstore in Manhattan, New York, in October 1998. Present was my Aunt Visalakshi, at whose home many years earlier I had received my first lessons in South Indian cooking. The circle was complete—I was back in New York for my book signing event!

As I reflect on the publication and the favorable reception of our first cookbook, I am filled with the deepest gratitude to the many people whose helpful suggestions and encouragements sustained my continued work with the recipes. The participants in various cooking classes conducted at community centers, hospitals, and gourmet clubs over the past three years inspired me greatly. The continued collaboration of my co-author Pat was invaluable in writing this new book. Pat is not only a scholar, but a natural cook who devoted many months to refining our recipes and perfecting her own South Indian cooking skills. Pat tested a wide variety of exquisite South Indian dishes on her own. My husband KV has observed that he has not found a match anywhere for Pat's coconut rice dish. Pat's crowning achievement as a South

Indian cook came when she prepared dosais to perfection together with truly authentic sambhar and kosamalli. I felt very much like a proud teacher who wanted to show off her pupil to the world. The more Pat and I worked together, the more we found the bonds of love and admiration between us grow.

I feel gratitude beyond words towards my beloved father A.V.M. Palaniappa Chettiar who, before his death in the spring of 1999, expressed enormous joy and pride in seeing our first cookbook in print. I remember during my childhood my dad fondly arranging for a broad array of delicious foods and skilled cooks who would indulge my every whim.

My preface would not be complete without mentioning again my dear husband KV who sustained my creativity, energy, perseverance, and passion throughout this project. Whether it was a book signing event, television appearance, or cooking class, KV inspired me greatly and gave me the confidence, love, and support I needed.

Most importantly, I would like to acknowledge the divine source of guidance and strength, which truly gave this project its wings and enabled me to accomplish an important goal.

I would like to suggest that readers approach South Indian cooking with an attitude of relaxation and enjoyment. Don't allow yourself to be burdened with concerns about the exactness of measurements or the lack of certain ingredients. Your dishes will be delicious, and family and guests will be delighted with your efforts. There is great joy to be found in sharing with others the food one has prepared. I hope that your cooking experiences will bring you much happiness that will extend to all areas of your life.

Alamelu Vairavan
Milwaukee, Wisconsin

✐

PREFACE
by Patricia Marquardt

The tantalizing aromas of Indian cooking emanating from the kitchen windows of my dear next-door neighbor Alamelu over 20 years ago beckoned me to a culinary journey and a treasured friendship. The first delicious tastes of lemon rice and beet vadas over the side fence in 1975 led to years of informal cooking sessions in Alamelu's kitchen, during which she generously shared with me not only her South Indian recipes but also her philosophy of cooking. Copious notes from our cooking sessions were incorporated in the text of our first book, *Art of South Indian Cooking*, which was published in November 1997. The enthusiastic reception of that book was most gratifying, and our cooking sessions continued with the testing of additional delicious recipes from the culinary tradition of South India. These sessions were enriched by the many comments we received from the readers of the first book and from participants in Alamelu's cooking demonstrations and our joint book-signing events.

Alamelu and I worked intensively on the second book during the summer of 2000, retesting and refining the recipes from the first book and adding numerous others. Always Alamelu was energized by a zeal to share her glorious culinary tradition through recipes that are as authentic as possible, clearly written, and accessible to everyone. The summer of 2000 proved to be a real learning experience for me as I cooked more South Indian dishes than ever before and read widely about the nutritional science that underlies the use of particular ingredients and spices in Indian dishes. The reward for my efforts came when KV, Alamelu's husband, commented that even a native of South India would believe that my cooking was the work of a true South Indian cook! That was rare praise, indeed, for one who has come to admire much about that rich culture.

Alamelu's enthusiasm for sharing her culinary tradition and for guiding others to a varied and healthful diet has been most inspirational. I learned from Alamelu not only techniques of food preparation and many delicious South Indian recipes, but also something of a true reverence for the act of cooking itself and the satisfaction one can find in serving the food to others. Alamelu and I visited South India in the winter of 1996, and there I personally experienced the cultural roots of that gracious hospitality that Alamelu embodies so beautifully. I am grateful that Alamelu has been my dearest friend and mentor for many years. How far I have traveled on my culinary journey!

I hope you, too, will begin a journey to a more varied and exciting cuisine, by way of South Indian cooking. I know that I shall continue on the cultural journey I began two decades ago with return trips to India, continued cooking sessions with Alamelu, and the inclusion of these extraordinarily delicious South Indian foods into my diet forever. I am equally certain that the treasured friendship with Alamelu will also be forever.

Patricia Marquardt
Milwaukee, Wisconsin

Dehli

Calcutta

Bay of
Bengal

Mumbai
(Bombay)

Arabian
Sea

ANDHRA PRADESH

KARNATAKA

Bangalore
Mysore

Chennai
(Madras)

KERALA

TAMIL NADU

India

Cochin

Madurai

Trivandrum

Indian Ocean

A Glimpse of South India

The term "South India" usually refers to the southern peninsula of the vast Indian subcontinent made up of the four states: Tamil Nadu and Andhra Pradesh on the east coast, and Karnataka and Kerala on the west coast. South Indian people from these states have distinct cultural characteristics and speak different languages: Tamil, Telugu, Kannada, and Malayalam respectively. These languages have rich and well-established literatures. Tamil is the most ancient of them with a great literature that dates back more than 2000 years. An important common feature of the South Indians is their Dravidian origin, in contrast to the predominantly Aryan origin of the people of the North. The vast majority of South Indians are Hindus, but Muslims and Christians form sizeable minorities and have also made significant contributions in the South. Since historically the northern part of India bore the brunt of foreign invasions, South India has been affected less by the outside influences. Thus the culture and religious practices, as well as the food, of the South tend to reflect long-standing traditions.

South India is known for its magnificent Hindu temples, some of which date back to ancient times. This region of India is also known for classical arts such as the Bharathanatyam dance and Carnatic music, each with long and great traditions. Also, some of the most ancient and beautiful sculptures in India can be found in this region.

South Indian geographical features include hill ranges, beautiful plateaus, dusty hot plains, rivers, and seacoasts populated by a large number of villages, towns, and many cosmopolitan cities. Two of the premiere cities of South India are Chennai (formerly known as Madras) in Tamil Nadu and Bangalore in Karnataka. Both of these cities have large industrial complexes, extensive cultural activities, centers of state governments, and highly regarded academic institutions. Because of its high-tech industries, Bangalore has come to be known as the Silicon Valley of India, and has attracted numerous multinational corporations. Chennai is on the East coast and has a tropical climate, while Bangalore is located about 200 miles to the west, on the Deccan plateau, and has a moderate climate. Interestingly, from the perspective of our cookbook, both cities boast of an exquisite variety of South Indian foods. Each of these cities offers a remarkably broad and wonderful array of restaurants that serve some of the best South Indian foods anywhere.

Other areas in the South noted for their outstanding cuisines include the

Chettinad region and the ancient cities of Tanjore and Madurai in Tamil Nadu; Udupi and Mysore in Karnataka; Cochin and Trivandrum in Kerala; and Hyderabad in Andhra Pradesh. Chettinad, the land of Chettiars, is a region located about 250 miles south of Chennai. The Chettiar community was historically known for its banking and business achievements, wealth, charitable pursuits, and hospitality. Chettinad cooking has always been distinctive, and recently has become especially popular in Chennai and in many other cities in India. Chettinad cuisine is characterized by thick delicious sauces, such as kulambu, and a dry stir-fry style of cooking vegetarian and nonvegetarian dishes called poriyal. This cuisine is also known for a wide variety of unique savories and sweets called palakaram usually served at breakfast, teatime, and the evening meal. Chettinad cooking techniques have influenced the cuisines of many other parts of South India. Conversely, other parts of South India, in particular Kerala and Karnataka, have influenced Chettinad cooking.

South India is known for the hospitality of its people. Guests at a private home are treated with much warmth and respect, and are welcome almost anytime. For example, it is not uncommon for people to drop by the homes of their friends and relatives, or even neighbors, casually and without invitation. Whether the visit is casual or is in response to a formal invitation, guests are received graciously and with eagerness, and are offered snacks and soft drinks or coffee. If the visit is close to a mealtime, the guests are often persuaded to stay on and have the meal with the hosts. During a meal it is very common for the host to focus attention on the guests' comfort and satisfaction. This special treatment of guests is a heartwarming and sometimes even an overwhelming experience.

A typical South Indian breakfast may include white fluffy idlis (steamed rice cakes) or crisp dosais (thin pancakes made with rice and urad dal) served with a chutney (savory accompaniment) or sambhar (a vegetable stew). Other possible breakfast items include uppuma (cream of wheat or rice cooked with spices), vadas (doughnut-shaped fritters made with lentils), and pongal (creamy spiced rice). A beverage often served with breakfast is a "latte"-like coffee made with steamed milk and sugar called Madras coffee or Mysore coffee. For lunch, plain rice is a staple food and is usually served in at least three courses. First, rice is served with sambhar or kulambu (a thick lentil or tamarind based vegetable sauce), then with rasam (a thin peppery soup), followed by plain yogurt or buttermilk to be mixed with rice. A variety of vegetable dishes, such as kootu and poriyal, are served in all three courses. If the meal is nonvegetarian, meat is served as a side dish or as a sauce served over plain rice. Pappadum, a crispy wafer-like accompaniment made from urad dal and spices, often enhances a meal. A South Indian dinner is usually a light meal and may consist of rice with vegetables, or idli or dosai served with sambhar or chutney. During meals people habitually drink plenty of water. Coffee or tea is not served with lunch or dinner. On special occasions, a dessert such as payasam (rice, tapioca, or vermicelli cooked in milk with saffron and cardamom) is served with a main meal.

It is interesting to note that a traditional way to eat a meal in South India is to use the right hand. Eating with the hand allows one to feel more connected to the food. Also a traditional South Indian way to serve the meals is on a banana leaf rather than a plate.

Foods play an important role in the South Indian life. Even most Hindu temples have kitchens associated with them, where only pure vegetarian foods are prepared and are used in religious ceremonies and then served to the devotees. In South India, many Hindus, as they get older, tend to become vegetarians for religious reasons and for health benefits.

South India is a remarkably interesting region of India with a wide range of characteristics, which include ancient arts, textiles and high-tech industries, many languages with rich literatures, and a cuisine that is among the best in the world.

NUTRITIONAL INTRODUCTION

Study after study of people's diets show that there is great benefit from eating a wide variety of foods in moderate amounts. Emphasis has been on increasing vegetables and legumes and decreasing total fat and sodium. The terms "phytochemical" and "functional foods" have become part of our language. We are learning that the foods we choose can make a difference in susceptibility to chronic disease or to the degree of genetic expression of disease or aging in our bodies.

The South Indian recipes in this book offer us a rich array of foods that include such phytochemicals as allium compounds, carotenoids, coumarins, and flavonoids. Examples of these are found in, but not limited to, garlic, onions, ginger, bell peppers, chili peppers, tomatoes and tomato products, broccoli and other cruciferous vegetables, nuts, eggplant, fenugreek, potatoes, and turmeric. The South Indian recipes also afford us functional foods such as wonderful sources of increased fiber, vitamins, and minerals. Minimal cooking oil, reduced salt, use of lean meats, and short cooking times round out the means to maintain good health through diet.

The authors include a nutritional analysis with each recipe in this book. Though it is good to be aware of the nutrients in each recipe, exclusive attention to particular nutrients can lead to an incomplete picture of the overall health benefits and enjoyment of food. For example, some vegetables by nature have a significant sodium content, but the overall nutritional value of vegetables in general is well understood.

If readers have concerns about sodium content, the amount of salt can be reduced or eliminated altogether, without sacrificing to any great extent the delicious flavors of these recipes. Do not lose sight of the fact that the recipes as written are authentic, delectable, and, once tried, will be forever remembered as truly wonderful.

South Indian food affects you in a good way. I hope you appreciate the good nutrition as well as the sumptuous aroma and taste.

Nutritional analysis in this book was performed using data found in *Bowes and Church's Food Values of Portions Commonly Used*, Jean A.T. Pennington, 17th Edition, Lippincott, 1998; United States Department of Agriculture (USDA) research publications; and the nutrition labels on some food products. The nutritional analysis for each recipe in this book is for a single serving unless the number of servings is unspecified as, for example, in the various appetizers and most bread items. In such cases, the nutritional analysis provided is for each food item.

Susan Sharer Dunn, (Suzie)
Registered Dietitian
Sedona, Arizona

MULTILINGUAL GLOSSARY OF
SPICES, DALS, AND FLOURS

The glossary shown below will be helpful in shopping for spices and lentils from Indian stores. Because spices are commonly labeled in Hindi in Indian groceries, the Hindi term is provided here. The Tamil term is also provided, as Tamil is one of the four major languages of South India.

English	Hindi	Tamil
Aniseed (Fennel)	Saunf (Sonf)	Perunjeeragam
Asafoetida	Hing	Perungayam
Bay Leaf	Tez Patta	Lavangilai
Black Pepper	Kalimirch	Milagu
Cardamom	Elachi	Ellakkai
Cinnamon	Dal Chini	Pattai
Chickpea (roasted)	Chana Dalia	Pottukadalai
Chilies (red)	Mirch	Milagaai
Cloves	Lavang	Krambu
Coriander seeds	Dhaniya	Kothamallivedai
Cumin seeds	Jeera	Jeerakam
Fenugreek seeds	Methi	Venthayam
Mustard seeds	Rai (Sarson)	Kadugu
Poppy seeds (white)	Khus Khus	Kus Kus
Saffron	Zaffran (Kesar)	Kungumappu
Tamarind	Imli	Puli
Turmeric	Haldi	Manjal

DALS AND FLOURS:

English	Hindi	Tamil
All-Purpose Flour	Maida	Maida Mavu
Almonds	Badam	Badam
Bengal Gram Dal	Channe-ki-dal	Kadalai Paruppu
Bengal Gram Flour (Chickpea Flour)	Besan (Gram flour)	Kadalai Mavu
Black Gram Dal (Split)	Urad Dal	Ulutham Paruppu
Chickpea	Kabuli Channa	Kondai Kadalai
Green Gram Dal (Split)	Moong Dal	Payatham Paruppu
Green Gram, Whole	Moong	Paasipayaru
Red Lentil	Masoor Dal	Mysoor Paruppu
Red Gram Dal	Toovar (Toor) Dal	Thuvaram Paruppu
Sago (Tapioca)	Sabudana	Javvarasi
Semolina	Sooji	Ravai
Vermicelli	Seviyan	Semiya
Wheat flour	Atta	Gothambai Mavu

THE INDIAN SPICE BOX

In an Indian spice box there are 7 small containers which usually contain the following spices for South Indian cooking:

1. Black mustard seeds
2. Urad dal
3. Cumin seeds
4. Fennel seeds
5. Fenugreek seeds
6. Dried red pepper
7. Cinnamon sticks

Under the cover of the spice box is another lid that holds the small containers in place. This lid is very convenient for storing bay leaves.

STORING SPICES AND DALS

Most spices keep best in covered glass bottles or containers. Spices will retain their quality for many months, tightly closed even for a year or two, provided they are stored in airtight containers. We highly recommend removing spices, powders, and dals from their plastic wraps and storing them in bottles with identifying labels. Spices kept in the kitchen cupboard in jars will retain flavor, aroma, and color. Dals can also be stored in glass or metal containers. There are various size jars available in spice shops and in discount stores.

If you purchase spices, rice, and dals in bulk, you will have more than what you will need for ready use in the kitchen. The remaining amount can be stored in a dry, airtight container on a cool pantry shelf.

SPICES AND OTHER BASICS

With very few exceptions, the spices used in South Indian cooking can be found in most American supermarkets. Other spices can be bought economically from Indian and Oriental grocery stores or from stores specializing in spices. One may also mail-order spices from many Indian grocery stores or websites in the United States and in Canada.

The long list of spices called for by some Indian recipes may at first be discouraging to the novice cook. Once a basic pantry of Indian spices is assembled, however, you will be able to use them time and again in numerous recipes that often call for the same ingredients in similar order.

SPICES USED IN SOUTH INDIAN COOKING

Asafoetida
A strongly scented resin used in small quantities in some vegetable and rice dishes, which imparts a flavor reminiscent of onion and garlic. Asafoetida is sold in lump or powdered form. The powdered form, available in Indian grocery stores, is recommended.

Bay Leaves
Long, dried-green leaves that add a subtle flavor to dishes. Only one or two leaves are needed to flavor a recipe of vegetables or nonvegetarian foods.

Black Mustard Seeds
Small, round, black seeds which impart fundamental flavor and texture to dishes. Mustard seeds are often used in combination with urad dal in vegetable, rice, and sambhar dishes.

Black Pepper
Used whole or in powdered form. Powdered black pepper and cumin, mixed in equal portion, can be used in chicken recipes, over fried eggs, and in yogurt salads to enhance the flavor of the dish. The combination of black pepper and cumin powder in soups and rasams helps to relieve cold symptoms.

Cardamom

A highly aromatic spice with a delicate sweetness, used primarily to flavor tea, soup, and dessert dishes. The seeds may be used whole or in powdered form. Cardamom is also used as a breath freshener.

Cayenne Powder

A hot ingredient made from the fruit of the pepper plant, nearly identical to red chili powder. Cayenne in powdered form is used in very small quantities. It enlivens a preparation and enhances the other seasonings.

Cinnamon

The aromatic reddish-brown bark of the cinnamon tree, it imparts a rich, sweet, pleasantly spicy flavor to foods. It is used, usually in stick form, in many vegetable and nonvegetarian dishes. Also available in powdered form.

Cloves

The aromatic unopened flower of the clove tree that imparts a rich and sweetly subtle flavor to rice and dessert dishes. Cloves are often chewed as mouth freshener after meals.

Coriander Seeds

Coriander seeds come from the same plant as coriander (cilantro) leaves. Coriander seeds can be used whole or ground. Usually a desired amount of coriander seeds is placed in an iron skillet, dry roasted over medium heat until dark brown, and then ground to a powder. Coriander seeds have a pleasant odor of sweetness with a bit of lemony taste. Coriander powder and cayenne powder are often combined together in equal portions in various dishes.

Cumin Seeds

An important spice that imparts a nutty, pleasantly bitter flavor to foods. Commonly used in whole or powdered form. Powdered cumin, in combination with black pepper, is used over fried eggs and in soup and yogurt dishes. The combination of cumin powder and cayenne powder enhances the flavor of many dishes.

Fennel Seeds

Larger in size than cumin seeds, they have a delicate flavor similar to anise. Commonly used in nonvegetarian cooking and in soups. Roasted fennel seeds are also used as a breath freshener.

Fenugreek Seeds

Small brown seeds that are slightly bitter. Used sparingly in sambhar dishes and in nonvegetarian dishes such as seafood to enhance flavor. Also used with dosai batter to give a distinct and special flavor.

Poppy Seeds (White)

The seeds from the poppy plant, used primarily as a thickening agent. White poppy seed is the only variety of poppy seed used in Indian cooking.

Red Chili Pepper

Pungent dried pods of the pepper plant can be added whole or in powdered form. The use of one or two pods will increase flavor level of dishes and enhance other seasonings. The perfect accompaniment for garnishing in hot oil with curry leaves and other seasonings, it enhances the flavor of chutneys and sambhar dishes.

Roasted Chickpeas

Also known as dhalia in Hindi and pottukadalai in Tamil, give a pleasing texture and flavor particularly to chutneys and kurma dishes. If unavailable, dry roasted unsalted peanuts can be substituted with similar results.

Saffron

A rare and aromatic spice from the stigmas of the crocus plant that adds an exotic flavor and orange-red color to rice dishes. Known as "the queen of all spices," saffron is also used widely in desserts. Often saffron is soaked in water or milk to develop color and aroma.

Tamarind

A bean with a sweet and sour taste that adds a certain tartness to dishes. It is known as "Indian date." Bottled tamarind paste is available in Indian grocery stores. Lemon juice may be substituted for tamarind.

Healthy South Indian Cooking

Tapioca

A beadlike starch obtained from the cassava root. It is used primarily in payasam (pudding) and is served as dessert.

Turmeric Powder

It is one of the great Indian spices. A yellow root-spice that has been dried and powdered. A natural food coloring that imparts a musty flavor and bright yellow color to any dish. Turmeric paste is reportedly good for the complexion and helps in digestion.

Vindaloo Curry Paste

Pastes are convenient blends of ground spices preserved in oil for freshness. Vindaloo paste is spicy and sour and can be used to make chicken, shrimp, and lamb dishes. Ingredients in this paste are vegetable oil, coriander, cumin, turmeric, chilies, ginger, garlic, and tamarind. Available in small jars at Indian grocery stores.

Rice and Oil In South Indian Cooking

I. RICE

Rice is a staple food of South India. Four types of rice are commonly used in our recipes for rice dishes:

A. Basmati rice
B. Jasmine rice
C. Extra Long-Grain rice
D. Uncle Ben's Parboiled Original Rice

A. **Basmati Rice:**

Basmati is a fragrant, high-quality rice used in making both plain and flavored rice dishes. Basmati rice has a nutlike flavor and is aromatic. It comes packaged under several brand names. When purchasing basmati rice, look for a quality brand, such as Dehradun or Tilda. It is available in natural food stores and Indian grocery stores. The grains of basmati rice are finer than the grains of other types of rice, and they separate beautifully after they are cooked. Basmati rice is unexcelled in making pulaoo and flavored rice dishes.

B. **Jasmine Rice:**

Jasmine rice is a delicate and aromatic pure white rice. It is excellent for making plain or flavored rice dishes. It is available in Indian and Oriental grocery stores.

C. **Extra Long-Grain Rice:**

Extra long-grain rice is used in making plain and flavored rice dishes. It lacks the aromatic quality of the basmati and jasmine rice, but it is a good all-purpose rice. It is available in regular supermarkets.

D. **Uncle Ben's Original Enriched Parboiled Long-Grain Rice:**

This type of rice is used in this book only for making idli, a South Indian breakfast specialty. Uncle Ben's Original Enriched Parboiled Long-Grain Rice gives the same authentic texture to idlis that is obtained from a specialty rice available in South India. Through experimentation, we found that Uncle Ben's Rice, when combined with other long-grain rice and urad dal, helps make delicious and soft idlis.

To cook any type of rice, we highly recommend an **automatic electric rice cooker**. Rice cookers are readily available in department stores and in Indian and Oriental stores. Rice cookers come in various sizes, ranging from a small, four-cup size to larger sizes.

Although white and basmati rice are commonly used in South Indian cooking, you may also prepare the recipes with **brown rice**. You may find that the nutty flavor and high fiber content of the brown rice compensates for its lack of lightness and delicacy.

II. COOKING OILS

Two types of light vegetable oils are preferred in preparing South Indian dishes. These are **Canola oil** (for its mild flavor) and **Corn oil** (for its rich corn taste). Both canola and corn oil provide a light cooking medium that will enhance the flavor of the dishes you are preparing. If you wish, you may also use **Olive oil** as a cooking medium, although it is not an authentic South Indian cooking medium and will alter the taste of the dish. The authors, therefore, recommend the more delicate canola and corn oils for South Indian cooking.

Coconut oil is used in only one recipe in this book, Kerala Aviyal. While coconut oil lends a deliciously rich flavor to foods, it is rather high in saturated fat. **Ghee**, clarified butter, is used in preparing delicious biriyani rice, chappati, and desserts. Ghee is made by melting butter and seasoning the melted butter with curry leaves and cumin. Allow the melted butter to cool. Then pour off the clear butter into a bottle and discard the residue. The residue from the butter with all its seasonings is often used for making delicious ghee rice. Store ghee, covered, at room temperature or in refrigerator. When you wish to use ghee, heat a small portion of ghee in a butter warmer and use as needed. Ghee is used very sparingly, but it adds a wonderful flavor to dishes.

Spice Powders

Black Pepper and Cumin Powder
Combine both spices in equal portion (for example, 1/4 cup to 1/4 cup) and grind to a fine powder. Delicious when used in nonvegetarian dishes and over fried eggs. It is also used in rasam preparation.

Cayenne Powder
Ground red pepper, readily available in regular and Indian grocery stores. Commonly used in both vegetarian and nonvegetarian dishes.

Chutney ("Podi") Powder
It is a blend of various spices such as curry leaves, red chilies, toor dal, and urad dal. It is readily available in Indian grocery stores, sometimes labeled as Chatney Powder. A recommended commercial preparation is the MTR brand.

A unique Chettinad variation of chutney powder is known as Podi. Podi is commonly served with such items as idli and dosai, but the authors have found podi, or alternately chutney powder, to be a delicious ingredient in vegetable dishes as well.

The following is an easy-to-make recipe for homemade Podi:
1/2 cup whole dried red chili peppers (about 16)
2 tablespoons urad dal
1 tablespoon toor dal
1/4 cup curry leaves
2 teaspoons corn oil
1/2 teaspoon asafoetida powder
1/2 teaspoon salt

1. Separately roast red chillies, urad dal, toor dal and curry leaves each in 1/2 teaspoon of oil over medium heat to a light golden color.
2. Combine the above roasted spices with asafoetida and salt.
3. In a spice (or coffee) grinder, grind the roasted ingredients together to a fine powder.

Makes 1/2 cup.

Coconut Powder

Available in Indian grocery stores and natural food stores as "unsweetened powdered coconut." It is easier to use powdered coconut rather than fresh coconut, which needs to be cracked and ground. Unsweetened coconut powder is used in various dishes. When coconut powder is ground with other seasonings to make kurma, it blends well with the vegetables, producing a smooth paste and allowing the flavors of the vegetables and meat to come through.

Cumin Powder

Powdered cumin is readily available in regular grocery stores. Cumin powder blends well with vegetables and has an aromatic flavor. Cumin powder blended with cayenne powder also lends distinctive flavor to any dish.

Curry Powder

A blend of many spices such as coriander, fenugreek, turmeric, cumin, black pepper, bay leaves, cloves, onion, red chilies, and ginger. Readily available in regular grocery stores, domestic curry powder is used in some vegetable and meat dishes.

Garam Masala Powder

A mixture of several spices. It can be purchased in Indian grocery stores, but has a fresher taste if you personally roast and grind the spices, such as cardamom, black peppercorns, cumin seeds, coriander, cinnamon, and cloves. Garam Masala powder is a spice mixture that is very aromatic. It is used in some nonvegetarian dishes.

Rasam Powder

An aromatic blend of many spices including coriander seeds, red chilies, cumin seeds, curry leaves, and asafoetida. It comes prepackaged. We prefer to use the MTR brand of rasam powder that is available in Indian grocery stores. MTR foods are made in Bangalore, India.

Sambhar Powder

An aromatic blend of many spices including red chilies, cumin, curry leaves, fenugreek, asafoetida, channa dal, and toovar dal. Commonly used in sambhar and kulambu dishes. MTR brand sambhar powder or any Madras brand sambhar powder is highly recommended. Readily available in Indian grocery stores.

HERBS AND FRESH INGREDIENTS

Coconut

The hard-shelled, edible nut of the coconut palm tree that is widely used as a garnish for cooked vegetables and as a base for kurmas and chutneys. Fresh coconut is available in general grocery stores. Crack open the coconut with a hammer. Food processors or electric mini choppers may be used to shred the fresh coconut. Shredded unsweetened powdered coconut is also available in natural food stores and in Indian grocery stores. The milk of the coconut is not used often in Indian cooking, but it is enjoyed as a cool, refreshing drink on a hot summer day.

Coriander

A distinctively aromatic herb of major importance, which may be purchased as leaves, seeds, or powder. Also called "cilantro" in Spanish and Mexican recipes, it is used both as a seasoning and as a garnish. Coriander chutney is a very popular accompaniment to vadai, idli, and dosai.

Curry Leaves

Dark green leaves of the curry plant that impart a savory taste and lingering aroma to South Indian dishes. They are one of the primary ingredients used in Madras sambhar and rasam powder. Curry leaves are dropped in hot oil before adding onions and other main ingredients or are used to flavor the oil that is poured over many dishes as a finishing step.

Garlic

A bulbous herb composed of individual cloves that is an essential ingredient in South Indian cooking. Used in most soups, vegetables, and meat dishes to enhance the flavor. Frequently sautéed in hot oil at the outset of a recipe, it infuses the entire dish with distinctively pleasing flavor. Garlic with ginger makes a delicious combination paste. Great curative powers are attributed to garlic.

Fresh Ginger Root

A root spice with a warm, fresh flavor that is used very often in Indian cooking both as a fundamental ingredient and as a garnish. Ginger in combination with garlic is very popular and adds wonderful flavor to any dish.

Ginger also aids in digestion. Ginger is available in powdered form, but fresh ginger is highly recommended for its flavor and healthful qualities. It is valued as a medicinal and culinary spice.

Green Chili Peppers

Fresh unripe chilies are a common ingredient that imparts a spicy, hot flavor to many Indian dishes. There are a wide variety of chili peppers and you may use any of the many types available. Chilies are used in virtually every savory dish in India. Chilies may be used sparingly, however, or omitted altogether depending on your taste. In general, the smaller the chili, the hotter it is.

Mint

Fragrant herb with a uniquely fresh flavor and aroma. Used primarily in cooling chutneys and relishes that balance the more spicy dishes.

Onion

Staple ingredient valued for its flavor and medicinal qualities. Onions sautéed in oil with various spices are the foundation of most dishes. Onions also appear raw in yogurt salad and as a garnish for other dishes.

DESCRIPTION OF DALS

Dals (lentils)

Legumes high in protein and fiber, which are a staple ingredient in many South Indian dishes. There are numerous varieties of dals. The dals most commonly used in the recipes in this book are as follows:

Toor Dal or Toovar Dal

A kind of yellow lentil that is split into two round halves. Sometimes toor dals are packaged in a slightly oiled form. Toor dal is cooked to a creamy consistency to make sambhars, kootus, and soups. It creates the rich base so characteristic of delicious sambhars. Toor dal is available in Indian grocery stores.

Yellow Split Peas

A familiar kind of legume, readily available in regular grocery stores. Yellow split peas appear often in the recipes in this book because of their distinctive texture and taste. Specifically yellow split peas are used to make dishes such as vadas, podimas, pachadis, and kootus.

Masoor Dal

An orange-red colored lentil, also known as **red lentil**, in split form, that is used in making sambhars. Masoor dal cooks faster than toor dal. Masoor dal can be substituted for toor dal in sambhars and other vegetable dishes. Masoor dal is available in natural food stores and Indian grocery stores.

Moong Dal

A golden yellow lentil used in split form. This most versatile of dals cooks quickly and is widely used in making vegetarian dishes. The whole moong bean, which is small, oval, and olive green in color, is called whole green gram dal. Available in Indian grocery stores.

Urad Dal

A creamy white split lentil. Fried urad dal gives a nutty, crunchy taste to dishes. Essential to South Indian cooking, urad dal is used both as a seasoning and as a base for vadas, idlis, and dosais. Urad dal, fried in oil with black mustard seeds and various seasonings, is an essential ingredient in many recipes. Available in Indian grocery stores. Urad dal, when whole, has a black skin and is known as black gram lentil. The recipes in this book use the split urad dal exclusively.

Channa Dal

A kind of yellow lentil, also called gram lentil, which resembles yellow split peas, but which is larger and coarser. When roasted, channa dal has a nutty taste and crunchy texture. Channa dal is used to make soondals, vadas, and kootus. Available in Indian grocery stores.

Note: Dals are very easy to cook. In each recipe, where dals are used, we have given easy-to-follow stovetop cooking instructions. Soaking toor dal and split peas in water for a few hours prior to cooking will reduce the cooking time. The use of pressure cooker can also reduce the cooking time considerably. Pressure cookers are often used in Indian households to cook all types of legumes. In case you prefer to use this method, the following instructions will be helpful.

Cooking dal in a pressure cooker of at least 2.5-quart-size:

1/2 cup dal (toor dal, yellow split peas, masoor dal, or moong dal)
1/4 teaspoon turmeric powder

1. Place 1 or 2 cups of water in a pressure cooker as specified by the manufacturer's instructions.

2. In a small stainless steel dish, place dal, the turmeric powder, and additional 1 cup of water.

3. Place the stainless steel dish in the bottom of the pressure cooker in the water. Pressure cook for 5 to 7 minutes in pressure cooker, according to manufacturer's instructions.

4. When the cooker is sufficiently cooled to open, remove dish with dal. Do not drain water.

Makes 1 cup cooked creamy dal

GLOSSARY OF NAMES FOR SOUTH INDIAN DISHES

Adai

A type of thick, fiber-rich pancake made from a variety of dals. Batter for adai does not require fermentation. Just soak dals, grind coarsely, and make adai immediately.

Aviyal

A delicious preparation of vegetables cooked with coconut, ginger, and green chilies. It has a consistency halfway between a thick kootu and a more liquid sambhar.

Bhaji

A vegetable fritter that can be made with potatoes, eggplant, or onions after dipping in a batter of besan flour and rice flour. Served as an appetizer or as a snack during teatime.

Bonda

Deep-fried dumplings coated with besan and rice flour and often filled with masala potatoes and peas. Served as an appetizer or as a snack during teatime.

Chappati

A flat, round unleavened thin wheat bread, common in North and South India.

Chutney

A savory sauce used as an accompaniment to appetizers and breakfast items. There are a variety of delicious chutneys featured in this book. Unlike their North Indian counterparts, the South Indian chutneys are not sweet.

Dosai

A South Indian thin pancake or crepe made from rice and urad dal, ground and allowed to ferment. Dosai is a South Indian breakfast specialty and can be prepared in a variety of ways. One favorite variety is Masala Dosai, which is dosai stuffed with a delicious filling of potato masala and coconut chutney.

Idiyappam

Steam-cooked thin noodles made from rice flour. Packages of dry rice sticks are available in Indian and Oriental stores. Rice sticks are cooked in boiling water like pasta and are drained. Then rice sticks are seasoned to make a delicious breakfast or a light supper.

Idli

Delicate steamed rice cake that is a South Indian specialty. Idli is made from a fermented batter similar to that used to make dosai. Idli, together with dosai, is a popular breakfast food usually served with sambhar and chutney.

Kesari

A dessert made with cream of wheat, milk, sugar, cardamom, raisins, saffron, and cashews.

Kootu

A thick, creamy textured and mildly flavored vegetable dish prepared with dal, ginger, and cumin. Thicker than sambhar, kootus are often served as side dishes in a main meal.

Kulambu

A thick vegetable sauce usually made without dals. Kulambu features numerous individual vegetables, and occasionally meats, cooked with tamarind paste and a variety of spices.

Kurma

Exquisitely flavorful vegetable (or meat) sauce made from coconut ground with many different spices to a milky consistency. A uniquely aromatic and delicious preparation.

Pachadi

Vegetables cooked with a variety of spices in tamarind paste. Similar to kootu, but less creamy in texture. Pachadi is a popular accompaniment to a meal.

Payasam

A sweet pudding-like dessert made with milk, cardamom, and saffron. Tapioca or vermicelli are the usual varieties. May be mixed with fruit cocktail or other fruit.

Podimas

A vegetable dish enhanced with coarsely ground and steamed split peas and spices.

Poori

A bread popular in both South and North India. Poori is made with unleavened wheat flour that puffs into airy rounds of bread when deep-fried.

Poriyal

A stir-fried vegetable without sauce that is served as a side dish in a main meal. Vegetables are cooked with seasonings and as a finishing touch combined with dals and coconut.

Pulaoo Rice

A kind of aromatic fried rice infused with the flavors of cinnamon and clove. Two pulaoo rice recipes are included in this book: vegetable pulaoo rice and chicken pulaoo rice.

Rasam

A thin peppery soup made from garlic, onions, and tomatoes. Usually served at mid-course in a meal with rice. May also be enjoyed at the beginning of a meal. Rasams are believed to be a potent remedy for colds and sore throats.

Sambhar

Vegetables and dals cooked with sambhar powder to make a hearty sauce of medium or thick consistency. There are a wide variety of sambhars to enjoy with idlis and dosais. Also served in main meals over plain rice.

Thuvaiyal

A kind of thick chutney made from coconut, chilies, and roasted dals. Sometimes made with vegetables such as eggplant.

Uppuma

A popular breakfast or snack item often made from cream of wheat, cream of rice, or cracked wheat seasoned with curry leaves, onions, and spices. Usually served with any of the many varieties of sambhars and chutneys.

Vadai

A fried doughnut-like patty made from urad dal or vegetables and yellow split peas ground with onions and chilies. Vadai is a popular breakfast and tea item. One particularly delicious variety is served marinated in seasoned yogurt and is called thayir vadai.

SOME GENERAL TIPS

1. Relax and enjoy South Indian cooking. Preparing the dishes does not require a precise measurement of the ingredients. If you add a little more or less than the amount specified in the recipe, you are not going to spoil the preparation. Most cooks in India do not use measuring cups or spoons. If you like a certain spice, such as cumin, you may use more than the quantity indicated in the recipe. Contrarily, if you dislike a particular spice, you may reduce the amount specified in the recipe or omit the ingredient altogether. There are very few absolutely essential spices or seasonings, given the wealth of spices and aromatic ingredients that make up almost every South Indian dish.

2. If you don't have a specific spice or other ingredient listed in the recipe, don't be disheartened. It is usually possible to substitute or omit ingredients and still produce a delicious dish although with a different taste. Instead of mustard seeds and urad dal, for example, you may use whole cumin seeds. In a very short time, you will become familiar with the spices and the possible substitutions.

3. Indian food is not always hot and spicy. It is the chili peppers and cayenne powder that give the "kick" to a dish. We have indicated only minimal amounts of chili peppers and cayenne powder in our recipes. You may add more or less chilies as you desire.

4. Use plump, ripened, round tomatoes. By adding more tomatoes, you can cut down on the tomato sauce if you prefer. In some recipes, however, tomato sauce enhances the flavor of the vegetable dish and should not be omitted.

5. Unsweetened coconut powder, available in Indian grocery stores, can be substituted for freshly ground coconut. The unsweetened coconut powder can be used as a garnish and also as a base for making chutneys and kurmas.

6. Most cities have Indian grocery stores. It is also possible to mail-order spices (an Internet search should provide you with retailers).

7. Some recipes in our cookbook will yield more servings than you may

wish to use in a single meal. That is no problem. The leftovers can be refrigerated or frozen with no detriment to flavor or nutritional value. Place leftovers in a plastic microwave dish or in a glass container. Just as wine tastes better with age, Indian food often tastes better after a day or two because of the rich blending of spices and seasonings. Most leftovers can be refrigerated for 3 to 5 days or kept frozen for weeks. Just reheat and enjoy.

8. Dals, such as toor dal and split peas, can be cooked in large quantities and can be kept frozen in one-cup portions for ready use any time. Freeze in a microwave container or any plastic container. Defrost, heat, and use as needed. Cooked dals can be frozen or refrigerated for many weeks with no loss of flavor or nutritional value.

9. Dal should be cooked on the stove or in a pressure cooker to achieve the creamy consistency so desirable for making delicious sambhars and kootus. For poriyals (stir-fry vegetables), however, dal should retain a firmer texture when cooked. Dals cooked in a microwave oven will take an excessive amount of time and will not attain a creamy consistency.

10. Our recipes are easy to follow. Once you have assembled all of your ingredients, it usually takes only 20 to 30 minutes to prepare a dish, sometimes even less. The more practiced you become in preparing a recipe, the easier it will become.

11. A word about vegetables: Even if you don't like a particular vegetable, you may be surprised at how much its taste is transformed and enhanced when prepared according to the recipes presented in this book. We have found that brussels sprouts, for example, have won new fans by being prepared in the South Indian style. Allow this book to expand your taste and that of your family to include a variety of nutritious vegetables in your daily diet.

12. Here is a hint on using tamarind paste that comes in a bottle: Open the plastic seal and lightly microwave the thick tamarind paste for 1 minute. The paste will be converted to a thick liquid. Now, cover the bottle and store bottle in the kitchen cupboard for any length of time. Tamarind paste, kept at room temperature in this way, is very easy to use.

13. If you are concerned about the amount of time you will need to prepare numerous Indian dishes for a big meal, you can always chop the vegetables ahead of time and keep them refrigerated in plastic wrap, ready for use.

14. You can also make the entire dinner early in the day and leave dishes at room temperature until dinnertime. Advance preparation actually enhances the flavor of the dishes. However, if a dish contains coconut or meat, it is important not to leave the cooked dish at a room temperature for an extended period of time. The dish must be refrigerated. Before serving, heat and enjoy.

15. Regular stainless steel heavy bottomed saucepans, nonstick pots and pans, cast-iron skillets, and woks can be used in Indian cooking. Electric rice cookers and woks are useful but not necessary. Electric blenders, however, are necessary.

16. Combining Indian and western dishes makes for a very interesting and pleasing dining experience. Combining grilled chicken or fish with an Indian rice and vegetable dish can be a pleasant change of pace for your family and friends. Be certain to see the section on Fusion meals, page 341.

17. If you are a beginner and you do not know what spices and dals you need to buy in order to get started, here is a short, initial shopping list: black mustard seeds; split urad dal, cumin powder; turmeric powder; chutney or cayenne powder; moong or masoor dal; and yellow split peas. With these spices and dals you can prepare many of the vegetable dishes in this book.

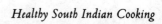

Appetizers

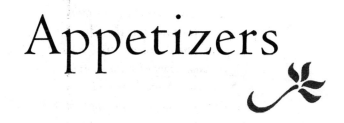

ᔆBEET VADASᔅ

Beet vadas are fried vegetable patties that can be served as appetizers or as an accompaniment to any meal.

1 cup yellow split peas
1 to 2 dried whole red chili peppers
3/4 teaspoon whole cumin seeds
1/2 teaspoon fennel seeds
1/4 cup finely shredded fresh beets
1 1/2 cups chopped yellow onion
1/2 cup chopped coriander
1 tablespoon minced fresh ginger root
1 to 2 green chili peppers (optional)
1/2 teaspoon salt
1 to 1 1/2 cups plain dry bread crumbs
Canola or corn oil for frying

1. Soak yellow split peas in approximately 2 cups of water for 2 to 3 hours. Drain and grind split peas with red chilies, cumin, and fennel seeds in a blender to a coarse texture (similar to cornmeal). Grind about 1/2 cup of soaked split peas at a time with only enough water added each time to facilitate the grinding process. Do not grind the split peas too finely. It is desirable to have the split pea mixture coarsely ground to lend a crunchy texture to the finished vadas.

2. Remove the split pea mixture from blender and place in a large bowl. Use your hand to blend the mixture of split peas and spices thoroughly.

3. Add the beets, onion, coriander, ginger, green chilies, and salt to the mixture. Blend thoroughly by hand.

4. Add bread crumbs to the mixture and blend by hand until mixture reaches a consistency sufficiently thick to form a ball. More bread crumbs may be added if the mixture is too watery.

ᔗ *Healthy South Indian Cooking*

5. Take a small portion of mixture (about 1 tablespoon) in the palm of the hand and form into a ball. With fingers, flatten ball into the shape of a patty, either in the palm of the hand or on a small plate. The patty should be about 1 inch in diameter.

6. Heat about 2 inches of oil in a skillet over medium heat. Fry a few patties at a time in the oil until golden brown. Remove vadas from hot oil with a perforated spatula and drain them on paper towels. Repeat the procedure until the desired number of vadas has been made.

Note: Any unused mixture may be refrigerated for further use, although it is advisable to use the refrigerated mix within a day or two.

Makes 50 small vadas

CALORIES 64; FAT 5g.; SATURATED FAT 1g.; PROTEIN 1g.; CARBOHYDRATE 5g.; FIBER 1g.; CHOLESTEROL 0mg.; SODIUM 42mg.

Variations: A number of different vegetables may substituted for the shredded beets in the basic recipe. These include 1 cup of finely chopped fresh spinach to make **Spinach Vadas** or 1/2 cup of shredded fresh carrots to make **Carrot Vadas**. Be sure to blend the vegetables thoroughly into the split pea mixture. Simple **Onion Vadas** may be made by following the basic recipe without the beets and doubling the amount of chopped onions.

⌣BHAJIS⌣

Bhajis are flat vegetable fritters that can be served warm as a snack with any type of chutney.

1 cup chickpea flour (gram flour or besan flour)
1/4 cup rice flour
1 teaspoon salt
1/4 teaspoon baking soda
1/2 teaspoon cayenne powder
1/2 teaspoon powdered asafoetida
1/4 teaspoon turmeric powder
30 thin potato slices with skin (about 3 inches in diameter), or eggplant slices, or onion slices
Canola or corn oil for frying

1. Mix together all of the dry ingredients by hand.

2. Add approximately 1 cup of water to dry ingredients to make a smooth, thick batter. Set aside for 1/2 hour.

3. Coat the potato or eggplant or onion slices by dipping them in the batter. Fry slices in a cast-iron skillet in about 2 inches of corn or canola oil. Fry until golden brown on both sides (2 to 3 minutes). Drain bhajis on paper towels.

Note: Instant pakora mix may be purchased and used in place of the dry ingredients.

Makes about 30 bhajis

CALORIES 100; FAT 7g.; SATURATED FAT 1g.; PROTEIN 1g.; CARBOHYDRATE 6g.; FIBER trace; CHOLESTEROL 0mg.; SODIUM 83mg.

৵: Bondas :৵

Bondas are deep-fried dumplings made with potatoes and mixed vegetables dipped in a batter of chickpea flour. They can be served warm as a snack with any type of chutney.

For Filling:
2 medium-size Idaho potatoes
3/4 teaspoon turmeric powder
1 teaspoon salt
1 cup chopped onion
1 teaspoon minced fresh ginger root
1/4 cup chopped tomato
1 green chili pepper, chopped
2 tablespoons corn oil
1/4 teaspoon asafoetida powder
1 teaspoon black mustard seeds
2 teaspoons urad dal
1/2 cup frozen green peas
1/4 cup roasted cashew halves
1/4 cup chopped coriander (cilantro)

For Batter:
1 cup besan flour (gram or chickpea flour)
1/4 cup rice flour
1/4 teaspoon baking soda
1/2 teaspoon turmeric powder
1/2 teaspoon cayenne powder
1/2 teaspoon salt
About 1 cup corn oil for frying

Instructions for Potato Filling:
1. Scrub potatoes. Cut in half and place in pressure cooker. Add enough water to cover potatoes, together with 1/2 teaspoon turmeric powder and 1/2 teaspoon salt. Cover and cook about 10 minutes until potatoes are tender. Or boil the potatoes in an uncovered saucepan. Peel the skin and set aside.

2. Mix onion, ginger, tomato, and green chilies. Set aside.

3. Mash potatoes coarsely.

4. Heat oil in skillet over medium heat. When oil is hot but not smoking, add asafoetida, mustard seeds, and urad dal. Cover and fry until mustard seeds pop and urad dal is golden brown, about 30 seconds.

5. Add onion mixture to skillet. Stir-fry for a few minutes. Add remaining 1/4 teaspoon turmeric powder and 1/2 teaspoon salt.

6. Add mashed potatoes and stir well. Add green peas, cashews, and coriander to potatoes and mix well. Set aside until batter is prepared.

Instructions for batter:

7. Mix besan flour, rice flour, baking soda, turmeric powder, cayenne powder, and salt.

8. Add about 1 cup warm water to dry ingredients to form a thick and smooth paste. Note: batter must be thick, so be careful to add only a little water at a time.

9. Shape the potato mixture into balls and coat balls with batter. Heat oil in a skillet over medium heat. Fry the coated balls in corn oil until golden brown. Drain on paper towels.

Note: Instant pakora mix may be used in place of the batter.

Makes 25 small bondas

CALORIES 124; FAT 11g.; SATURATED FAT 1g.; PROTEIN 1g.; CARBOHYDRATE 6g.; FIBER 1g.; CHOLESTEROL 0mg.; SODIUM 147mg.

ᔾPAKORASᔿ

Pakoras are vegetable fritters that are served warm with any type of chutney.

1 cup besan flour (gram flour or chickpea flour)
1/2 cup rice flour
1/4 teaspoon baking soda
1/2 teaspoon turmeric powder
1/2 teaspoon cayenne powder
1/2 teaspoon salt
1 cup chopped onion
1 cup chopped bell pepper
1 tablespoon minced fresh ginger root
2 green chili peppers
1/4 cup chopped coriander
1 cup corn oil for frying
1/2 cup roasted cashew halves (optional)

1. Mix together besan flour, rice flour, baking soda, turmeric powder, cayenne powder, and salt.

2. Add onion, bell pepper, ginger, green chili, and coriander to the dry mixture.

3. Add 1/2 cup of water to the mixture. Use your hand to blend the ingredients into a smooth batter. Batter should be thick and should coat the vegetables thoroughly.

4. Add the corn oil to a small wok over medium heat. When oil is hot, but not smoking, drop spoonfuls of thick batter into oil and fry until golden yellow to brown. Drain on paper towels.

Note: You may add 1/2 cup of cashew halves to the batter and mix well before frying. It will enhance the taste.

Instant pakora mix may be purchased and used in place of the dry ingredients.

Makes 25 to 30 pakoras

CALORIES 41; FAT trace; SATURATED FAT trace; PROTEIN 2g.; CARBOHYDRATE 8g.; FIBER 2g.; CHOLESTEROL 0mg.; SODIUM 52mg.

⌁ PAPPADUMS ⌁

There are several varieties of the pappadum (called appalam in South India) which is essentially a wafer made from urad dal. Pappadums can be bought in grocery stores in spiced or unspiced forms. Madras pappadums are usually small and plain. When fried, they don't absorb much oil and are very crisp. Spiced pappadums vary from jeera (cumin) to garlic to black pepper-flavored pappadums. Pappadums can be deep-fried in hot oil and served as appetizers or as accompaniments to a meal. The frying takes just a few seconds. For convenience, pappadums can be broken in half before frying.

10 pappadums
Corn oil for deep-frying

1. Set a large platter, lined with paper towels, beside the stove to drain the pappadums.

2. Heat about 1 to 2 inches oil in a heavy skillet or wok over medium heat.

3. When oil is hot, but not smoking, put one pappadum in skillet. As the oil sizzles the pappadum will expand.

4. Turn pappadum over once and remove in a few seconds with slotted spoon. Note: If pappadum becomes brown, then your cooking oil is too hot. Reduce the temperature to medium or low and then continue the frying.

5. Prepare as many pappadums as you like, but fry only one at a time.

Makes 10 pappadums.

CALORIES 131; FAT 8g.; SATURATED FAT trace; PROTEIN 5g.; CARBOHYDRATE 15g.; FIBER 4g.; CHOLESTEROL 0mg.; SODIUM 57mg.

Variation: To make pappadum without deep-frying:

Place one pappadum in the microwave. Cook on high heat for 30 seconds to 1 minute depending on power of microwave.

You may also cook pappadum, lightly brushed with oil, in a toaster oven or regular oven for 40 seconds to a minute depending on the temperature of your oven.

Nutritional analysis, prepared without added fat:
CALORIES 86; FAT 1g.; SATURATED FAT trace; PROTEIN 5g.; CARBOHYDRATE 15g.; FIBER 4g.; CHOLESTEROL 0mg.; SODIUM 57mg.

᭙ SAMOSAS ᭙

Samosas are crispy savories stuffed with vegetables or meat that can be served warm as an appetizer or as a snack with any type of chutney.

1 package of 10 flour tortillas (6-to 7-inch)
1 recipe Potato Masala (page 265) or Tuna Masala (page 58)
1 cup corn oil for frying

1. Bring tortillas to room temperature before using so they will be softer and easy to fold.

2. Lightly moisten one side of the tortilla with warm water.

3. Cut tortillas into quarters.

4. Take each quartered tortilla and fold it into a cone shape by bringing the two ends of tortilla together. In other words, take one quarter and make a triangular pocket by folding diagonally.

5. Take about a teaspoonful of masala and stuff into a cone, being careful not to overfill.

6. Moisten the edges of tortilla cone and fold down to seal tightly into a triangular shape.

7. Heat the oil in a small wok over medium heat. When the oil is hot, but not smoking, place one filled samosa into oil and deep-fry over medium heat to golden brown.

8. Set the fried samosas on paper towels to drain excess oil.

Make about 40 samosas

Variations: Instead of deep-frying, brush each folded samosa on both sides with corn or canola oil or use cooking oil spray and broil for about 5 minutes on each side.

Samosas may also be prepared by using egg roll wrappers instead of flour tortillas.

The pastry for samosas can also be prepared from scratch according to the following recipe:

1 cup all-purpose flour
1 tablespoon butter
1/4 teaspoon salt

1. Mix together all the above ingredients with fingers, adding only enough water to form a soft dough. Knead it well to make smooth dough.

2. Allow the dough to settle for 1 hour at room temperature before filling with mixture.

3. Divide the dough equally into about 10 smooth balls. Roll each ball evenly with a rolling pin into a circular shape as far as it can spread (about 4 inches in diameter).

4. Place a small spoonful of filling into the middle of circle pastry. Lightly moisten the edge of circle with water. Fold in half and seal the edge tightly with the tip of a fork before frying.

5. Frying can be avoided completely by using frozen crescent dinner rolls as a covering for the potato filling and baking them.

Nutritional analysis per samosa using flour tortillas and Tuna Masala filling:
CALORIES 175; FAT 8g.; SATURATED FAT 2g.; PROTEIN 5g.; CARBOHYDRATE 20g.; FIBER 1g.; CHOLESTEROL 3mg.; SODIUM 259mg.

⌒STUFFED MUSHROOMS⌒

Mushrooms baked with spinach or tuna filling.

12 mushroom caps
Spinach Poriyal (page 272) or Tuna Masala (page 58)
2 tablespoons butter

1. Preheat oven to 350 degrees. Wash and dry mushrooms. Remove stems and hollow out mushroom pulp to form cups.

2. Fill mushroom cups with Spinach Poriyal or Tuna Masala.

3. Dot filled mushrooms with butter and bake, uncovered (or lightly tented) on a greased cooking sheet, for 15 to 20 minutes.

Note: Grated Parmesan cheese, if desired, may be sprinkled over tops of mushrooms.

Makes 12 stuffed mushrooms

Nutritional analysis of one mushroom stuffed with Tuna Masala:
CALORIES 26; FAT 2g.; SATURATED FAT 1g.; PROTEIN 1g.; CARBOHYDRATE 2g.; FIBER trace; CHOLESTEROL 5mg.; SODIUM 21mg.

⌣ Tuna Masala ⌣

Cooked with onions, tomatoes, and garlic with mild seasonings, Tuna Masala is an innovative and flavorful side dish which can be served over cocktail rye bread or with crackers as an appetizer. It can also be used to make delicious Tuna Balls or as a filler for Samosas.

2 tablespoons corn oil
3 to 4 very small pieces cinnamon stick
1/4 teaspoon fennel seeds
1/2 teaspoon cumin seeds
2 teaspoons urad dal
1 cup chopped yellow onions
1/4 cup finely chopped tomato
1/4 cup minced garlic (less, if desired)
1 green chili pepper, chopped (more, if desired)
1/4 teaspoon turmeric powder
2 teaspoons curry powder
1/4 cup tomato sauce
1 can (12 ounces) tuna in oil
1/4 cup plain bread crumbs
1/2 teaspoon salt
1/4 cup minced coriander

1. Heat corn oil in an iron skillet over medium heat. When oil is hot, but not smoking, add cinnamon stick, fennel seeds, cumin, and urad dal.

2. When urad dal is golden, add the onions, tomato, garlic, and green chili pepper. Cook for 1 minute. Add turmeric, curry powder, and tomato sauce. Mix and cook for another minute.

3. Drain oil from tuna can.

4. Add tuna and mix thoroughly. Add bread crumbs and salt and blend well with other ingredients and cook for another 7 to 10 minutes over medium heat.

5. Add coriander and mix well.

Optional step: A slight amount of corn oil (I to 2 teaspoons) may be added to skillet while cooking tuna masala over low heat for a few extra minutes to add crispiness.

Note: You may use tuna packed in water instead of tuna in oil.

Serves 6

CALORIES 145; FAT 7g.; SATURATED FAT 1g.; PROTEIN 9g.; CARBOHYDRATE 13g.; FIBER 3g.; CHOLESTEROL 4mg.; SODIUM 362mg.

⌇TUNA BALLS⌇

Fried savories made with Tuna Masala, Tuna Balls are a delicious appetizer with beer or any beverage. Tuna Balls also make a unique side dish.

2 tablespoons all-purpose flour
3 teaspoons cumin powder
1/4 teaspoon garam masala powder (optional)
1/4 cup plain bread crumbs
1 recipe Tuna Masala (page 58)
1 cup corn oil for frying

1. Add all-purpose flour, cumin powder, garam masala, and plain bread crumbs to the cold tuna masala.

2. Mix the above ingredients together with hand or with a spoon. Add sufficient bread crumbs to form a firm ball. You may need to add more bread crumbs if the tuna mixture is not firm.

3. Form the tuna mixture into small balls (about 1 inch in diameter). Heat 2 inches of corn oil in a heavy skillet over medium heat. Deep-fry 2 to 4 balls at a time until golden brown on all sides (about 2 minutes).

4. Drain on paper towels and serve either warm or cold.

Reheat in toaster oven before serving.

Makes about 24 tuna balls

CALORIES 104; FAT 7g.; SATURATED FAT 1g.; PROTEIN 5g.; CARBOHYDRATE 6g.; FIBER 1g.; CHOLESTEROL 3mg.; SODIUM 132mg.

⌣:VEGETABLE CUTLETS:⌣

Vegetable cutlets are made from a variety of colorful, mildly seasoned vegetables that are pleasing to the palate. Serve vegetable cutlets plain or with Tomato Chutney as an appetizer or snack.

For Filling:
2 to 3 Idaho potatoes (enough for 2 cups mashed)
1 1/2 teaspoons salt
1/4 teaspoon turmeric powder
1 tablespoon butter
1 tablespoon corn oil
4 to 6 curry leaves, chopped
1/2 teaspoon cumin seeds
1 cup chopped onion
2 tablespoons minced fresh ginger root
1 green chili pepper, finely chopped
1/2 cup peeled and shredded carrots
1/4 cup peeled and shredded fresh beets
1/2 cup chopped coriander
1/4 cup frozen green peas
1/4 cup crushed peanuts
1/4 cup freshly ground or unsweetened powdered coconut
1/4 teaspoon garam masala powder

For Coating:
1/2 cup plain bread crumbs
1/2 cup 100% grated Parmesan cheese
2 eggs
1/4 teaspoon turmeric powder
4 to 6 tablespoons corn oil

1. Cut potatoes in half and place in pressure cooker with 1/2 teaspoon salt, turmeric powder, and enough water to cover potatoes. Cook until tender, about 10 minutes. Potatoes may also be cooked in a regular, covered kettle. When potatoes are tender, mash and set aside.

2. Place butter and oil in an iron skillet over medium heat. When oil is hot, but not smoking, immediately add curry leaves and cumin seeds. Add onion, ginger, and green chili. Stir-fry for about a minute.

3. Add carrots and beets and stir well for 1 minute. Add mashed potatoes, coriander, and green peas. Stir well. Cook mixture over medium heat.

4. Add peanuts, coconut, garam masala powder, and 1 teaspoon salt to the vegetables. Mix the seasonings well with potatoes and vegetables and cook over medium/low heat. Remove from heat and allow the vegetable mixture to cool.

5. Form vegetable mixture (about 1/4 cup each) into small oval patties.

6. For coating: Mix bread crumbs with cheese on a plate. Set it aside.

7. Beat eggs in a bowl with turmeric powder. Set aside.

8. Dip vegetable patties into egg batter and coat the patties with bread crumb mixture. Set aside the coated vegetable patties on a platter.

9. Place oil in an iron skillet over medium heat. When oil is hot, but not smoking, cook the vegetable patties until golden brown and crisp.

Makes 12 cutlets

CALORIES 161; FAT 11g.; SATURATED FAT 3g.; PROTEIN 5g.; CARBOHYDRATE 12g.; FIBER 2g.; CHOLESTEROL 37mg.; SODIUM 393mg.

Variation:
If you do not wish to use egg batter, coat the vegetable patties in the bread crumbs and Parmesan mixture, or in a simple corn or all-purpose flour batter coating, before browning in skillet.

Soups and Rasam

✌BEET SOUP✌

A thin dal-based soup with beets and delicate seasonings, Beet Soup is a great option as a first course or as part of a light lunch.

1/4 cup toor dal
1/2 teaspoon turmeric powder
2 tablespoon corn oil
2 to 3 small pieces cinnamon stick
1/2 bay leaf
4 to 6 curry leaves (optional)
1/4 teaspoon fennel seeds
1/4 teaspoon cumin seeds
1/4 cup onion, cut lengthwise
1/2 cup chopped tomatoes
1/2 green chili pepper, finely chopped (more, if desired)
1/4 cup peeled and thinly sliced beets
1/2 cup tomato sauce
1 teaspoon salt
1/2 teaspoon cardamom powder
1/2 teaspoon cumin powder
1/4 cup finely chopped fresh coriander

1. Boil 3 cups of water in a tall saucepan. Add toor dal and 1/4 teaspoon turmeric powder. Reduce heat to medium and cook, uncovered, for about 30 minutes until dal becomes creamy. Set aside.

2. Place corn oil in tall saucepan and heat over medium heat. When oil is hot, but not smoking, add cinnamon stick, bay leaf, curry leaves, fennel, and cumin seeds. Stir and heat until seeds are golden brown (about 30 seconds).

3. Add onion, tomato, and green chili. Stir and cook for a few minutes. Add sliced beets and remaining 1/4 teaspoon turmeric powder. Stir well to blend the seasonings with beets.

4. Add tomato sauce and cook over medium heat for another 1 to 2 minutes.

5. Add the dal mixture and additional 5 cups of warm water to the saucepan.

6. Add salt, cardamom, and cumin powder to saucepan. Stir well. Cook, uncovered, over medium heat until mixture begins to boil.

7. Add coriander and let simmer for a few minutes until beets are tender.

8. Remove from heat. Serve immediately or cover and briefly reheat before serving.

Serves 6

CALORIES 99; FAT 5g.; SATURATED FAT 1g.; PROTEIN 3g.; CARBOHYDRATE 12g.; FIBER 4g.; CHOLESTEROL 0mg.; SODIUM 490mg.

Variation: To make **Carrot Soup**, add 1/4 cup peeled and thinly sliced carrots instead of beets and follow the above recipe.

⌣ CAULIFLOWER SOUP ⌣

Thin dal-based soup with cauliflower and aromatic seasonings.

1/4 cup toor dal
1/2 teaspoon turmeric powder
2 tablespoons corn oil
2 to 3 small pieces cinnamon stick
1/2 bay leaf
4 to 6 curry leaves (optional)
1/4 teaspoon fennel seeds
1/4 teaspoon cumin seeds
1/4 cup onion, cut lengthwise
1/2 cup chopped tomatoes
1/2 green chili pepper, finely chopped (more if desired)
1/2 cup tomato sauce
1 teaspoon salt
1/2 teaspoon cardamom powder
1/2 teaspoon cumin powder
1 cup cauliflower, in 1-inch florets
1/4 cup finely chopped fresh coriander

1. Boil 3 cups of water in a tall saucepan. Add toor dal and 1/4 teaspoon turmeric powder. Reduce heat to medium and cook, uncovered, for about 30 minutes until dal becomes creamy. Set aside.

2. Place corn oil in tall saucepan and heat over medium heat. When oil is hot, but not smoking, add cinnamon stick, bay leaf, curry leaves, fennel, and cumin seeds. Stir quickly. Cover and heat until seeds are golden brown (about 30 seconds).

3. Add onion, tomato, and green chili. Stir. Add remaining 1/4 teaspoon turmeric powder. Stir well and cook, uncovered, until onions are tender.

4. Add tomato sauce and cook over medium heat for another 2 to 3 minutes. Stir until the ingredients in the saucepan reach a creamy consistency.

5. Add the dal mixture and additional 5 cups of warm water to the saucepan.

6. Add salt, cardamom, and cumin powder to saucepan. Stir well. Cook, uncovered, over medium heat until mixture begins to boil.

7. Add cauliflower and cook, uncovered, until just tender (about 2 minutes). Be careful not to overcook cauliflower.

8. Add coriander and let simmer for a few minutes with cauliflower.

9. Remove from heat. Serve immediately or cover and briefly reheat before serving.

Serves 6

CALORIES 100; FAT 5g.; SATURATED FAT 1g.; PROTEIN 3g.; CARBOHYDRATE 12g.; FIBER 3g.; CHOLESTEROL 0mg.; SODIUM 490mg.

Variation: To make plain **Tomato Soup**, skip Step 7 in the above recipe. Add 3/4 cup chopped tomatoes instead of 1/2 cup chopped tomatoes.

ᴄCHETTINAD CHICKEN SOUP:ᴠ

A flavorful chicken soup with ginger, garlic and other herbs, this dish is a perfect starter at dinner or over rice as a main course. It's also a great remedy for colds!

1/4 cup toor dal
3/4 teaspoon turmeric powder
4 cloves garlic
2 tablespoons corn oil
1 bay leaf, broken
2 small pieces cinnamon stick
2 to 4 curry leaves
1/2 teaspoon cumin seeds
1/4 teaspoon fennel seeds
1/2 cup onion, cut lengthwise
1/4 cup chopped tomatoes
1 teaspoon minced fresh ginger root
1/2 green chili pepper, chopped
1 cup chopped skinless chicken pieces
1/2 teaspoon curry powder
1/2 teaspoon salt (more, if desired)
1/4 cup chopped fresh coriander
1/2 teaspoon black pepper and cumin powder

1. Boil 3 cups of water in a tall saucepan. Add toor dal and 1/4 teaspoon turmeric powder. Reduce heat to medium and cook, uncovered, for about 30 minutes until dal becomes creamy. Set aside.

2. Peel 3 cloves garlic and cut into halves or quarters.

3. Heat corn oil in a tall saucepan over medium heat. When oil is hot, but not smoking, add bay leaf, cinnamon stick, curry leaves, cumin, and fennel. Immediately add onions, garlic pieces, tomato, ginger, and green chili. Stir for a few seconds until onions are tender.

4. Add chicken and stir-fry with onions over medium heat. Add remaining 1/2 teaspoon turmeric powder and curry powder. Stir well and cook, uncovered, for 3 to 5 minutes. Add salt.

5. Add toor dal mixture and 4 cups of warm water to chicken.

6. Add coriander and allow the soup to come to a boil. Crush the remaining 1 garlic clove and add along with the black pepper and cumin powder. Stir well.

7. After soup has come to a boil, reduce heat and allow to simmer until the chicken is tender. Stir frequently. If soup thickens, add a cup or two of water to thin it. When chicken is cooked, remove from heat.

Serves 6

CALORIES 140; FAT 6g.; SATURATED FAT 1g.; PROTEIN 12g.; CARBOHYDRATE 12g.; FIBER 3g.; CHOLESTEROL 22mg.; SODIUM 210mg.

⚭ Lemon Rasam ⚭

A thin peppery soup with lemon, Lemon Rasam is delightful when served over plain rice. Many claim it to be an effective cold remedy.

1/4 cup toor dal
1/2 teaspoon turmeric powder
1/4 cup chopped tomatoes
1/4 teaspoon minced fresh ginger root
1/2 green chili, finely chopped
1/4 cup chopped fresh coriander
1 teaspoon rasam powder
1/2 teaspoon salt (more, if desired)
1 teaspoon corn oil
1/4 teaspoon asafoetida
2 to 4 curry leaves
1 dried red pepper
1 teaspoon mustard seeds
2 tablespoons fresh lemon juice

1. Boil 3 cups of water in a tall saucepan. Add toor dal and 1/4 teaspoon turmeric powder. Reduce heat to medium and cook, uncovered, for about 30 minutes until dal becomes creamy. Set aside.

2. Transfer creamy dal to a saucepan over medium heat with 3 cups of warm water and add remaining 1/4 teaspoon turmeric powder. Let it boil.

3. Add tomatoes and let cook for 2 to 4 minutes. Cooked tomatoes will blend well with creamy dal.

4. Add ginger, green chili, and coriander to the dal mixture. Let simmer for about 2 minutes.

5. Add rasam powder and salt and let them blend with the seasonings for another minute or two.

⚜ *Healthy South Indian Cooking*

6. Heat oil in a small butter warmer. When oil is hot, but not smoking, add asafoetida, curry leaves, red pepper, and mustard seeds. When mustard seeds burst add to the above rasam mixture. Let rasam mixture come to a boil.

7. Immediately remove from heat. Add the lemon juice and stir well.

Serves 6

CALORIES 54; FAT 1g.; SATURATED FAT trace; PROTEIN 3g.; CARBOHYDRATE 9g.; FIBER 2g.; CHOLESTEROL 0mg.; SODIUM 181mg.

Variation: Another traditional rasam is the **Paruppu Rasam** (Dal Rasam) which can be made using the above recipe but omitting step 7.

ᔉ PINEAPPLE RASAM ᔊ

A thin peppery soup with the sweetness of pineapple, this rasam can be
served hot as a first course, or over rice at dinner.

1/4 cup chopped tomatoes
1/4 teaspoon minced fresh ginger root
1/2 teaspoon rasam powder
1/4 teaspoon black pepper and cumin powder
1/4 cup tomato sauce
1/2 teaspoon salt (more, if desired)
1/4 cup chopped fresh coriander
1 cup freshly cut small pineapple chunks

Garnish:
1/2 teaspoon ghee
1 dried red pepper
2 to 4 curry leaves
1/2 teaspoon mustard seeds
1/2 teaspoon cumin seeds

1. Boil 4 cups of water. Add tomato, and let it simmer, uncovered, in
water for 5 minutes.

2. Add ginger. Simmer over medium heat for another 2 to 3 minutes.

3. Stir rasam powder and black pepper and cumin powder into boiling
water.

4. Add tomato sauce, salt, and coriander. Stir well. Let all the ingredients
simmer for 5 to 6 minutes.

5. Heat ghee in a butter warmer. When ghee is hot, but not smoking, add
all of the garnish items. When mustard seeds pop, pour ingredients into
rasam mixture.

ᔉ   *Healthy South Indian Cooking*

6. Add pineapple chunks to the rasam mixture and let them simmer for a few minutes before serving.

Serves 4

CALORIES 28; FAT trace; SATURATED FAT trace; PROTEIN 1g.; CARBOHYDRATE 7g.; FIBER 1g.; CHOLESTEROL 0mg.; SODIUM 361mg.

◝ Shrimp Soup ◝

This light, easy-to-make soup with shrimp and carefully blended seasonings will warm you up on cold winter nights!

1/2 cup coarsely chopped tomatoes
1/4 cup tomato sauce
1/4 teaspoon black pepper and cumin powder
1/2 teaspoon rasam powder
1/4 teaspoon salt (more, if desired)
3 tablespoons chopped green onion tops, plus additional for garnish
3 tablespoons chopped coriander, plus additional for garnish
1/4 teaspoon minced fresh ginger root
1 clove garlic, crushed
1/2 pound fresh raw shrimp (shelled and cleaned), cut in half

1. Boil 6 cups of water. Add tomato and cook, uncovered, until tender.

2. Add tomato sauce, cumin and black pepper powder, rasam powder, and
salt. Stir well and let it simmer over medium-low heat.

3. Add green onion tops, coriander, ginger, and garlic. Let it cook over
medium heat for 2 to 3 minutes.

4. When the mixture begins to boil, add shrimp. Let shrimp cook over
medium heat until they turn pink (2 to 3 minutes).

5. Freshen the soup by garnishing with additional chopped green onion
tops and chopped coriander.

Serves 6

CALORIES 38; FAT trace; SATURATED FAT trace; PROTEIN 7g.; CARBOHYDRATE
58g.; FIBER trace; CHOLESTEROL 58 mg.; SODIUM 219 mg.

~:TOMATO RASAM:~

A thin delicious traditional soup with garlic and cumin, Rasam is thought to be an excellent remedy for colds and sore throats. Serve hot as a first course or over plain rice as a main course.

1 cup chopped tomatoes
1/4 teaspoon minced fresh ginger root
1/4 cup chopped fresh coriander
1 teaspoon rasam powder
1/4 teaspoon black pepper and cumin powder
1/4 cup tomato sauce
2 cloves garlic, crushed
1/2 teaspoon salt (more, if desired)

1. Boil 4 cups of water. Add tomato and let it simmer, uncovered, for 5 minutes.

2. Add ginger and coriander. Simmer over medium heat for another 2 to 3 minutes.

3. Stir rasam powder and black pepper and cumin powder into boiling water.

4. Add tomato sauce. When the mixture begins to boil, add the garlic and salt and stir well. Let all the ingredients simmer for 5 to 6 minutes.

Serves 6

Per 1/2 cup portion:
CALORIES 16; FAT trace; SATURATED FAT trace; PROTEIN 1g.; CARBOHYDRATE 3g.; FIBER 1g.; CHOLESTEROL 0mg.; SODIUM 245mg.

Variation: For enhanced flavor, heat 1 teaspoon oil in a small saucepan. When oil is hot, but not smoking, add 1 dried red pepper, 1/4 teaspoon asafoetida, 2 to 4 curry leaves, 1 teaspoon mustard seeds and 1 teaspoon urad dal. When mustard seeds pop and urad turns golden, add the seasonings to the above mixture. Let rasam simmer for a couple of minutes with the seasonings.

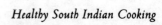

Breads

◁ Adai ▷

Adais are pancakes made with lentils, rice, and spices that can be served with any type of chutney or kosamalli, usually for breakfast or for tea. Adai batter does not require fermentation.

1/4 cup urad dal
1/4 cup yellow split peas
1/4 cup toor dal
1/4 cup moong dal
1 cup extra long-grain rice
3 red chili peppers
1 teaspoon cumin seeds
1 teaspoon fennel seeds
1/4 cup ground fresh coconut
1/2 teaspoon asafoetida powder
1/2 teaspoon turmeric powder
1 teaspoon salt
1 cup chopped onion
1/4 cup chopped fresh coriander

1. Soak the urad dal, split peas, toor dal, moong dal, and rice with red pepper and cumin for 3 hours. Grind the chili, cumin, and fennel with the soaked ingredients and about 2 cups of water to a coarse and thick consistency in the blender.

2. Add fresh coconut, asafoetida, turmeric, salt, onion, and coriander to the ground mixture.

3. Mix all the ingredients well. Now the batter is ready for making adai.

4. Spray the iron skillet with the nonstick cooking oil spray.

5. Heat iron skillet over medium heat. Spread about 1/3 cup of batter over the skillet in a circular pattern (like a thick pancake). Spread a small amount of oil (1/2 teaspoon) around each adai. Cook until adai becomes

golden brown and crunchy. With a stainless steel spatula turn it over and cook the other side. When adai is crunchy and golden brown on both sides take it out of skillet and serve hot.

Makes about 10 adais

CALORIES 160; FAT 1g.; SATURATED FAT 1g.; PROTEIN 8g.; CARBOHYDRATE 31g.; FIBER 5g.; CHOLESTEROL 0mg.; SODIUM 235mg.

～·Chappati·～

Thin, flat wheat breads, chappatis are a staple of Indian cooking. They can be served with any kind of vegetable, kurma, or chutney.

1 cup wheat flour
1/4 teaspoon salt
1/4 teaspoon oil

1. Place the flour in a large mixing bowl. Add salt and oil. Mix well.

2. Gradually add approximately 1/4 cup warm water to flour mixture, all the while working the dough with the hands. Knead with the hand or with a food processor to make dough elastic and pliable.

3. Moisten the palms of the hands with a small amount of corn oil and work with dough to make it soft. Shape the dough into 6 small balls.

4. Dust each of the balls of dough with flour and on a floured board roll out evenly into a thin, flat, circular shape, 4 to 5 inches in diameter. At this point, chappatis are ready for cooking.

(OR)
For more fluffy, flaky chappatis: Brush half of the rolled, circular chappati lightly with corn oil. Fold dough over oiled half. Next, brush the other half of the folded dough lightly with oil. Again, fold over oiled half. The dough should now be roughly triangular in shape. Dust well with additional chappati flour and roll out again evenly into a thin, flat, fanlike shape.

5. For cooking, place chappatis, one at a time, in a nonstick skillet or iron skillet over medium heat. When the skillet is hot, add chappati and cook both sides until slightly brown. Press the edge of the chappati lightly with spatula until it puffs up. Remove chappati from skillet and brush lightly with butter or margarine, if desired. Serve hot.
Makes 6 chappatis

CALORIES 69; FAT 1g.; SATURATED FAT trace; PROTEIN 3g.; CARBOHYDRATE 15g.; FIBER 2g.; CHOLESTEROL 0mg.; SODIUM 90mg.

‍⁀CRACKED WHEAT UPPUMA‍⁀

Cracked wheat with shredded carrots and cashews, this uppuma can be served for breakfast or tea with any type of chutney or sambhar.

2 tablespoons corn oil
4 to 6 curry leaves
1 dried red chili pepper
1 teaspoon black mustard seeds
2 teaspoons urad dal
1 cup cracked wheat
1 teaspoon salt
1 green chili, chopped (optional)
1/4 cup shredded carrots
1/4 cup freshly ground coconut or unsweetened powdered coconut

1. Place corn oil in a skillet over medium heat. When oil is hot, but not smoking, add curry leaves, red chili pepper, mustard seeds, and urad dal. Wait for mustard seeds to pop and urad to turn golden.

2. Add cracked wheat and roast, uncovered, over medium heat for a few minutes.

3. Add salt and 4 cups of warm water. Blend carefully with ingredients in the skillet.

4. Add green chili and carrots. Stir and cook briefly over low heat, covered, until water evaporates.

5. Stir in coconut and mix well. Serve warm.

Serves 4

CALORIES 305; FAT 14g.; SATURATED FAT 3g.; PROTEIN 10g.; CARBOHYDRATE 40g.; FIBER 8g.; CHOLESTEROL 0mg.; SODIUM 541mg.

~:Dosai:~

Dosai, a thin, unsweetened pancake made of rice and urad dal, is a delicious breakfast item that is also served for afternoon tea or for a light evening meal. Unique to South India, dosai can be made plain or as onion dosai or masal dosai. Serve any variety hot with chutney or sambhar.

The batter for dosai needs fermentation. Grind the batter for the dosai a day before you intend to prepare dosai in order for fermentation to take place. After you make the batter, you must wait 6 to 8 hours for fermentation to occur.

You may make a few dosais at a time. Save the remaining batter in the refrigerator for making dosais at a later time. The batter can be kept for several days in the refrigerator, but do not freeze.

There are 4 steps to making dosai:
1. Soaking the ingredients for about 6 hours.
2. Grinding for less than 15 minutes.
3. Fermenting for 6 to 8 hours.
4. Cooking dosai (only 3 minutes at most).

2 cups raw extra long-grain rice
1/3 cup urad dal
1 teaspoon fenugreek seeds
1/2 cup cooked plain rice
1 teaspoon salt

1. Place raw rice, urad dal, and fenugreek in enough warm water to cover generously. Soak at room temperature for about 6 hours.

2. Drain water and place rice and dal mixture in an electric blender. Add about 1 1/2 cups of water to facilitate the grinding process.

3. Grind dal mixture on high power for several minutes. Add cooked rice a little at a time to the above mixture, as it is being ground. Cooked rice is added to improve the texture of the batter. Grind to a fine paste.

4. Pour the creamy fine batter into a tall mixing bowl. Add the salt and mix well with the hand. It is essential to use the hand for mixing, and not a spoon, because the warmth of the hand initiates the fermentation process.

5. Cover bowl with a plate and place it overnight in a warm place in the kitchen. Do not use direct heat. The rice batter will begin to ferment and will double in quantity. Be certain that the bowl you are using will allow the batter to double its quantity.

Note: Sometimes, because of cold weather, the batter will not ferment. You may place the bowl in a warmed oven. Just heat oven to 350 degrees for 10 minutes and then turn off the oven. Wait 10 to 15 minutes, then place the bowl with batter, still covered, in the oven.

6. The next morning the fermented batter will be frothy. Stir the batter with a large spoon for a few minutes and set aside.

Note: Depending upon the temperature and humidity, the batter might ferment in a shorter time and may overflow from the mixing bowl. This will still result in good dosais. Discard the overflow (it cleans up easily) and work with the batter in the bowl. Now you are ready to make dosai.

To Make Plain Dosai

1. Place about 1/2 cup of batter into the center of a hot, nonstick skillet.

2. Spread the batter by moving the batter spoon in concentric circles, starting at the inside of the circle and working towards the outside. The purpose of this step is to spread out the batter thinly and evenly.

3. Cover and cook over medium heat for 1 to 2 minutes. When tiny bubbles appear on the dosai in skillet place about 1/2 to 1 teaspoon corn oil around dosai if added crispiness is desired. Otherwise make plain, soft dosai without oil. To make soft, plain dosai, it is necessary to cook only one side.

4. Lift dosai with a spatula and turn over in skillet if both sides of dosai are to be cooked. After both sides are cooked evenly, transfer dosai to a serving plate.

Often dosai is served folded in a semicircular shape.

Makes 16 dosais

Nutritional analysis of dosai cooked without additional oil:
CALORIES 292; FAT 1g.; SATURATED FAT trace; PROTEIN 8g.; CARBOHYDRATE 62g.; FIBER 3g.; CHOLESTEROL 0mg.; SODIUM 361mg.

Nutritional analysis of Crispy Dosai:
CALORIES 332; FAT 5g.; SATURATED FAT 5g.; PROTEIN 8g.; CARBOHYDRATE 62g.; FIBER 3g.; CHOLESTEROL 0mg.; SODIUM 361mg.

To Make Onion Dosai
Following Step 2 as stated above, add about 1 teaspoon finely chopped onions over the batter spread in the skillet. Follow the remaining steps as for crispy dosai.

Makes 16 dosais

CALORIES 333; FAT 5g.; SATURATED FAT 1g.; PROTEIN 8g.; CARBOHYDRATE 63g.; FIBER 3g.; CHOLESTEROL 0mg.; SODIUM 361mg.

To Make Masala Dosai

This dosai is stuffed with coconut chutney and potato masala.

1 recipe Coconut Chutney (page 103)
1 recipe Potato Masala (page 265)
1/4 to 1/2 teaspoon butter or margarine, melted

1. Make plain dosai. With a spoon, spread coconut chutney evenly over top side of dosai. Place 1 to 2 tablespoons of potato masala over coconut chutney, on one half of dosai only. Fold the dosai up over the potato mixture and pat down with spatula. The dosai should now have a semicircular shape.

2. Lightly brush both halves of dosai with melted butter and brown evenly one side at a time until desired crispness is reached.

3. Remove dosai to serving platter as you repeat the same procedure with other dosai. Be certain to wipe all butter from skillet with a paper towel before you start making the next dosai, otherwise the batter will not spread evenly in the skillet.

Makes 16 dosais

CALORIES 477; FAT 13g.; SATURATED FAT 5g.; PROTEIN 11g.; CARBOHYDRATE 79g.; FIBER 6g.; CHOLESTEROL 0mg.; SODIUM 968mg.

⌣IDIYAPPAM⌣

This is a delicate dish made from rice sticks, onions, and chili peppers. Serve idiyappam with sambhar, chutney, or kosamalli as a breakfast item or for a light supper.

1 pound thin rice sticks
2 teaspoons salt
4 tablespoons plus 1/2 teaspoon corn oil
5 to 6 curry leaves
3 teaspoons black mustard seeds
3 teaspoons urad dal
2 onions, chopped
2 green chili peppers, chopped
1/4 cup low-fat buttermilk
1/4 cup chopped fresh coriander

1. Remove rice sticks from package and break into small pieces. Set aside.

2. Boil 6 to 8 cups of water in a large saucepan.

3. When water is boiling vigorously, add salt, 1/2 teaspoon corn oil, and rice sticks. Boil, uncovered, for about 5 minutes. Do not overcook. (Oil is added to the boiling water to prevent rice sticks from sticking together.)

4. When noodles are tender, drain thoroughly in a colander. Set aside.

5. Place remaining 4 tablespoons corn oil in a largeskillet and heat over medium heat. When oil is hot, but not smoking, add curry leaves, mustard seeds, and urad dal. Cover and cook until mustard seeds pop and urad dal is golden brown, about 30 seconds.

6. Add onions and chilies to skillet. Stir-fry for few minutes.

7. Add rice sticks from the colander to ingredients in skillet. Mix rice sticks with onions and chilies. Reduce heat to low while mixing well.

⚘ *Healthy South Indian Cooking*

8. Add buttermilk to moisten noodles slightly. Stir delicately and add more salt, if desired.

9. Add coriander and stir.

Serves 6

CALORIES 526; FAT 11g.; SATURATED FAT 1g.; PROTEIN 2g.; CARBOHYDRATE 104g.; FIBER 2g.; CHOLESTEROL trace; SODIUM 881mg.

⌒IDLI:~
(TRADITIONAL)

An idli is a light, steamed rice-cake. To make idli you need an idli cooker, which is available in Indian stores. Plan to soak, grind, and ferment the batter a day in advance.

Extensive testing has shown us that the use of a parboiled rice, such as Uncle Ben's, along with extra long-grain rice, most closely approximates the specialty rices used in South India for making traditional idlis.

1 cup Uncle Ben's Original Enriched Parboiled Long-Grain Rice
5 cups extra long-grain white rice
1 1/2 cups urad dal
1 cup cooked rice
2 teaspoons salt

1. Soaking: You will need 3 separate bowls for soaking. Soaking takes about 6 hours or overnight. Soak the Uncle Ben's rice in 4 cups of boiling water. Cover and set aside. Soak extra long-grain rice in enough warm water to cover. Cover and set aside. Soak the urad dal in warm water to cover. Cover and set aside.

2. Grinding:
▪ Add drained Uncle Ben's rice to blender with enough water to facilitate grinding (about 1 1/2 cups). Grind to a coarse cornmeal-like texture. Transfer ground Uncle Ben's rice to a tall container.

▪ Drain water and grind long-grain rice, a little at a time, with just enough water to cover rice, which will facilitate the grinding process. Grind to a creamy, coarse cornmeal-like consistency. Add to the above tall container.

▪ Drain water from soaked urad dal and place urad dal in blender. Add just enough water about (1 1/2 cups) to facilitate grinding. Grind to a fine smooth paste. Transfer ground dal to the above tall container.

⚘ *Healthy South Indian Cooking*

3. When all the above three ground mixtures are together in the tall container, add salt. With your hand, mix the batters and the salt thoroughly. It is important to use your hand, and not a spoon, because the warmth from the hand will initiate or start the fermentation process of the batter.

4. Cover the bowl and set aside overnight. Do not use direct heat.

Note: Sometimes, because of cold weather, the batter may not readily ferment. To encourage the batter to ferment, place the tall container in a warmed oven. Just heat oven to 350 degrees for 10 minutes and then turn off the oven. After a 10 to 15 minute wait, the bowl with batter can be placed, still covered, in the oven.

5. The following morning or about 6 hours later depending upon the outside temperature and humidity, you will notice that the batter has risen in the container and has a foamy appearance. This is fermentation. Sometimes, depending upon the climate, the batter may over ferment and overflow the container. Discard spillage and just use the batter in the container to make idli.

6. It is important not to stir the batter after fermentation. Make idli with an idli cooker as explained below for about 10 minutes.

Idli Cooker: A special type of vessel that is used to make idlis. It has a bottom pan to hold water and a plate insert with 5 to 7 mold sections, similar in appearance to an egg poacher. A wet cloth is draped over idli plate and the batter is poured into each mold over the the steamed cloth. The steamed cloth is necessary to hold the batter from flowing into the water in the bottom vessel. The vessel has a tight cover to steam cook the idlis. Steam cook for 8 to 10 minutes.

Makes about 60 idlis

CALORIES 73; FAT trace; SATURATED FAT trace; PROTEIN 2g.; CARBOHYDRATE 15g.; FIBER 2g.; CHOLESTEROL 0mg.; SODIUM 65mg.

A normal serving is about 4 idlis per person. Unused idlis from the above recipe can be refrigerated and used later. Refrigerated idlis can be warmed in microwave for 1 to 2 minutes before serving. Idlis can be kept in the refrigerator for up to 4 weeks.

Idli from Ready Made Mix: Ready made plain or rava (special cream of wheat) idli mix is available in Indian grocery stores. Follow the instructions on package and enjoy.

◟ POORI ◞

A wheat bread that puffs like a balloon when deep-fried in oil.

1 cup graham (pastry) wheat flour
1 tablespoon cream of wheat
1/2 teaspoon salt
Canola or corn oil for frying

1. Place the first three ingredients in large bowl and mix well by hand.

2. Add approximately 1/3 cup warm water to flour mixture a little at a time. Work ingredients with hand until they form a firm dough without sticking to the fingers.

3. Knead dough well with lightly oiled hand. Pound dough vigorously into bowl several times. (A food processor may also be used to form the dough.)

4. Roll the dough into a long, cord-like shape using the palms of both hands. Break off a small piece of dough from the long shape and form a small, smooth ball, approximately the size of a walnut. If large pooris are desired, the dough should be formed into larger equal size balls.

5. Dab a very small amount of oil on a flat board or work surface. Place ball of dough on oiled surface and roll evenly into a circular shape approximately 3 inches in diameter. After evenly rolling out balls of dough, keep pooris separate by placing them between grease-proof paper or on the top of wax paper.

6. Heat about 2 inches of corn oil in a small wok or electric fry pan until a poori dropped into the oil immediately sizzles and rises to the surface. Fry the pooris one at a time. The poori will puff up only if the oil is hot enough but not smoking. Using a slotted spoon, turn the poori over and fry both sides evenly for 30 to 45 seconds. Lift pooris out from the pan, drain off the excess oil on paper towels, and serve hot.

Makes approximately 15 small pooris

CALORIES 97; FAT 7g.; SATURATED FAT 1g.; PROTEIN 1g.; CARBOHYDRATE 7g.; FIBER trace; CHOLESTEROL 0mg.; SODIUM 71mg.

CREAM OF WHEAT UPPUMA

This is cream of wheat cooked with onions and spices. Serve uppuma with sambhar or chutney.

1 tablespoon corn oil
1 dried red pepper
1 teaspoon black mustard seeds
1 teaspoon urad dal
1/4 cup finely chopped onions
1 cup quick or regular cream of wheat
1/2 teaspoon salt
1/2 teaspoon finely minced fresh ginger
1/4 cup minced fresh coriander
1 teaspoon butter or margarine
2 tablespoons roasted cashew halves (optional)

1. Place corn oil in a skillet over medium heat.

2. When oil is hot, but not smoking, add red pepper, mustard seeds, and urad dal.

3. When urad dal turns golden, add chopped onions and cook for 1 minute. Add cream of wheat and stir for a minute. Add salt and ginger.

4. Add 2 cups of warm water gradually to cream of wheat while stirring.

5. Cover and cook over low heat, stirring frequently for about 2 minutes. Add coriander and butter. Stir well.

6. Add cashews, if desired, and mix well.

Serves 4

CALORIES 213; FAT 5g.; SATURATED FAT 1g.; PROTEIN 5g.; CARBOHYDRATE 35g.; FIBER 2g.; CHOLESTEROL 0mg.; SODIUM 285mg.

Tomatobhath (Tomato Uppuma): Follow the same recipe as above. After adding onions, add 1/4 cup chopped tomatoes and 1/4 teaspoon finely chopped green chilies. Stir well.

CALORIES 448; FAT 13g.; SATURATED FAT 2g.; PROTEIN 11g.; CARBOHYDRATE 72g.; FIBER 5g.; CHOLESTEROL 0mg.; SODIUM 595mg.

Vegetable Uppuma: Follow the same recipe as above. After adding water to cream of wheat, add 4 ounces frozen mixed vegetables and stir (OR) add 1/4 cup of shredded carrots together with 1/4 cup of cooked green peas and stir. Cook and cover over low heat, stirring frequently.

CALORIES 463; FAT 13g.; SATURATED FAT 2g.; PROTEIN 12g.; CARBOHYDRATE 74g.; FIBER 6g.; CHOLESTEROL 0mg.; SODIUM 618mg.

⌁ Soji Uppuma ⌁

Soji is a special type of coarse cream of wheat that has a unique texture and taste when cooked. Soji is available in Indian grocery stores and can be prepared in less than 15 minutes. This dish is wholesome, delicious, and satisfying. Soji can be served for breakfast, tea, or as a light evening meal, with any chutney and sambhar.

1 teaspoon corn oil
4 to 6 curry leaves
1 teaspoon black mustard seeds
1 teaspoon urad dal
1 cup soji
3/4 teaspoon salt
1 teaspoon minced fresh ginger root (optional)
1 teaspoon minced green chili
1/4 cup shredded carrots
1 teaspoon butter
2 tablespoons roasted cashew halves (optional)

1. Boil 2 cups of water in a saucepan. Set aside.

2. In a skillet or wok heat corn oil and butter together over medium heat. When oil is hot, but not smoking, add curry leaves, mustard seeds, and urad dal. Wait for mustard seeds to pop and urad to turn golden.

3. Add soji and salt to skillet and roast with spices over medium/low heat for a minute.

4. Add ginger, green chili, and carrots to soji and mix well over low heat.

5. Slowly add the hot water to soji in skillet and keep stirring often, over low heat, for 2 to 4 minutes. Add butter to soji with vegetables and mix well.

6. Stir cashew halves into soji. Serve warm.

Serves 4

CALORIES 270; FAT 11g.; SATURATED FAT 2g.; PROTEIN 6g.; CARBOHYDRATE 37g.; FIBER 3g.; CHOLESTEROL 3mg.; SODIUM 420mg.

⚘

◆ URAD DAL VADAI ◆

Urad dal vadai, a donut-shaped snack made of lentils, is a unique South Indian food. It is also known as Medhu vadai. Urad dal vadai is commonly served in South India for breakfast and tea. It is delicious served with coconut chutney.

1/2 cup urad dal
2 tablespoons urad flour (optional)
1/4 cup finely chopped onion
1 green chili pepper, finely chopped
1/2 teaspoon salt
1/4 cup chopped fresh coriander
1 cup corn oil for frying

1. Soak urad dal in water to cover for 2 hours.

2. Drain water from urad dal. Transfer soaked urad dal to blender and grind with 1/4 cup of water to facilitate the grinding process. Add urad flour to thicken batter if desired. Caution: Do not make the batter too watery, otherwise the vadai will become oily when fried.

3. Add onion and green chilies to batter and mix well. The quantity of onion and chilies may be adjusted to taste.

4. Add salt and coriander to batter and mix well.

5. Heat oil in a wok. Oil must be hot, but not smoking. Take about 1 1/2 tablespoons of batter in hand. Form into a doughnut shape over a wet cloth (to prevent sticking to hands) and transfer directly to the hot oil. Deep-fry; when one side is cooked, turn with a slotted spoon to the other side until vadai becomes golden brown.

If the above method seems complicated, you may also drop batter by the spoonfuls directly into the oil, as though making dumplings. Fry until golden brown and drain on paper towels.

Makes 12 small vadais

CALORIES 71; FAT 4g.; SATURATED FAT trace; PROTEIN 3g.; CARBOHYDRATE 7g.; FIBER 3g.; CHOLESTEROL 0mg.; SODIUM 94mg.

Variation: Thayir Vadai (vadai soaked in yogurt): First, soak the vadais in hot water for 3 to 5 minutes in a wide-bottomed bowl. Scoop vadais without water to a deep platter. Blend 2 cups of fat-free plain yogurt with 1 tablespoon minced ginger, 1/2 green chili, and 1/2 teaspoon cumin in a blender. Pour the ground mixture over vadais and let them soak in the yogurt mixture for an hour before serving. Garnishing: Fry 1/2 teaspoon mustard seeds, 1/2 teaspoon urad dal with 2 to 4 curry leaves in a teaspoon of oil in a small saucepan and and pour it over thair vadai. Leftover thair vadais can be refrigerated and served at a later time.

Makes 12 thayir vadai

CALORIES 97; FAT 4g.; SATURATED FAT trace; PROTEIN 5g.; CARBOHYDRATE 11g.; FIBER 3g.; CHOLESTEROL 1mg.; SODIUM 125mg.

↬Uthappam↫
(South Indian Pancake)

Uthappam is a thick variety of dosai. Follow the recipe for making dosai batter (soaking, grinding, fermenting) (page 82).

1. Heat nonstick skillet or iron skillet over medium heat. If you are using iron skillet, spray with nonstick cooking spray.

2. Pour 1/2 cup of the batter in the middle of the hot skillet and spread it like a small thick pancake of about 6 inches in diameter.

3. When tiny bubbles appear on uthappam in the skillet place 1/2 to 1 teaspoon corn oil around uthappam.

4. Spread chopped onions over uthappam as it cooks. After about a minute, turn the uthappam to the other side and cook until uthappam becomes golden brown.

Makes 12

Nutritional analysis based on Crispy Dosai with onions recipe:
CALORIES 313; FAT 5g.; SATURATED FAT 1g.; PROTEIN 7g.; CARBOHYDRATE 58g.; FIBER 3g.; CHOLESTEROL 0mg.; SODIUM 361mg.

Variation:
Uthappam can also be topped with other ingredients such as finely chopped tomatoes, chopped coriander, shredded carrots or finely chopped chilies.

Uthappam goes extremely well with any chutney, thuveyal, sambhar, or kulambu.

Chutney

ᴄᴏᴄᴏɴᴜᴛ ᴄʜᴜᴛɴᴇʏ

A condiment-like sauce with fresh coconut, Coconut Chutney is a delicious accompaniment to a number of dishes, including many listed as appetizers and breads in this book. Coconut chutney is one of the outstanding specialties of South Indian cuisine.

1 heaping cup fresh coconut, cut in small chunks (or) 1 heaping cup unsweetened
powdered coconut
3 green chili peppers or 3 dried red chili peppers (more if desired)
2 small slices fresh ginger root
1 tablespoon roasted chickpeas (chana dalia), or dry roasted peanuts
1/2 teaspoon salt (more, if desired)

Grind the above ingredients in blender with 1 cup of hot water to create a smooth paste. Transfer chutney paste from blender to a bowl before serving.

A delicious optional enhancement:
1 tablespoon canola or corn oil
1/4 teaspoon powdered asafoetida
4 curry leaves (optional)
1 whole dried red chili pepper (more, if desired)
1 teaspoon black mustard seeds
1 teaspoon urad dal

Heat oil over medium heat in a butter warmer or in a small saucepan. When oil is hot, but not smoking, add asafoetida, curry leaves, and red pepper. Add mustard seeds and urad dal. Fry until mustard seeds burst and urad dal is golden. Pour over chutney and mix well.
Note: Always keep coconut chutney refrigerated.

Makes 2 1/2 cups

Per Tablespoon:
CALORIES 16; FAT 1g.; SATURATED FAT 1g.; PROTEIN trace; CARBOHYDRATE 1g.;
FIBER trace; CHOLESTEROL 0mg.; SODIUM 49mg.

❧Coconut Thuveyal☙

Thuveyal is a thick variation of chutney. It is a finely ground paste-like accompaniment for various appetizers, breads, and rice dishes. Thuveyal goes particularly well with idli, dosai, yogurt rice, lemon rice, and tamarind rice.

1 tablespoon canola or corn oil
1/2 teaspoon asafoetida powder
4 to 6 curry leaves (optional)
1 teaspoon black mustard seeds
1 teaspoon urad dal
1 heaping cup fresh coconut, cut in small pieces, (or) 1 heaping cup unsweetened powdered coconut
2 tablespoons roasted chickpeas (chana dalia), or dry roasted peanuts
4 dried red chili peppers (more, if desired)
1/4 cup chopped onions
1/4 teaspoon tamarind paste
1/2 teaspoon salt (more, if desired)

1. Heat oil in a skillet over medium heat. When oil is hot, but not smoking, add asafoetida, curry leaves, mustard seeds, and urad dal. Cover and cook over medium heat until mustard seeds burst and urad dal is golden.

2. Add coconut and the remaining ingredients (except salt) to the skillet. Stir-fry for 2 minutes.

3. Grind ingredients in a blender with 1 1/2 cups of hot water and salt for 2 to 3 minutes to create a smooth thick paste.

Makes 2 cups

Per Tablespoon:
CALORIES 27; FAT 2g.; SATURATED FAT 1g.; PROTEIN 1g.; CARBOHYDRATE 2g.; FIBER trace; CHOLESTEROL 0mg.; SODIUM 44mg.

⌁CORIANDER CHUTNEY I⌁

A chutney with sautéed spices, fresh coriander, and ginger.

1 teaspoon corn oil
1 teaspoon asafoetida powder
1/2 teaspoon black mustard seeds
1/2 teaspoon urad dal
3 cups washed and chopped fresh coriander
2 green chili peppers (more, if desired)
2 to 3 small slices fresh ginger root
1/3 cup roasted chickpeas (chana dalia), (or) roasted peanuts
1/4 teaspoon tamarind paste
1/2 teaspoon salt (more, if desired)

1. Place oil in a wok or skillet over medium heat. When oil is hot, but not smoking, add asafoetida, mustard seeds, and urad dal. Cover and fry until mustard seeds pop and urad dal is golden brown.

2. Add coriander, chilies, ginger, and chana. Stir-fry for a few minutes.

3. Transfer all ingredients to a blender. Add tamarind paste and 1 cup hot water (enough water to grind ingredients smoothly).

4. Grind all the ingredients to a smooth consistency. Add salt to taste.

Makes 2 cups

Per Tablespoon:
CALORIES 14; FAT trace.; SATURATED FAT trace; PROTEIN 1g.; CARBOHYDRATE 2g.; FIBER 1g.; CHOLESTEROL 0mg.; SODIUM 35mg.

ᴄᴏʀɪᴀɴᴅᴇʀ ᴄʜᴜᴛɴᴇʏ II

An easy-to-prepare chutney with fresh coriander and coconut.

2 cups washed and chopped fresh coriander
1 to 2 green chili peppers (more, if desired)
1 tablespoon minced fresh ginger root
1/4 cup freshly ground coconut or 1 tablespoon unsweetened powdered coconut
1/3 cup roasted chickpeas (chana dalia), or 1/3 cup dry roasted peanuts
1/4 teaspoon tamarind paste
1 teaspoon salt

1. Place all the above ingredients, except salt, in a blender.

2. Add 1 cup of hot water to grind ingredients to a smooth paste.

3. Add salt to taste and mix well.

Makes 2 cups

Per Tablespoon:
CALORIES 10; FAT trace; SATURATED FAT trace; PROTEIN 1g.; CARBOHYDRATE 2g.; FIBER trace; CHOLESTEROL 0mg.; SODIUM 47mg.

⌁Eggplant Chutney⌁

A condiment-like sauce made from eggplant, tomatoes, and garlic, Eggplant Chutney is served as an accompaniment to many Indian breads and appetizers.

1/4 cup fresh or unsweetened powdered coconut
1/2 cup coarsely chopped tomato
1 cup coarsely chopped onion
4 cloves garlic, chopped
1 tablespoon minced fresh ginger root
3 tablespoons corn oil
1/4 teaspoon asafoetida powder
1 teaspoon black mustard seeds
1 teaspoon urad dal
2 cups unpeeled chopped fresh eggplant
2 to 3 dried red chili peppers (more, if desired)
1/4 teaspoon tamarind paste
2 tablespoons tomato sauce
1 teaspoon salt

1. Set aside coconut, tomato, onion, garlic, and ginger on a plate.

2. Heat the oil in a skillet over medium heat. When the oil is hot, but not smoking, add asafoetida, mustard seeds, and urad dal. Cover and fry until mustard seeds pop and urad dal is golden brown.

3. Add eggplant, coconut, tomato, onions, and garlic to skillet. Stir-fry for 5 to 7 minutes. Add red chili peppers, tamarind paste, tomato sauce, and 1 cup of hot water to the above mixture in the skillet. Add salt and mix well. Cover and cook eggplant over medium heat until it becomes somewhat soft, about 3 minutes.

4. Transfer ingredients from skillet to a blender and grind coarsely. Transfer eggplant chutney to a bowl and serve.

Makes 3 cups

Per Tablespoon:
CALORIES 13; FAT 1g.; SATURATED FAT trace; PROTEIN trace; CARBOHYDRATE 1g.; FIBER trace; CHOLESTEROL 0mg.; SODIUM 49mg.

∽KOSAMALLI∽

This is an eggplant dish with onions and tomatoes cooked in tamarind paste. Serve with adai, idli, dosai, or idiyappam.

3 cups chopped eggplant
1 cup chopped onion
1/4 cup chopped tomatoes
1 green chili pepper, chopped (more, if desired)
2 tablespoons canola or corn oil
4 to 6 curry leaves
1/4 teaspoon asafoetida
1 teaspoon black mustard seeds
1 teaspoon urad dal
1/4 teaspoon turmeric powder
1/2 teaspoon cayenne powder
1/2 teaspoon cumin powder
1 teaspoon salt
1/2 teaspoon tamarind paste
1/4 cup chopped fresh coriander

1. In a saucepan add enough water to cover the eggplant and cook, uncovered, for a few minutes until it is somewhat soft. Use a masher to mash the eggplant. Set aside.

2. Combine onion, tomatoes, and green chili pepper and set aside.

3. Heat oil in a saucepan over medium heat. When oil is hot, but not smoking, add curry leaves, asafoetida, mustard seeds, and urad dal. Fry until mustard seeds pop and urad dal turns golden.

4. Immediately add onion, tomatoes, and green chili and cook until onions are tender. Add turmeric powder and mix well.

5. Add the mashed eggplant and stir into the mixture. Add cayenne powder, cumin powder, salt, and tamarind paste.

6. Add 2 cups of water and stir. When the mixture begins to boil, add coriander and let it simmer over low heat for 7 to 10 minutes.

Serves 6

CALORIES 39; FAT 3g.; SATURATED FAT trace; PROTEIN 1g.; CARBOHYDRATE 4g.; FIBER 1g.; CHOLESTEROL 0mg.; SODIUM 181mg.

⌁Masoor Dal Supreme⌁

A hearty sauce made from tomatoes and masoor dal (also known as red lentils) which can be served with poori, chappati, or with any Indian bread. It can also be served over any plain or basmati rice. Masoor dal cooks quickly and has a delicate texture.

1/4 cup masoor dal (red lentils)
1/2 teaspoon turmeric powder
2 tablespoons corn oil
4 to 6 curry leaves
1 dried red chili pepper
1 teaspoon black mustard seeds
1 teaspoon urad dal
1 cup chopped onion
1 cup chopped tomatoes
1 minced green chili pepper
1 teaspoon minced fresh ginger root
1/2 teaspoon cumin powder
1/2 teaspoon salt (more, if desired)
1/2 cup chopped fresh coriander

1. Boil 2 cups of water. Add masoor dal with 1/4 teaspoon turmeric powder. Cook, uncovered, over medium heat for about 15 minutes until it becomes soft and well cooked. Mash cooked masoor dal. Set aside.

2. Place corn oil in a saucepan over medium heat. When oil is hot, but not smoking, add curry leaves, red chili pepper, mustard seeds, and urad dal. Fry until mustard seeds pop and urad dal turns golden.

3. Add onion, tomatoes, green chili pepper, and ginger. Cook until onion is tender.

4. Add remaining 1/4 teaspoon turmeric powder and mashed masoor dal. Stir well with the seasonings in the saucepan. Add about 3/4 cup of warm water and mix well.

5. Add cumin powder and salt. When the mixture begins to boil, add coriander and let it slow cook for about 3 minutes.

Makes 4 cups (1/2 cup serving size)

Note: Instead of 2 tablespoons of corn oil, the dish can be enhanced in flavor by adding 1 tablespoon of ghee (clarified butter) and 1 tablespoon of oil in Step 2, if you desire.

CALORIES 71; FAT 4g.; SATURATED FAT trace ; PROTEIN 3g.; CARBOHYDRATE 8g.; FIBER 3g.; CHOLESTEROL 0mg.; SODIUM 138mg.

Variation: For a delicious variation in flavor, you may substitute moong dal for masoor dal in step 1 to create **Moong Dal Supreme.**

⌇MINT CHUTNEY⌇

A refreshing condiment-like sauce with fresh mint, Mint Chutney is an accompaniment to any appetizer and goes well with yogurt rice.

1 tablespoon corn oil
1/4 teaspoon asafoetida
1 teaspoon black mustard seeds
1 teaspoon urad dal
1/2 cup of chopped onion
1 green chili pepper (more, if desired)
1 cup fresh mint leaves
1 tablespoon fresh (or) unsweetened powdered coconut
1 tablespoon roasted chickpeas (chana dalia) (or) 1 tablespoon roasted peanuts
1/4 teaspoon tamarind paste
1/2 teaspoon salt (more, if desired)

1. Heat oil in a heavy skillet until hot, but not smoking. Add asafoetida, mustard seeds, and urad dal. Cover and fry until mustard seeds pop and urad dal is golden brown.

2. Add onion and green chili to skillet and stir-fry for a few minutes.

3. Add mint, coconut, and roasted chickpeas to skillet and stir-fry for at least 2 minutes. Mix well.

4. Transfer ingredients to blender and grind finely. Add 1/2 cup of hot water to facilitate the grinding.

5. Add tamarind paste and salt and continue grinding until ingredients reach a fine medium-thick consistency.
Makes 1 cup

Per Tablespoon:
CALORIES 11; FAT 1g.; SATURATED FAT trace; PROTEIN trace; CARBOHYDRATE 1g.; FIBER trace; CHOLESTEROL 0mg.; SODIUM 35mg.

⌁ONION AND POTATO KOSE⌁

A thick tomato-based sauce with onion and potatoes, Kose is an excellent accompaniment to chappati, poori, idli, dosai, or tortillas.

2 tablespoons corn oil
2 to 4 small pieces cinnamon stick
1 bay leaf, crumbled
1 teaspoon black mustard seeds
1 teaspoon urad dal
1/2 cup chopped onion
1/2 cup chopped tomato
1 cup Idaho potatoes with skins, cut in small oblong pieces
1/4 teaspoon turmeric powder
1/2 teaspoon cayenne powder
1 1/2 teaspoon cumin powder
1/2 cup tomato sauce
1/2 teaspoon salt
1/4 cup chopped fresh coriander

1. Heat oil in a medium saucepan over medium heat. When oil is hot, but not smoking, add cinnamon stick and bay leaf. Immediately add mustard seeds and urad dal. Cover and fry until mustard seeds burst (listen for popping sound) and urad dal is golden.

2. Immediately add onion, tomato, and potatoes to saucepan. Add turmeric powder and stir well. Cook, uncovered, over medium-low heat for 1 to 2 minutes.

3. Add cayenne powder, cumin powder, tomato sauce, and salt. Blend well. Add 2 cups of water and blend well with ingredients in saucepan. When the ingredients start to boil, add coriander. Cook, covered, over medium-low heat until potatoes are tender (8 to 10 minutes). Stir frequently.

Serves 6

Per 1/2 cup serving:
CALORIES 69; FAT 4g.; SATURATED FAT trace; PROTEIN 1g.; CARBOHYDRATE 9g.;
FIBER 2g.; CHOLESTEROL 0mg.; SODIUM 232mg.

Variation:

- In a spice grinder or coffee grinder, grind together 1 teaspoon unsweetened powdered coconut, 1 dried red chili pepper, 1/2 teaspoon fennel seeds, and 1/2 teaspoon cumin seeds. Stir into cooked potato sauce. Simmer over low heat for an additional 2 to 3 minutes.

- For a lighter version, omit potatoes and increase both onions and tomatoes to 1 cup each to create a delicious **Onion and Tomato Kose.**

ᴐ᷈Onion and Tomato Chutney᷉ᴑ

Onion and Tomato Chutney can be served with any bread and is an excellent accompaniment to dosai, adai, and idli. This chutney is also delicious with pakora and bhaji.

1 cup coarsely chopped onion
1 cup chopped tomato
3 cloves garlic
2 tablespoons corn oil
1/4 teaspoon asafoetida powder
4 to 5 curry leaves
2 to 4 dried red chili peppers (more, if desired)
1 teaspoon black mustard seeds
1 teaspoon urad dal
1/4 teaspoon tamarind paste
1/2 teaspoon salt

1. Mix onion and tomato and set aside. Peel garlic and set aside.

2. Heat corn oil in a small skillet or wok over medium heat. When oil is hot, but not smoking, add asafoetida, curry leaves, red chili peppers, mustard seeds, and urad dal. Wait for mustard seeds to pop and urad dal to turn golden brown.

3. Add onions, tomatoes, and garlic cloves to skillet and stir-fry until tender.

4. Add tamarind paste and salt. Stir and cook for a few minutes until mixture is well blended. Remove from heat.

5. Transfer ingredients from skillet to a blender. Add 1/2 cup of warm water.

Healthy South Indian Cooking

6. Grind on high speed for few minutes until the ingredients are ground thoroughly and have reached a thick consistency.

Makes 2 1/2 cups

Per tablespoon:
CALORIES 11; FAT 1g.; SATURATED FAT trace; PROTEIN trace; CARBOHYDRATE 1g.; FIBER trace; CHOLESTEROL 0mg.; SODIUM 27mg.

↜Paruppu Thuveyal↝

A thick condiment-like sauce made from lentils, coconut, and garlic, this thuveyal can be served with buttered plain rice, yogurt rice, or as a spread over any bread.

1/2 cup moong dal
1/4 cup unsweetened powdered coconut
2 cloves garlic
2 dried red chili peppers
1/4 teaspoon salt (more, if desired)

1. Dry roast moong dal for about 2 minutes over medium heat.

2. Mix roasted moong dal with coconut, garlic, red chili pepper, salt, and 1/2 cup of warm water and grind in the blender.

Makes 1 cup

Per Tablespoon:
CALORIES 35; FAT 1g.; SATURATED FAT trace; PROTEIN 2g.; CARBOHYDRATE 5g.; FIBER 2g.; CHOLESTEROL 0mg.; SODIUM 38mg.

◡ TOMATO CHUTNEY ◡

A salsa-like South Indian chutney! This easy-to-prepare chutney may be served with many appetizers or Indian breads.

1 cup finely chopped tomato
1 cup finely chopped onion
2 tablespoons corn oil
1/4 teaspoon asafoetida powder
1 teaspoon black mustard seeds
2 teaspoons urad dal
3 to 4 curry leaves (optional)
1/4 teaspoon turmeric powder
1/4 teaspoon cayenne powder
1 teaspoon cumin powder
1 cup tomato sauce
1/4 cup minced fresh coriander
3/4 teaspoon salt (more, if desired)

1. Mix tomato and onion. Set aside.

2. Place corn oil in a small saucepan or a small skillet over medium heat. When oil is hot, but not smoking, add asafoetida powder, mustard seeds, urad dal, and curry leaves. Fry, covered, until mustard seeds pop and urad dal is golden.

3. Add tomato and onion. Sauté for a few minutes.

4. Add turmeric powder, cayenne pepper, and cumin powder and stir well into the mixture.

5. Add tomato sauce, coriander, and salt. Cook, covered, over low heat for approximately 10 minutes. The tomato will blend with other ingredients over low heat to become somewhat smooth and thickened.

Makes 2 cups

Per Tablespoon:

CALORIES 10; FAT 1g.; SATURATED FAT trace; PROTEIN trace; CARBOHYDRATE 1g.; FIBER trace; CHOLESTEROL 0mg.; SODIUM 65mg.

Rice

BASMATI RICE WITH GREEN PEAS

An aromatic rice dish flavored with saffron and cardamom.

2 cups basmati rice
2 tablespoons butter
4 to 5 small pieces cinnamon stick
2 bay leaves
1 tablespoon broken cashew nuts (more, if desired)
1/4 teaspoon saffron (optional)
2 whole cloves (optional)
1/4 teaspoon turmeric powder
1/4 teaspoon ground cardamom (or 2 whole cardamoms)
1/2 teaspoon salt (more, if desired)
1/2 cup frozen peas

1. Wash basmati rice well and rinse thoroughly.

2. Bring 4 cups of water to a boil in a microwave oven or on stovetop and set aside.

3. Heat butter over medium heat in a saucepan. When butter is hot, but not smoking, add cinnamon stick, bay leaves, and cashews. Fry over medium heat until cashew pieces become golden brown.

4. Add rice to saucepan and stir well to mix all ingredients.

5. Add saffron, cloves, turmeric powder, cardamom, and salt. Mix well. Fry for a minute or two.

6. Pour hot water over rice.

7. Stir and wait until water with rice begins to boil.

8. Reduce heat to low. Then cover and cook for 20 minutes or until rice is fluffy and water has evaporated.

9. Cook green peas for 2 minutes in microwave oven until just tender. Drain peas and set aside to add to cooked rice.

Serves 6

CALORIES 271; FAT 6g.; SATURATED FAT 3g.; PROTEIN 6g.; CARBOHYDRATE 48g.; FIBER 3g.; CHOLESTEROL 10mg.; SODIUM 277mg.

↭ Bell Pepper and Tomato Rice with Cashews ↝

This hearty, flavorful, and nutritious rice dish is filling and delicious by itself. It also can be served with chicken or turkey. This recipe uses a large quantity of rice and keeps well in the refrigerator for many days. If a smaller quantity is desired, you may prepare the dish with half the stated amount of ingredients.

> 2 cups basmati rice
> 1 box (10 ounces) frozen baby lima beans
> 3/4 teaspoon turmeric powder
> 4 tablespoons corn oil
> 4 to 5 small pieces cinnamon stick
> 1 bay leaf, crumbled
> 1/2 teaspoon cumin seeds
> 1/2 teaspoon fennel seeds
> 1 cup onion, cut lengthwise
> 1 cup tomato, cut in small chunks
> 1 green chili pepper, finely chopped
> 2 cups coarsely chopped green bell peppers
> 1 cup tomato sauce
> 1 tablespoon curry powder
> 2 teaspoons salt
> 1/2 cup cashew halves

1. Cook rice in 4 cups of water in a rice cooker, or cook rice in 4 cups of water following directions on rice package for fluffy rice but omitting salt and oil if included in the directions. Transfer cooked rice into a bowl and let it cool for about 15 minutes so grains do not stick together.

2. Cook lima beans in a saucepan in 1 cup of water with 1/4 teaspoon turmeric powder. When beans are tender, drain and set aside to cool.

3. Heat oil in a wok or large fry-pan over medium heat. When oil is hot, but not smoking, add cinnamon stick, bay leaf, cumin, and fennel seeds.

Brown for a few seconds.

4. Add 3/4 cup of the onion, tomato, and chili. Stir-fry for 1 minute.

5. Add bell pepper and cooked lima beans with remaining 1/2 teaspoon turmeric powder. Mix well.

6. Add tomato sauce. Blend ingredients well in wok. Cook, covered, over medium heat, until bell pepper becomes slightly tender (approximately 1 minute), stirring occasionally. Do not overcook bell pepper.

7.Stir in curry powder and salt.

8. Add cooked rice to wok and blend well with sauce. Immediately reduce heat to low.

9. Stir in cashew halves.

10. Sprinkle remaining 1/4 cup onion over rice. Fluff and mix the rice gently. Turn off heat.

Serves 12

CALORIES 443; FAT 13g.; SATURATED FAT 2g.; PROTEIN 12g.; CARBOHYDRATE 74g.; FIBER 6g.; CHOLESTEROL 0mg.; SODIUM 618mg.

ᘒ Black Pepper Rice with Cashews ᘒ
(Milagu Saathum)

A distinctly savory rice dish, Black Pepper Rice goes well with both vegetable and meat dishes and also with yogurt salad.

2 cups extra long-grain white rice or basmati rice
2 tablespoons corn oil
4 to 6 curry leaves (optional)
1 dried red chili pepper
2 teaspoons black mustard seeds
3 teaspoons urad dal
1 cup chopped yellow onion
2 teaspoons black pepper and cumin powder
1 teaspoon salt (more, if desired)
1/4 cup dry roasted cashews

1. Cook rice in rice cooker, or cook rice in 4 cups of water following directions for fluffy rice but omitting salt and oil if included in the directions. Cool rice about 1 hour, so grains do not stick together.

2. Heat oil in a wok or in a large skillet over medium-high heat. When oil is hot, but not smoking, add curry leaves and red peppers. Stir briefly. Add mustard seeds and urad dal. Cover and heat until mustard seeds burst (listen for popping sound) and urad dal is golden brown.

3. Add onion and cook for a minute.

4. Add cooked rice to the onion mixture and stir well with spoon.

5. Add black pepper and cumin powder to rice. Add salt and mix well.

6. Add cashews and stir well into rice.
Serves 8

CALORIES 238; FAT 5g.; SATURATED FAT 1g.; PROTEIN 5g.; CARBOHYDRATE 41g.; FIBER 1g.; CHOLESTEROL 0mg.; SODIUM 274mg.

ᵔCAULIFLOWER RICEᵔ

A unique cauliflower-based adaptation of South Indian flavored rice dishes.

1 cup basmati rice
1 tablespoon butter (plus 1 teaspoon, optional)
1 tablespoon corn oil
4 to 6 curry leaves
1 bay leaf, crumbled
2 to 4 very small cinnamon sticks
1 teaspoon cumin seeds
1 teaspoon urad dal
1 cup onion, chopped lengthwise
2 cups cauliflower florets
1/2 teaspoon black pepper and cumin powder
1 teaspoon salt
1/4 cup peanuts or cashews
1/2 cup chopped fresh coriander

1. Rinse and cook basmati rice in 2 cups of water. Let it cool for few minutes. Set aside.

2. Melt 1 tablespoon butter in a wok or wide-bottomed skillet. Add corn oil and heat over medium heat. When oil is hot, but not smoking, add curry leaves, bay leaf, and cinnamon sticks.

3. Add cumin seeds and urad dal and fry over medium heat until cumin are golden brown.

4. Add onion and cauliflower and stir-fry for a few minutes.

5. Add black pepper and cumin powder and salt. Continue cooking, covered, over medium heat until cauliflower is tender. About 1 tablespoon of water should be added to facilitate the cooking of the cauliflower.

6. Add cooked basmati rice. Stir well into cauliflower mixture. Cover and

allow to steam over low heat until rice becomes softer and absorbs the flavor of the cauliflower.

7. Add peanuts and coriander and fluff the rice gently.

8. Optional step: I teaspoon of melted butter or ghee may be added to rice to enhance flavor. Mix well.

Serves 4

Nutritional Analysis without optional butter or ghee:
CALORIES 314; FAT 13g.; SATURATED FAT 3g.; PROTEIN 8g.; CARBOHYDRATE 43g.; FIBER 5g.; CHOLESTEROL 10mg.; SODIUM 622mg.

Nutritional Analysis with optional butter or ghee:
CALORIES 342; FAT 16g.; SATURATED FAT 5g.; PROTEIN 8g.; CARBOHYDRATE 43g.; FIBER 5g.; CHOLESTEROL 19mg.; SODIUM 622mg.

ᴄ᷍Coconut Rice:᷍᷍

This exquisite dish is served on auspicious occasions and even in temples in South India.It goes well with light vegetable dishes, such as Cauliflower Poriyal (page 222) and Green Beans Podimas (page 204). Be careful not to overpower this delicate dish with heavy sauces.

2 cups long-grain rice (or) basmati rice
1 coconut
1/4 cup corn oil
1/2 teaspoon asafoetida
2 dried red chili peppers (more, if desired)
6 to 8 curry leaves (optional)
1 1/2 teaspoons black mustard seeds
1 1/2 teaspoons urad dal
1/4 cup cashew halves (raw or roasted)
1 teaspoon salt (more if desired)
1/4 cup chopped fresh coriander

1. Cook rice in 4 cups of water. Cool and set aside.

2. Finely grind coconut in a blender to make 3 cups.

3. Roast the shredded coconut by itself in a wok, stirring constantly, until golden (approximately 3 minutes). Remove coconut from wok and set aside.

4. Heat oil in wok over medium heat. When oil is hot, but not smoking, add asafoetida, red chili peppers, and curry leaves. Add mustard seeds and urad dal. Fry until mustard seeds pop and urad dal turns golden.

5. Add cashews (raw) to the wok and fry for 2 to 3 minutes.

6. Add cooked rice to the wok and mix well with roasted nuts and spices.

Healthy South Indian Cooking

7. Stir in the roasted coconut and mix rice well.

8. Add salt and coriander. Mix well.

Serves 8

CALORIES 365; FAT 19g.; SATURATED FAT 10g.; PROTEIN 5g.; CARBOHYDRATE 44g.; FIBER 4g.; CHOLESTEROL 0mg.; SODIUM 278mg.

ᨳ Lemon Rice ᨳ

This popular rice dish is served on special social and religious occasions. Indeed, lemon is considered a very auspicious fruit. Lemon rice goes particularly well with Potatoes Roasted with Garlic and Tomatoes (page 267). It keeps well at room temperature and can be packed for lunch.

2 cups jasmine rice (or) extra long-grain rice
1/3 cup dry yellow split peas
1/2 cup lemon juice
2 teaspoons salt
1 1/2 teaspoons turmeric powder
3 tablespoons corn oil
1 dried red chili pepper
1/2 teaspoon asafoetida powder
4 to 6 curry leaves (optional)
2 teaspoons black mustard seeds
2 teaspoons urad dal
1 teaspoon chutney powder
2 tablespoons dry roasted unsalted peanuts (more, if desired)
2 tablespoons minced fresh coriander leaves

1. Cook rice in 4 cups of water, following directions for fluffy rice but omitting salt and oil if included in directions. Cool rice about 1 hour, so grains do not stick together. If time is limited, a little of the lemon juice mixture can be stirred into the cooling rice to help separate the grains.

2. Soak split peas in 1 cup warm water for about 30 minutes. Drain water and set aside.

3. Combine lemon juice, salt, and turmeric powder; set aside. (If fresh lemon juice is used, use only 1/4 cup of pure juice and dilute with 1/4 cup of water.)

4. Heat oil in a large skillet or wok over medium heat. When oil is hot, but not smoking, add red chili pepper, asafoetida powder, and curry

leaves. Immediately stir in mustard seeds and urad dal. Cover and heat until mustard seeds burst (listen for popping sound) and urad dal is golden.

5.Immediately stir in soaked split peas. Cook, uncovered, for 2 to 3 minutes, reducing heat until the mixture starts to bubble.

6. Immediately stir in lemon juice mixture and chutney powder. Simmer 2 to 4 minutes, reducing heat if mixture starts to boil.

7. Reduce heat to low. Add cooked rice and stir the rice gently into lemon juice mixture.

8. Taste and add additional seasonings, if desired. Serve garnished with peanuts and coriander.

Serves 8

CALORIES 248; FAT 5g.; SATURATED FAT 1g.; PROTEIN 6g.; CARBOHYDRATE 45g.; FIBER 6g.; CHOLESTEROL 0mg.; SODIUM 546mg.

∽ SAVORY MUSHROOM RICE ∾

This rice dish with mushrooms is a variation of basmati rice with peas. It can be served with turkey, chicken, fish, or any meat during the holidays. It also makes a good accompaniment to any potato, vegetable, or chicken kurma sauce.

1 tablespoon butter (plus 1 tablespoon, optional)
1 tablespoon corn oil
1 bay leaf, crumbled
1 teaspoon cumin seeds
1/2 cup onion, chopped lengthwise
3 cups chopped mushrooms (portobello, cremini, etc.)
1 cup basmati rice, rinsed and drained
1 teaspoon black pepper and cumin powder
1/2 teaspoon salt

1. Heat 1 tablespoon butter with corn oil. When oil is hot, but not smoking, add bay leaf.

2. Add cumin seeds and heat until golden brown.

3. Add onions and sauté for a few minutes.

4. Add mushrooms and sauté for a few additional minutes over medium-high heat until mushrooms become brown and aromatic.

5. Add basmati rice and blend well.

6. Add black pepper and cumin powder and salt.

7. Add 3 cups of hot water to the rice mixture in the pan. Bring to a boil and then reduce to low heat. Cook, covered, for 20 to 30 minutes until rice becomes fluffy.

Healthy South Indian Cooking

8. *Optional step:*When rice is cooked, you may add 1 tablespoon butter and mix well to enhance the flavor.

Serves 6

CALORIES 156; FAT 5g.; SATURATED FAT 2g.; PROTEIN 4g.; CARBOHYDRATE 24g.; FIBER 1g.; CHOLESTEROL 5mg.; SODIUM 220mg.

᭞SPINACH RICE᭞

Spinach rice with split peas or moong dal is another variety of flavored rice. It is delicious by itself and also an excellent accompaniment to any chicken or fish recipe, vegetable side dish, or yogurt salad.

1 recipe Basmati Rice with Peas, omitting peas (page 123)
1 recipe Spinach Poriyal, using split peas or moong dal (page 272)
1 teaspoon salt
1 teaspoon cumin powder
1 green chili, minced (optional)
1/4 cup unsalted roasted cashews

1. In a large heavy bottomed saucepan or skillet over medium heat, mix rice with 1 1/2 cups of spinach poriyal.

2. Add salt and cumin powder to the spinach rice and fluff rice gently. Add green chili, if desired.

3. Garnish rice with cashews.

Serves 8

CALORIES 264; FAT 10g.; SATURATED FAT 3g.; PROTEIN 6g.; CARBOHYDRATE 39g.; FIBER 3g.; CHOLESTEROL 8mg.; SODIUM 625mg.

ᴥ Sweet Pongal Rice ᴥ

Cooked in milk with brown sugar, cardamom and saffron, Sweet Pongal Rice is often served during religious holidays or on special social occasions as a dessert.

1 cup extra long-grain rice or jasmine rice
3 cups 2% milk
2 cups packed dark brown sugar
1/4 teaspoon saffron threads
1/2 teaspoon powdered cardamom
2 very small pieces crystalline camphor (optional)
2 tablespoons raisins (more, if desired)
1/4 cup raw cashews
1/2 tablespoon butter (plus 2 tablespoons, optional)

1. Cook rice to a creamy consistency in either a saucepan or rice cooker. 1 cup of rice to 4 cups water will result in a creamy consistency.

2. As soon as rice is cooked, use a masher to mash the rice. Transfer the mashed rice to a saucepan if rice has been cooked in a rice cooker.

3. Add milk to rice. Stir for about 2 minutes over medium/low heat.

4. Add the dark brown sugar together with the saffron, cardamom, camphor, and raisins. Stir all ingredients and let simmer. Cook mixture, covered, over low heat, stirring frequently.

5. Fry raw cashews to a golden brown in 1/2 tablespoon butter and add to rice mixture when it is cooked.

6. You may add 2 additional tablespoons of butter to the rice while simmering to enhance the flavor of sweet pongal rice.

Serves 8

CALORIES 368; FAT 4g.; SATURATED FAT 2g.; PROTEIN 5g.; CARBOHYDRATE 70g.; FIBER 1g.; CHOLESTEROL 7mg.; SODIUM 69mg.

~:Tamarind Rice:~

Made from the fruit of the tamarind tree, which is indigenous to tropical countries, this rice is served on auspicious occasions and even in temples in South India. Tamarind rice is often taken for lunch during trips. It keeps well for several days in the refrigerator.

2 cups extra long-grain white rice or jasmine rice
1/4 cup yellow split peas
3 teaspoons tamarind paste
2 teaspoons salt
1/4 cup corn oil
6 to 8 curry leaves
1 to 2 dried red chili peppers
1/2 teaspoon asafoetida powder
1 1/2 teaspoons black mustard seeds
1 1/2 teaspoons urad dal
3/4 teaspoon turmeric powder
1 pinch brown sugar (optional)
1 teaspoon chutney powder
1/4 cup unsalted roasted peanuts

1. Cook rice with 4 cups of water in a rice cooker or in an open saucepan over medium heat. Transfer cooked rice into a bowl and cool rice for about 15 minutes.

2. Soak yellow split peas in 1 cup of water for about 30 minutes.

3. Add tamarind paste and salt to 1/4 cup of warm water. Stir to achieve a smooth consistency.

4. Place oil in wok over medium heat. When oil is hot but not smoking, add curry leaves, red peppers, asafoetida, mustard seeds, and urad dal. Cover and fry over medium heat until mustard seeds pop and urad dal is golden brown.

❧ *Healthy South Indian Cooking*

5. Drain water from split peas and stir peas into hot oil in wok.

6. Stir-fry for 30 seconds. Add tamarind mixture to wok.

7. Add turmeric powder and mix well.

8. Add brown sugar if desired.

9. Add chutney powder.

10. When the mixture begins to boil, add rice and blend thoroughly. Add peanuts and stir into rice.

Serves 8 to 10

CALORIES 258, FAT 8g.; SATURATED FAT 1g.; PROTEIN 6g.; CARBOHYDRATE 41g.; FIBER 3g.; CHOLESTEROL 0mg.; SODIUM 481mg.

☙Tomato Rice with Cashews☙

Basmati rice cooked with tomato in and aromatic mixture of coconut, garlic, and ginger, this dish is particularly delicious served with Potato Kurma (page 259) or Chicken Kurma (page 291).

1/4 cup fresh coconut, cut into small pieces
4 green chili peppers (more, if desired)
5 garlic cloves
4 small slices fresh ginger root
2 cups basmati rice
3 tablespoons ghee or butter
3 to 4 small pieces cinnamon stick
1 bay leaf, crushed
1 cup onion, cut lengthwise (plus additional for garnish, optional)
1 cup chopped tomato
1/2 cup chopped fresh coriander
1 tablespoon lemon juice
2 teaspoons salt
1 cup cashews

1. Grind coconut, chilies, garlic, and ginger in a blender with a 1/4 cup warm water (only enough to facilitate the grinding process).

2. Wash rice thoroughly and drain.

3. Add 2 tablespoons ghee in a large wide-bottomed saucepan and melt over medium heat. Add pieces of cinnamon stick and bay leaf to melted ghee.

4. Add rice to saucepan and fry until golden brown. Transfer rice to a bowl and set aside.

5. Add remaining 1 tablespoon of ghee in a large wide-bottomed saucepan. When ghee is hot, but not smoking, add onion, tomato, and 1/4 cup of coriander and cook until tender.

6. Add the contents from the blender and the lemon juice. Simmer for a few minutes.

7. Add 2 cups of water and the salt. Continue to simmer.

8. When the mixture is ready to boil, add the browned rice. Cover and cook over low heat until rice is cooked (approximately 10 minutes).

9. As soon as rice is cooked, turn off heat. Gently stir well and add cashews and remaining 1/4 cup of coriander.

10. You may add raw onions, chopped lengthwise, to garnish.

Serves 8

CALORIES 316; FAT 14g.; SATURATED FAT 5g.; PROTEIN 8g.; CARBOHYDRATE 42g.; FIBER 2g.; CHOLESTEROL 12mg.; SODIUM 617mg.

⌁ TOMATO RICE WITH GREEN ONIONS ⌁

This easy-to-prepare rice dish in a seasoned tomato base may be served with any vegetable dish, cucumber yogurt salad, Potato Kurma, or any grilled or baked meat.

1 cup basmati rice (or) extra long-grain rice (or) jasmine rice
2 tablespoon corn or canola oil
1 bay leaf, crumbled
3 to 4 small pieces cinnamon stick
1/2 teaspoon cumin seeds
1/2 cup chopped onion
1/2 cup chopped tomato
1/4 cup chopped fresh coriander
1/4 teaspoon turmeric powder
1/2 cup tomato sauce
1/4 teaspoon ground cloves (optional)
1/2 teaspoon garam masala powder
1/2 teaspoon salt
1/2 cup chopped green onion tops
1/2 cup roasted cashews

1. Cook rice in 2 cups of water in a rice cooker or covered saucepan over low heat. Set aside to cool for about 10 minutes.

2. Place corn oil in a wok or wide-bottomed skillet and heat over medium heat.

3. When oil is hot, but not smoking, add bay leaf, cinnamon sticks, and cumin seeds. Fry until cumin seeds are golden.

4. Add onion, tomato, and coriander to wok and sauté for a few minutes.

5. Add turmeric powder, tomato sauce, ground cloves, and garam masala powder. Stir well and reduce heat to low. Continue cooking uncovered.

6. Add salt and mix well with ingredients in wok.

7. Add rice and stir carefully into above mixture.

8. Add green onions to rice and stir gently.

9. Add cashew nuts and stir well.

Serves 4

CALORIES 353; FAT 16g.; SATURATED FAT 2g.; PROTEIN 8g.; CARBOHYDRATE 47g.; FIBER 4g.; CHOLESTEROL 12mg.; SODIUM 494mg.

~:Vegetable Pulaoo Rice:~

Made from mixed vegetables and basmati rice, Vegetable Pulaoo Rice can be served with onion and cucumber salad, and Chicken or Potato Kurma.

2 cups basmati rice
2 tablespoons butter or ghee
1 bay leaf, crumbled
2 to 3 small pieces cinnamon stick
1 1/2 cups onion, chopped lengthwise
1/2 cup chopped tomato
1 green chili, chopped
3/4 teaspoon turmeric powder
2 teaspoons garam masala powder
1 tablespoons minced fresh ginger root
1 teaspoon cardamom powder
2 cups peeled and cubed potatoes
1 cup frozen lima beans
2 teaspoons salt
1/4 cup coarsely shredded beets
1/4 cup coarsely shredded carrots
1/2 cup roasted cashews

1. Rinse rice thoroughly in cold water. Drain rice and set aside.

2. Heat 1 tablespoon butter over medium heat in a saucepan. When butter is hot, but not smoking, add bay leaf and cinnamon sticks.

3. Immediately add 1 cup onions, tomatoes, and green chili. Add rice and fry over medium heat for 1 to 2 minutes to brown the rice. Stir frequently.

4. Add 1/4 teaspoon turmeric powder and the garam masala powder. Mix well.

5. Pour 4 cups of hot water over rice in saucepan. Stir well and add ginger and cardamom powder.

6. When mixture begins to boil, reduce heat to low and cover saucepan. Cook until the water evaporates and the rice is fluffy (about 10 minutes). Remove saucepan from heat and allow to cool, uncovered.

7. In a separate saucepan add potatoes and lima beans with remaining 1/2 teaspoon turmeric powder and about 1 cup of water to cover the vegetables.

8. Add 1 teaspoon salt to saucepan and cook vegetables, uncovered, over medium heat until just tender. Be careful not to overcook the vegetables. Set aside.

9. Place remaining 1 tablespoon butter in wok or skillet and allow to melt.

10. Add cooked rice to wok and stir briefly to separate rice grains. Add the drained potatoes and limas to rice and mix gently.

11. Add remaining 1/2 cup onion and the beets and carrots to rice.

12. Add the remaining 1 teaspoon salt to rice and stir gently.

13. Sprinkle roasted cashews over the top of rice.

Serves 8

CALORIES 281; FAT 8g.; SATURATED FAT 3g.; PROTEIN 7g.; CARBOHYDRATE 46g.; FIBER 3g.; CHOLESTEROL 8mg.; SODIUM 604mg.

ᵥ:YOGURT RICE:ᵥ
(THAYIR SAATHAM)

Cooling and satisfying Yogurt Rice, also known as Curd Rice, is traditionally served as a final course in a South Indian meal. It can accompany any vegetable dish or Indian pickles (lime or mango, for example), which are available in Indian grocery stores. Nutritious and tasty, Yogurt Rice can be packed for lunch at work or for an outing and is very soothing to the stomach.

1/2 cup long-grain rice or jasmine rice
1 1/2 cups fat-free plain yogurt
1/4 teaspoon salt
1 teaspoon minced fresh ginger root

1. Cook rice in 2 cups of water to achieve a creamy consistency.

2. You might use a masher to soften the rice to ensure a creamy consistency. Add yogurt and be certain to mix very well. More yogurt may be added, if desired.

3. Add salt and ginger and mix well.

Note: If you already have 1 cup precooked plain rice, you could start directly from Step 2. Also, taste may be enhanced by adding up to 1/4 cup buttermilk in Step 2.

Serves 2

CALORIES 136; FAT trace; SATURATED FAT trace; PROTEIN 7g.; CARBOHYDRATE 26g.; FIBER trace; CHOLESTEROL 2mg.; SODIUM 205mg.

♨ *Healthy South Indian Cooking*

Variations:

Yogurt Rice with Cucumber and Carrots:
To enhance the Yogurt Rice as prepared above, add 1 tablespoon minced cucumbers, 1 tablespoon shredded carrots, and 1 tablespoon minced coriander. Mix well.

CALORIES 137; FAT trace; SATURATED FAT trace; PROTEIN 7g.; CARBOHYDRATE 26g.; FIBER trace, CHOLESTEROL 2mg.; SODIUM 206mg.

Seasoned Yogurt Rice:
Place 1 teaspoon oil in a small saucepan or butter warmer over medium heat. When oil is hot, but not smoking, add 4 to 6 curry leaves, 1 teaspoon mustard seeds, and 1 teaspoon urad dal. When mustard seeds pop and urad dal is golden brown, pour mixture over yogurt rice. Mix well. Add 1/4 cup chopped coriander. Add 1/4 cup of 2% milk to prevent the yogurt rice from turning sour. Leave rice at room temperature until you are ready to serve.

CALORIES 162; FAT 2g.; SATURATED FAT trace; PROTEIN 8g.; CARBOHYDRATE 27g.; FIBER 1g.; CHOLESTEROL 3mg.; SODIUM 213mg.

❦

Sambhar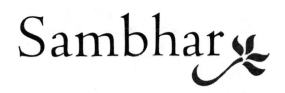

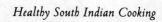

ᛩ Acorn Squash Pulikulambu ᛩ

A unique dish of assorted vegetables cooked with spices in tamarind sauce.

1 acorn squash
1 tablespoon corn oil
1/4 teaspoon asafoetida
4 to 6 curry leaves
1/2 teaspoon fenugreek
1 teaspoon black mustard seeds
1 teaspoon urad dal
1/2 cup chopped onion
1/4 cup chopped tomato
1/4 teaspoon turmeric powder
2 teaspoons sambhar powder
1 cup tomato sauce
1/4 teaspoon tamarind paste
1 teaspoon salt
1/4 chopped fresh coriander

1. Acorn squash has a tough skin. Cut squash in half and cook one half in microwave for 2 to 3 minutes so that it is easy to cut the squash. Remove the seeds and skin. Cut squash into small cubes. Save the other half in the refrigerator for later use.

2. In a small saucepan heat corn oil over medium heat. When oil is hot, but not smoking, add asafoetida, curry leaves, fenugreek, mustard seeds, and urad dal. Fry until mustard seeds pop and urad dal turns golden.

3. Add onion and tomato and cook for a minute or two.

4. Add squash and stir. Add turmeric powder and mix well over medium heat.

5. Add sambhar powder, tomato sauce, tamarind paste, and salt. Stir in the saucepan. Add 1 cup of water to the mixture.

6. Add coriander. Cook, covered, over low heat, stirring often until squash becomes tender.

Serves 4

CALORIES 79; FAT 4g.; SATURATED FAT trace; PROTEIN 2g.; CARBOHYDRATE 12g.; FIBER 2g.; CHOLESTEROL 0mg.; SODIUM 907mg.

ᵥ:Bangalore Sambhar:ᵥ

A mixture of vegetables and spices cooked in a base of creamy dal, this sambhar should be served over plain rice as an accompaniment to a meal.

1/2 cup toor dal
1/4 teaspoon turmeric powder
1 cup peeled and cubed Idaho potato
1 cup frozen Fordhook (large size) lima beans
1/4 cup coconut, fresh or powdered
5 dried red chili peppers
2 garlic cloves
1 teaspoon cumin
1 teaspoon salt (more, if desired)
1/4 cup tomato sauce
1/4 cup chopped fresh coriander
1 tablespoon corn oil
1/4 teaspoon asafoetida powder
4 to 6 curry leaves (optional)
1 teaspoon black mustard seeds
1 teaspoon urad dal

1. Boil 4 cups of water in a tall saucepan over medium heat. Add toor dal and turmeric powder. Reduce heat to medium and cook, uncovered, for about 30 minutes until dal becomes creamy. If water evaporates during the cooking process, add another cup of water and cook until dal becomes creamy.

2. When dal is cooked, place creamy dal in a saucepan and add potatoes and lima beans with 2 cups of water to cover the vegetables.

3. Cook over medium heat until vegetables are tender, about 10 minutes.

4. Place coconut, 4 red chili peppers, garlic, and cumin in blender. Add about 1/2 cup of warm water to facilitate the grinding. Grind until smooth.

5. Pour contents of blender into saucepan. Add salt and tomato sauce. Stir well.

6. Add coriander and continue to simmer, covered, until potatoes are tender.

7. Place corn oil in a small skillet and heat oil over medium heat. When oil is hot, but not smoking, add asafoetida, curry leaves, remaining 1 red chili pepper, mustard seeds, and urad dal. Fry until mustard seeds pop and urad dal is golden brown. Pour fried mustard seeds and urad dal into sambhar. Stir and let it simmer for a few minutes. If sambhar seems too thick, add 1/2 to 1 cup of warm water as desired and stir. Let it simmer for another minute or two.

Serves 6

CALORIES 179; FAT 4g.; SATURATED FAT 1g.; PROTEIN 8g.; CARBOHYDRATE 30g.; FIBER 6g.; CHOLESTEROL 0mg.; SODIUM 445mg.

Idli, Coconut Chutney, Vadai, Green Beans Sambhar

Pappadum, Chickpea Soondal, Spinach Kootu,
Eggplant Masala, Lemon Rice

Lemon Rice

Thayir Vadai, Plain Vadai

Yogurt Rice, Tamarind Rice

Poori, Potato Curry for Poori

Beets Vadai

Brussels Sprouts Kulambu

Spinach Poriyal

Eggplant and Potato Masala

*Mushroom Masala, Potato Moong Dal Pachadi,
Cabbage with Coconut Poriyal*

*Meal served on a Banana Leaf: Chickpea Soondal,
Potato Moong Dal Pachadi, Cabbage with Coconut Poriyal, Pappadum,
Carrot Sambhar, Plain Rice, Mushroom Masala*

Carrot Sambhar

Plain Vadai, Bell Pepper and Radish Sambhar, Eggplant Chutney, Uppuma, Coriander Chutney, Dosai

Cauliflower Masala Poriyal

Green Beans Poriyal

Fresh Curry Leaves, Dried Curry Leaves,
Fresh Ginger Root, Turmeric Powder (in center)

Fresh Coconut Half, Freshly Ground Coconut,
Chopped Fresh Coconut

Spice Box with 7 Containers: Fenugreek, Fennel, Cumin Seed, Black Mustard Seed, Urad Dal, Dried Red Chili Pepper, Cinnamon Stick (in center)

Moong Dal, Yellow Split Peas, Masoor Dal, Toor Dal (starting from top and going clock-wise)

Green Beans Podimas (variation of Broccoli Podimas), Coconut Rice

Tuna Balls, Tuna Masala

Samosas, Bhajis, Bondas with 3 Chutneys (left to right): Tomato Chutney, Coconut Chutney, Coriander Chutney

Broccoli with Coconut Poriyal, Acorn Squash Masala Poriyal, Madras Vegetable Medley

Bell Pepper and Tomato Rice, Onion and Tomato Salad, Carrots Poriyal

Okra Masala

Bell Pepper and Tomato Rice, Chicken Kurma, Shrimp Masala

*Okra Masala, Broccoli with Coconut Poriyal, Madras Vegetable Medley,
Acorn Squash Masala Poriyal*

Chicken Biriyani Rice

Tamarind Rice, Yogurt Rice, Bell Pepper and Tomato Rice

Assorted South Indian Dishes Surrounding Tamarind Rice

~:BEANS KULAMBU:~

Green beans cooked with tomatoes and spices in a creamy dal base, Beans Kulambu is delicious served over plain rice, with idli and dosai, or with toasted bread.

1/4 cup toor dal
1/2 teaspoon turmeric powder
1 cup green beans
2 tablespoons corn oil
1/8 teaspoon asafoetida powder
4 to 6 curry leaves
1 dried red chili pepper
1 teaspoon black mustard seeds
1 teaspoon urad dal
1/2 cup chopped tomatoes
1 teaspoon sambhar powder
1/2 teaspoon salt (more, if desired)
1/4 teaspoon tamarind paste
1/4 cup tomato sauce
1/4 cup chopped coriander

1. Boil 3 cups of water in a tall saucepan. Add toor dal and 1/4 teaspoon turmeric powder. Reduce heat to medium and cook, uncovered, for about 30 minutes until dal becomes creamy. If water evaporates during the cooking process, add another cup of water and cook until dal becomes creamy. Set aside.

2. Wash and cut the ends of green beans. Cut each bean in half. Place in a bowl and set aside.

3. In a saucepan place corn oil over medium heat. When oil is hot, but not smoking, add asafoetida, curry leaves, red pepper, mustard seeds, and urad dal. Fry until mustard seeds pop and urad dal turns golden.

4. Add tomatoes and green beans and cook for a minute.

5. Add remaining 1/4 teaspoon turmeric powder, sambhar powder, and salt. Blend the seasonings well with vegetables in the saucepan.

6. Add cooked creamy dal, tamarind paste, and tomato sauce to the mixture in the saucepan. Add 1 cup of warm water. Stir and let mixture come to a boil.

7. Add coriander and let it simmer for few minutes.

Serves 4

CALORIES 146; FAT 8g.; SATURATED FAT 1g.; PROTEIN 5g.; CARBOHYDRATE 15g.; FIBER 7g.; CHOLESTEROL 0mg.; SODIUM 367mg.

⌣ BELL PEPPER AND RADISH SAMBHAR ⌣

Bell peppers and radishes cooked with spices in a creamy dal base, this sambhar is best served over plain rice.

1/2 cup toor dal
3/4 teaspoon turmeric powder
3 tablespoons corn oil
1/4 teaspoon asafoetida powder
1 whole dried red chili pepper
1/2 teaspoon fenugreek seeds
1 teaspoon black mustard seeds
1 teaspoon urad dal
1/2 cup chopped onion
1/2 cup coarsely chopped tomatoes
1 cup thinly sliced white or red radish
1/2 teaspoon tamarind paste
2 teaspoons sambhar powder
1 1/2 teaspoons salt
1 cup tomato sauce
1/4 cup chopped coriander
2 cups coarsely cut green bell peppers

1. Bring 4 cups of water to a boil in a tall saucepan. Add toor dal and 1/4 teaspoon turmeric powder. Reduce heat to medium and cook, uncovered, for about 30 minutes until dal becomes creamy. If water evaporates during the cooking process, add another cup of water and cook until dal becomes creamy. Set aside.

2. Place corn oil in a saucepan over medium heat. When the oil is hot, but not smoking, add asafoetida, red chili pepper, fenugreek seeds, mustard seeds, and urad dal. Fry, covered, until mustard seeds pop and other ingredients are a golden brown.

3. Add the onion and tomato. Cook for a minute. Add the remaining 1/2 teaspoon turmeric powder and radish. Cook over medium heat, stirring

constantly.

4. Add the creamy toor dal mixture, plus 2 cups of water, to the ingredients in the saucepan.

5. Add the tamarind paste, sambhar powder, and salt. Cook, covered, over low heat for 10 minutes.

6. Add tomato sauce and coriander. When the mixture begins to boil add bell pepper. Cover and cook over low heat for 5 to 7 minutes. Do not overcook the green pepper.

Note: If the finished sambhar is very thick, add an additional cup of warm water.

Serves 6

CALORIES 194; FAT 9g.; SATURATED FAT 1g.; PROTEIN 8g.; CARBOHYDRATE 27g.; FIBER 9g.; CHOLESTEROL 0mg.; SODIUM 527mg.

ᨄBLACK-EYED PEAS SAMBHARᨂ

A blend of black-eyed peas cooked with tomatoes, garlic, and spices in a creamy dal base, this sambhar is best served over plain rice or with idlis and dosai.

1/4 cup toor dal
3/4 teaspoon turmeric powder
1 cup dry black-eyed peas or 1 cup frozen black-eyed peas
1 onion
1 tomato
2 tablespoons canola or corn oil
1/4 teaspoon asafoetida powder
1 whole dried red chili pepper
1/2 teaspoon fenugreek seeds
1 teaspoon black mustard seeds
1 teaspoon urad dal
2 teaspoons sambhar powder
1 1/2 teaspoons salt
1/2 cup tomato sauce
2 cloves garlic, crushed
1/4 cup chopped fresh coriander

1. Boil 3 cups of water in a tall saucepan. Add toor dal and 1/4 teaspoon turmeric powder. Reduce heat to medium and cook, uncovered, for about 30 minutes until dal becomes creamy. If water evaporates during the cooking process, add another cup of water and cook until dal becomes creamy. Set aside.

2. To 4 cups of boiling water, add dried or frozen black-eyed peas and 1/4 teaspoon turmeric powder. Cook black-eyed peas, uncovered, until they are tender. When beans are tender, rinse well in a colander and set aside.

3. Chop onion and tomato and set aside.

4. In a saucepan, heat oil over medium heat. When oil is hot, but not smoking, add asafoetida, red chili pepper, fenugreek, mustard seeds, and urad dal. Cover and cook over medium heat until mustard seeds pop and urad dal is golden brown.

5. Add onion and tomato to saucepan and stir well. Add 1/4 teaspoon turmeric powder.

6. Add sambhar powder and salt. Stir well. Add tomato sauce.

7. Add cooked creamy dal and 2 additional cups of water.

8. When mixture is ready to boil, add cooked black-eyed peas and let the sambhar simmer for about 5 minutes.

9. Add garlic and coriander and allow to simmer for another 5 to 7 minutes. If sambhar seems too thick, add additional (1 cup) warm water and let simmer.

Note: Black-eyed peas sambhar can also be prepared without toor dal. In that case, omit Step 1 and increase the quantity of tomato sauce by 1 cup in Step 6.

Serves 6

CALORIES 191; FAT 5g.; SATURATED FAT 1g.; PROTEIN 11g.; CARBOHYDRATE 30g.; FIBER 7g.; CHOLESTEROL 0mg.; SODIUM 637mg.

ᴥBRUSSELS SPROUTS KULAMBUᴥ

These brussels sprouts are cooked with onions and tomatoes and simmered in tamarind sauce with spices. This kulambu is best served over
plain rice or with such items as idli and dosai.

2 tablespoons corn oil
1/4 teaspoon asafoetida powder
4 to 6 curry leaves (optional)
1/2 teaspoon fenugreek seeds
1 teaspoon black mustard seeds
1 teaspoon urad dal
1/2 cup chopped onion
1/2 cup chopped tomato
1/4 teaspoon turmeric powder
2 teaspoons sambhar powder
1 cup tomato sauce
1 teaspoon salt
1/4 teaspoon tamarind paste
1 1/2 cups fresh brussels sprouts, cut in half (if large, cut in quarters)

1. Place corn oil in a saucepan over medium heat. When the oil is hot,
but not smoking, add asafoetida, curry leaves, fenugreek, mustard seeds,
and urad dal. Cover and fry over medium heat until the mustard seeds
pop and urad dal is golden brown.

2. Add onion, tomato, and turmeric powder to hot oil, stirring constantly.

3. Add sambhar powder, tomato sauce, and salt. Stir well. Add 1 cup of
water to saucepan. Stir and cook for few minutes.

4. Add tamarind paste and mix all the ingredients thoroughly.

5. When the mixture in saucepan begins to boil, add brussels sprouts.
Cover and cook over low heat until brussels sprouts are just tender
(about 10 minutes). Be careful not to overcook.

Serves 4

CALORIES 120; FAT 8g.; SATURATED FAT 1g.; PROTEIN 3g.; CARBOHYDRATE 12g.; FIBER 3g.; CHOLESTEROL 0mg.; SODIUM 649mg.

◌∴Carrot Sambhar∴◌

Carrots cooked with spices in a creamy dal base, this sambhar is delicious served over plain rice and with idli, dosai, and chappati.

1/2 cup toor dal
3/4 teaspoon turmeric powder
2 tablespoons corn oil
1 whole dried red chili pepper
1/4 teaspoon asafoetida powder
4 to 6 curry leaves (optional)
1/4 teaspoon fenugreek seeds
1 teaspoon black mustard seeds
1 teaspoon urad dal
1/2 cup chopped onion
1/4 cup chopped tomato
1 cup peeled and sliced fresh carrots (thin rounds)
2 teaspoons sambhar powder
1/4 teaspoon tamarind paste
1/2 cup tomato sauce
1 teaspoon salt (more, if desired)
1/4 cup chopped coriander

1. Boil 4 cups of water in a tall saucepan. Add toor dal and 1/4 teaspoon turmeric powder. Reduce heat to medium and cook, uncovered, for about 30 minutes until dal becomes creamy. If water evaporates during the cooking process, add another cup of water and cook until dal becomes creamy. Set aside.

2. Place corn oil in a large saucepan over medium heat. When oil is hot, but not smoking, add the whole red pepper, asafoetida, curry leaves, fenugreek seeds, mustard seeds, and urad dal. Fry, covered, until mustard seeds burst (listen for popping sound) and other ingredients are a golden brown.

3. Add the onion and tomato. Add the remaining 1/2 teaspoon turmeric

powder and stir-fry for 1 to 2 minutes.

4. Add the carrots and stir-fry for a minute.

5. Add sambhar powder, tamarind paste, tomato sauce, and salt. Cook, covered, over medium-low heat for 3 minutes, stirring occasionally.

6. Add the toor dal mixture plus 2 cups of warm water, to the mixture in the saucepan. Add coriander. Cook, covered, over medium-low heat for another 5 to 7 minutes, until carrots are tender.

Note: You may substitute masoor dal (also known as red lentil) for toor dal and follow the above recipe. Cooking instructions for masoor dal are on page 173, Step 1.

Serves 6

CALORIES 129; FAT 5g.; SATURATED FAT 1g.; PROTEIN 6g.; CARBOHYDRATE 21g.; FIBER 7g.; CHOLESTEROL 0mg.; SODIUM 504mg.

~:Eggplant Pulikulambu:~

Eggplant is cooked with onions, tomatoes, and tamarind to make a delicious sauce.

2 tablespoons corn oil
1 dried red chili pepper
3 to 4 curry leaves (optional)
1/4 teaspoon asafoetida powder
1/2 teaspoon fenugreek seeds
1 teaspoon black mustard seeds
1 teaspoon urad dal
1 small onion, chopped
1 small tomato, chopped
2 cups eggplant, cut into small chunks
1/4 teaspoon turmeric powder
1/2 teaspoon cayenne powder (more, if desired)
1 teaspoon salt
1 cup tomato sauce
1/2 teaspoon tamarind paste

1. Place corn oil in a saucepan or a pressure cooker over medium heat. When oil is hot, but not smoking, add red pepper, curry leaves, asafoetida, fenugreek, mustard seeds, and urad dal.

2. Fry, covered, for a few minutes until mustard seeds pop and urad dal becomes golden. Add onion and tomato and sauté for a few minutes.

3. Add eggplant chunks and stir-fry for a few minutes.

4. Add turmeric, cayenne powder, and salt. Stir the seasonings into the mixture over medium heat.

5. Add tomato sauce and 1 1/2 cups of warm water. Add tamarind paste. Blend the ingredients well in saucepan.

6. Cook, covered, over low heat until eggplant becomes soft and blends well with other ingredients in the saucepan to become a delicious thickened kulambu.

Note: You may follow the above recipe up to Step 5, cover and then pressure cook, if you prefer.

Serves 4

CALORIES 125; FAT 7g.; SATURATED FAT 1g.; PROTEIN 3g.; CARBOHYDRATE 14g.; FIBER 3g.; CHOLESTEROL 0mg.; SODIUM 910mg.

～Eggplant and Potato Pulikulambu～

Simmered in a rich tamarind-based sauce, Eggplant and Potato Pulikulambu (without dal) takes only 15 minutes to prepare using a pressure cooker. At least a 2.5-quart-size pressure cooker is necessary. This pulikulambu can be served over plain rice, yogurt rice, idli, dosai, uthappam, or with any Indian bread.

2 tablespoons corn oil
1/8 teaspoon asafoetida powder
4 to 6 curry leaves (optional)
1 whole dried red chili pepper
1/4 teaspoon fenugreek seeds
1 teaspoon black mustard seeds
1 teaspoon urad dal
2 cups chopped eggplant
1 cup chopped potato, cut into small cubes (slightly bigger than eggplant)
1/2 cup onion, cut lengthwise
1/2 cup chopped tomato
1/2 teaspoon turmeric powder
2 teaspoons sambhar powder
1 cup tomato sauce
1/4 teaspoon tamarind paste
1 teaspoon salt (more, if desired)
1/4 cup chopped fresh coriander

1. Place corn oil in a pressure cooker or saucepan over medium heat. When oil is hot, but not smoking, add asafoetida, curry leaves, red pepper, fenugreek, mustard seeds, and urad dal.

2. Cover and fry until mustard seeds pop and urad dal is golden brown.

3. Add eggplant, potato, onion, and tomato.

4. Add turmeric powder and stir-fry for a few minutes over medium heat.

5. Add sambhar powder, tomato sauce, tamarind paste, salt, and coriander. Blend the seasonings well into the vegetables.

6. Add about 2 cups of water to the mixture. Be sure that there is enough liquid to cover the vegetables.

7. If cooking in a saucepan, cover and cook over medium heat, stirring often, until potatoes and eggplant are cooked. (Or) Cover pressure cooker and cook over medium heat for 10 minutes. Check for doneness. If the potatoes are not tender, cook the sambhar for few additional minutes, uncovered, in the pressure cooker over low heat (Or) transfer the sambhar to a saucepan and cook over low heat until the potatoes are tender.

Serves 6

CALORIES 105; FAT 5g.; SATURATED FAT 1g.; PROTEIN 2g.; CARBOHYDRATE 14g.; FIBER 3g.; CHOLESTEROL 0mg.; SODIUM 608mg.

⌒GARLIC KULAMBU⌒

Garlic is delicious when slow-cooked with onion, tomatoes, and spices in tamarind sauce. Garlic Kulambu is wonderful served over plain rice. It goes well with any Indian bread and is believed to be very healthful.

3 tablespoons corn oil
1/4 teaspoon asafoetida powder
4 to 6 curry leaves (optional)
1/2 teaspoon fenugreek seeds
1 teaspoon black mustard seeds
1 teaspoon urad dal
1/2 cup chopped onion
1/2 cup chopped tomato
1/2 cup whole garlic cloves
1/2 teaspoon turmeric powder
2 teaspoons sambhar powder
1/4 teaspoon tamarind paste
1/2 teaspoon salt (more, if desired)
1 cup tomato sauce
1/2 cup minced fresh coriander

1. Place corn oil in a saucepan over medium heat. When oil is hot, but not smoking, add asafoetida powder and curry leaves.

2. Immediately add fenugreek, mustard seeds, and urad dal. Stir quickly and cover. Fry until mustard seeds burst (listen for popping sound) and urad dal is golden (about 30 seconds).

3. Add onion, tomato, and garlic. Stir-fry for a minute. Add turmeric powder and mix well. Cook, covered, over medium-low heat, for approximately 3 minutes, until onion is tender.

4. Add sambhar powder, tamarind paste, and salt. Mix all the ingredients thoroughly while cooking over medium heat.

5. Add tomato sauce and 1 cup of warm water and coriander. Continue to cook, covered, until garlic is tender. The cooking time will vary with the size of the garlic cloves (4 to 6 minutes).

Serves 4

CALORIES 162; FAT 11g.; SATURATED FAT 1g.; PROTEIN 3g.; CARBOHYDRATE 15g.; FIBER 2g.; CHOLESTEROL 0mg.; SODIUM 644mg.

·ᴄKOHLRABI SAMBHAR:ᴠ

Kohlrabi sambhar is cooked with kohlrabi, tomato, and toor dal. It is light, flavorful, and easy to prepare. This sambhar is delicious served over plain rice, with uppuma, idli, dosai, or with any Indian bread.

1/2 cup toor dal
1/2 teaspoon turmeric powder
2 tablespoons corn oil
1/4 teaspoon asafoetida powder
1 whole dried red chili pepper
1/2 teaspoon fenugreek seeds
1 teaspoon black mustard seeds
1 teaspoon urad dal
1/4 cup chopped onions
1/2 cup chopped tomato
1 cup peeled and thinly sliced kohlrabi
1 teaspoon sambhar powder
1/4 cup tomato sauce
1/4 teaspoon tamarind paste
1 teaspoon salt
2 tablespoons chopped fresh coriander

1. Boil 4 cups of water to a boil in a saucepan. Add toor dal and 1/4 teaspoon turmeric powder. Reduce heat to medium and cook, uncovered, for about 30 minutes until dal becomes creamy. If water seems to evaporate during the cooking process, add another cup of water and cook until dal becomes creamy.

2. In a saucepan, heat oil over medium heat. When oil is hot, but not smoking, add asafoetida, whole red pepper, fenugreek, mustard seeds, and urad dal. Cook, covered, until mustard seeds pop and urad dal is golden brown.

3. Add chopped onion and tomato. Cook 2 to 3 minutes, until onion is tender. Add kohlrabi and the remaining 1/4 teaspoon turmeric powder.

Stir well.

4. Add sambhar powder and tomato sauce. Stir and add toor dal mixture, plus 2 cups of warm water, to the mixture in the saucepan. Stir well.

5. Add tamarind paste and salt. When mixture begins to bubble, reduce heat and cook kohlrabi until tender (4 to 6 minutes).

6. Add coriander and simmer for an additional few minutes.

Serves 6

CALORIES 135; FAT 5g.; SATURATED FAT 1g.; PROTEIN 6g.; CARBOHYDRATE 18g.; FIBER 5g.; CHOLESTEROL 0mg.; SODIUM 428mg.

ᴀᴍᴀsᴏᴏʀ Dᴀʟ Vᴇɢᴇᴛᴀʙʟᴇ Sᴀᴍʙʜᴀʀᴧ

This sambhar takes only few minutes to cook, as masoor dal cooks quickly. Potatoes, bell pepper, and tomatoes are cooked in masoor dal to make a delicious sambhar, which is very satisfying served over plain rice.

1/4 cup masoor dal (red lentils)
1/2 teaspoon turmeric powder
1 cup Idaho potato, peeled and cut lengthwise
1/4 cup chopped tomato
1 teaspoon sambhar powder
1 teaspoon salt
1/4 cup chopped coriander
1/2 cup chopped bell pepper

1. In a medium saucepan, boil 2 cups of water and add masoor dal with 1/4 teaspoon turmeric powder. Cook, uncovered, over medium-low heat until dal becomes soft, about 15 minutes. If water evaporates during the cooking process, add another 1/2 cup water and cook until dal becomes creamy. Set aside.

2. After dal is cooked, add potato, tomato, and the remaining 1/4 teaspoon turmeric powder to dal mixture in saucepan.

3. Add sambhar powder, salt, coriander, and an additional 2 cups of warm water to the vegetables. Cook over medium-low heat, covered, until potatoes are tender.

4. When potatoes are almost cooked, add bell pepper and let simmer for a few minutes until bell pepper is cooked to desired degree of doneness.

Serves 4

CALORIES 80; FAT trace; SATURATED FAT trace; PROTEIN 5g.; CARBOHYDRATE 16g.; FIBER 5g.; CHOLESTEROL 0mg.; SODIUM 539mg.

Variation:

To enhance the flavor of this sambhar, heat 1 tablespoon corn oil in a butter warmer. When oil is hot, but not smoking, add 2 to 4 curry leaves, 1/4 teaspoon asafoetida, 1 red chili pepper, 1 teaspoon mustard seeds, and 1 teaspoon urad dal. Cover and wait until mustard seeds pop and urad dal turns golden. Add this garnish to above sambhar in the saucepan and let it simmer over low heat for about 2 minutes before serving.

⌁Mixed Vegetable Sambhar⌁

Potatoes, bell peppers, and tomatoes are cooked in a creamy dal base. In this preparation, roasted and ground aromatic spices are added to the sambhar. Serve with plain rice, idli, or dosai.

1/2 cup toor dal
3/4 teaspoon turmeric powder
2 1/2 tablespoons corn oil
3 dried red chili peppers
1 teaspoon coriander seeds
1/2 teaspoon whole cumin seeds
3/4 teaspoon yellow split peas
1 tablespoon unsweetened coconut powder
1/4 teaspoon asafoetida powder
1 teaspoon black mustard seeds
1 teaspoon urad dal
1/2 cup onion, cut lengthwise
1/2 cup chopped tomatoes
2 small Idaho potatoes, washed, peeled, and cut into cubes
1 teaspoon salt
1/2 teaspoon sambhar powder (more, if desired)
2 green bell peppers, cut into small pieces
1/4 cup chopped coriander leaves

1. Boil 4 cups of water in a tall saucepan. Add toor dal and 1/4 teaspoon turmeric powder. Reduce heat to medium and cook, uncovered, for about 30 minutes until dal becomes creamy. If water evaporates during the cooking process, add another cup of water and cook until dal becomes creamy. Set aside.

2. Place 1/2 tablespoon corn oil in a cast-iron skillet and heat over medium heat. When oil is hot, but not smoking, add 2 red chili peppers, coriander seeds, cumin, and yellow split peas. Fry over low heat until golden brown. Add coconut powder and stir 1 minute.

3. Put all the above fried ingredients in a spice or coffee grinder and grind (without water) to a powdery consistency. Set aside.

4. Heat remaining 2 tablespoons corn oil in a saucepan over medium heat. When oil is hot, but not smoking, add asafoetida powder and the remaining red chili pepper. Immediately add mustard seeds and urad dal.

5. When urad dal turns golden, add onion and tomatoes. Stir-fry briefly. Add potatoes together with remaining 1/2 teaspoon turmeric powder. Stir well, uncovered, over medium heat.

6. Add creamy dal, 3 additional cups of water, and salt. Cook potatoes, covered, over medium heat about 5 minutes (until partially cooked).

7. Add ground spices to the mixture in the saucepan. Stir and cook, covered, over medium heat. When potatoes are cooked, add bell peppers and fresh coriander.

8. Cook over low heat until vegetables are tender.

Serves 6

CALORIES 185; FAT 6g.; SATURATED FAT 1g.; PROTEIN 7g.; CARBOHYDRATE 29g.; FIBER 6g.; CHOLESTEROL 0mg.; SODIUM 369mg.

~MOORE KULAMBU~

This buttermilk sauce, similar to a sambhar, is blended with coconut, cumin, ginger, and chili pepper. Vegetables of your choice can be added to this dish. Moore Kulambu is delicious served over plain rice.

2 teaspoons corn oil
1 tablespoon cumin seeds
1 tablespoon chana dal
1 tablespoon white rice
1/4 cup chopped fresh coconut
1 tablespoon sliced fresh ginger root
1 green chili pepper (more, if desired)
1 1/2 cups buttermilk
1/4 teaspoon asafoetida powder
1 dried red chili pepper
4 to 6 curry leaves
1 teaspoon mustard seeds
1 teaspoon urad dal
1/4 cup onion, cut lengthwise
1/4 cup tomato, chopped
1/4 cup cucumber, unpeeled and cut lengthwise into thin slices
1/2 teaspoon salt
1/4 cup chopped fresh coriander

1. Place 1 teaspoon corn oil in a small skillet over medium heat.

2. When oil is hot, but not smoking, add cumin seeds, chana dal, and rice. Fry to a golden brown. Turn off heat. Add coconut, ginger, and green chili to the seasonings in skillet.

3. Transfer all the ingredients from the skillet to a blender. Add buttermilk to cover the ingredients and 1 cup of water.

4. Grind the ingredients to create a smooth mixture.

5. Heat remaining 1 teaspoon corn oil in a saucepan over medium heat.

6. When oil is hot, but not smoking, add asafoetida, red chili pepper, curry leaves, mustard seeds, and urad dal.

7. Cover and fry until mustard seeds pop and urad dal is golden brown. Add onion and tomato and stir-fry for a minute. Add cucumber, salt, and coriander.

8. Add buttermilk mixture to the saucepan and stir well.

9. When the mixture begins to boil remove from heat. Do not let buttermilk simmer as it will begin to curdle.

Makes about 3 cups (1/2 cup per serving)

Serves 6

CALORIES 79; FAT 4g.; SATURATED FAT 1g.; PROTEIN 3g.; CARBOHYDRATE 9g.; FIBER 2g.; CHOLESTEROL 1mg.; SODIUM 228mg.

Variation:
Skip the first 4 steps in the above recipe.

1. In a grinder blend 1 cup of buttermilk with 1 tablespoon sliced ginger, 1 green chili, and 2 teaspoons cumin seeds. Grind the ingredients to create a smooth paste.

2. Follow the above recipe from Step 5 through Step 10.

ᵕ Okra Sambhar ᵕ

Okra cooked with tomatoes in a creamy dal, this nutritious and satisfying sambhar is best served over plain rice.

1/4 cup toor dal
1/2 teaspoon turmeric powder
2 tablespoons corn oil
1/2 teaspoon asafoetida powder
1 dried red chili pepper
4 to 6 curry leaves (optional)
1/4 teaspoon fenugreek seeds
1 teaspoon black mustard seeds
1 teaspoon urad dal
1/3 cup chopped onion
1/4 cup chopped tomato
2 cups frozen cut okra
2 teaspoons sambhar powder
1/2 cup tomato sauce
1 teaspoon salt

1. Boil 3 cups of water in a tall saucepan over medium heat. Add toor dal with 1/4 teaspoon turmeric powder. Reduce heat to medium and cook, uncovered, for about 30 minutes until dal becomes creamy. If water evaporates during the cooking process, you may add another cup of water and cook until dal becomes creamy. Set aside.

2. In a saucepan, place corn oil over medium heat. When oil is hot, but not smoking, add asafoetida, red pepper, curry leaves,fenugreek, mustard seeds, and urad dal. Cover and cook over medium heat until mustard seeds pop and urad dal is golden.

3. Add onion and tomato to saucepan and stir well.

4. Add okra and the remaining 1/4 teaspoon turmeric powder to saucepan and sauté for 2 to 3 minutes over medium heat.

5. Add sambhar powder, tomato sauce, and salt. Stir well.

6. Add cooked creamy dal with about 2 cups of water to the saucepan. Stir the mixture well. Let okra continue to cook over medium-low heat for 3 to 5 minutes.

Note: You may also use fresh cut okra for making okra sambhar. Cut the ends off fresh okra and slice in 1/2- inch to 3/4-inch slices. Follow the above recipe. The authors prefer to use frozen cut okra, because it is cut evenly and cooks faster than fresh okra.

Serves 6

CALORIES 107; FAT 5g.; SATURATED FAT 1g.; PROTEIN 4g.; CARBOHYDRATE 13g.; FIBER 3g.; CHOLESTEROL 0mg.; SODIUM 483mg.

❧ Pearl Onion and Tomato Sambhar ❧

This aromatic sambhar is a popular and traditional dish. Pearl Onion Sambhar is served over plain rice with any vegetable kootu, poriyal, and pappad. It can also be served with idli and dosai during breakfast.

1/4 cup toor dal
1/2 teaspoon turmeric powder
1/2 cup (about 12) fresh pearl onions
3 tablespoons corn oil
1/4 teaspoon asafoetida powder
4 to 6 curry leaves
1 dried red chili pepper
1/4 teaspoon fenugreek
1 teaspoon black mustard seeds
1 teaspoon urad dal
1 cup chopped tomatoes
2 teaspoons sambhar powder
1 teaspoon salt
1/4 cup tomato sauce
1/4 teaspoon tamarind paste
1/4 cup chopped fresh coriander

1. Boil 3 cups of water in a tall saucepan. Add toor dal and 1/4 teaspoon turmeric powder. Reduce heat to medium and cook, uncovered, for about 30 minutes until dal becomes creamy. If water evaporates during the cooking process, add another cup of water and cook until dal becomes creamy. Set aside.

2. Peel pearl onions and set aside.

3. Place corn oil in a saucepan and heat over medium heat. When the oil is hot, but not smoking, add asafoetida, curry leaves, red pepper, fenugreek, mustard seeds, and urad dal. Fry, covered, until mustard seeds pop and urad turns golden.

4. Add onions and tomatoes to saucepan. Cook, covered, for about 2 minutes until onions are tender.

5. Add remaining 1/4 teaspon turmeric powder and blend well. Add sambhar powder and salt. Blend the seasonings well with onions and tomatoes. Cook for a minute.

6. Add cooked creamy dal to the above mixture with about 2 and 1/2 cups of warm water. Stir well.

7. Add tomato sauce, tamarind paste, and coriander to the sambhar mixture. Let onions cook with sauce over low heat, covered, for about 3 minutes.

Serves 6

CALORIES 118; FAT 7g.; SATURATED FAT 1g.; PROTEIN 3g.; CARBOHYDRATE 11g.; FIBER 3g.; CHOLESTEROL 8mg.; SODIUM 442mg.

ᴖ Potato Sambhar ᴖ

This quick and easy-to-prepare recipe for potato sambhar uses a pressure cooker (at least a 2.5-quart-size pressure cooker is necessary for this recipe.) This sambhar may be served with idli, dosai, uppuma, or idiyappam.

1/2 cup toor dal
2 whole dried red chili peppers
1/4 teaspoon turmeric powder
2 cups unpeeled chopped potatoes
1/2 cup chopped tomato
1 green chili pepper, chopped
1 teaspoon salt
1 teaspoon sambhar powder
1/2 teaspoon asafoetida powder
3 to 4 curry leaves (optional), or 1/4 cup chopped fresh coriander
2 tablespoons corn oil
1 red chili pepper
1 teaspoon mustard seeds
1 1/2 teaspoons urad dal

1. Place toor dal, 1 red pepper, turmeric powder, and 3 cups of water in a medium-size stainless steel mixing bowl that will fit into the pressure cooker

2. Add potatoes, tomato, and green chili to the bowl.

3. Add salt, sambhar powder, and 1/4 teaspoon asafoetida powder with several curry leaves or chopped coriander, if desired, to the mixing bowl.

4. Place 1 or 2 cups of water in bottom of pressure cooker according to manufacturer's direction and size of pressure cooker. Place the bowl containing all the above ingredients in the pressure cooker.

5. Cook in pressure cooker for 10 to 15 minutes.

6. Place oil in a medium-size saucepan over medium heat. When oil is hot, but not smoking, add remaining 1 red chili pepper, 1/4 teaspoon asafoetida powder, mustard seeds, and urad dal. Cover and fry until mustard seeds pop and urad dal is golden brown.

7. Pour ingredients from pressure cooker plus 2 cups warm water into a saucepan.

8. Heat for a few minutes over low heat to blend all the ingredients thoroughly.

Serves 6

CALORIES 170; FAT 5g.; SATURATED FAT 1g.; PROTEIN 7g.; CARBOHYDRATE 26g.; FIBER 5g.; CHOLESTEROL 0mg.; SODIUM 365mg.

᭡THANNIR KULAMBU᭡

A Chettinad favorite featuring onions and tomatoes in a mildly flavored tomato base, this light kulambu is best served over plain rice or uppuma.

2 tablespoons corn oil
1/4 teaspoon asafoetida powder
4 to 5 curry leaves
1 dried red chili pepper
1/4 teaspoon fenugreek seeds
1 teaspoon black mustard seeds
1 teaspoon urad dal
1/2 cup chopped onion
1/2 cup chopped tomato
1/4 teaspoon turmeric powder
1/2 teaspoon sambhar powder (more, if desired)
1/4 cup tomato sauce
2 cloves garlic, crushed
1/2 teaspoons salt
2 tablespoons minced fresh coriander

1. Heat corn oil in a saucepan over medium heat.

2. When oil is hot, but not smoking, add asafoetida powder, curry leaves, and red pepper.

3. Add fenugreek, mustard seeds, and urad dal. Cover and fry until mustard seeds pop and urad dal is golden.

4. Add onion and tomato. Sauté for a few minutes.

5. Add turmeric powder.

6. When onion and tomatoes are tender, add sambhar powder. Blend well.

7. Add tomato sauce and 2 cups of water.

8. Simmer over medium heat. When kulambu begins to boil, add garlic, salt, and coriander.

9. Simmer for a few more minutes.

Serves 4

CALORIES 96; FAT 7g.; SATURATED FAT 1g.; PROTEIN 2g.; CARBOHYDRATE 7g.; FIBER 2g.; CHOLESTEROL 0mg.; SODIUM 364mg.

ᴠ:ZUCCHINI SAMBHAR:ᴠ

This sambhar is made from zucchini, onion, and tomatoes in a creamy dal base. It is delicious served over plain rice, with uppuma, idli, dosai, or with any Indian bread.

1/2 cup toor dal
1/2 teaspoon turmeric powder
2 tablespoons corn oil
1/2 teaspoon asafoetida powder
1 whole dried red chili pepper
1/2 teaspoon fenugreek seeds
1 teaspoon black mustard seeds
1 teaspoon urad dal
1/2 medium onion, cut lengthwise
1 small tomato, chopped
2 teaspoons sambhar powder
1/4 cup tomato sauce
1/4 teaspoon tamarind paste
1 teaspoon salt (more, if desired)
2 cups peeled and cubed zucchini
2 to 3 tablespoons chopped fresh coriander

1. Boil 4 cups of water in a tall saucepan. Add toor dal and 1/4 teaspoon turmeric powder. Reduce heat to medium and cook, uncovered, for about 30 minutes until dal becomes creamy. If water evaporates during the cooking process, add another cup of water and cook until dal becomes creamy. Set aside.

2. In a saucepan, heat oil over medium heat. When oil is hot, but not smoking, add asafoetida, whole red pepper, fenugreek, mustard seeds, and urad dal. Cook, covered, until mustard seeds pop and urad dal is golden brown.

3. Add onion and tomato. Cook 2 to 3 minutes, until onions are tender. Then add remaining 1/4 teaspoon turmeric powder and sambhar powder

and stir well.

4. Add tomato sauce. Add toor dal mixture, plus 3 cups of warm water, to the mixture in the saucepan. Stir mixture well.

5. Add tamarind paste and salt. When mixture begins to bubble, add zucchini and cook, covered, over low heat, until zucchini is tender.

6. Add coriander and simmer for an additional few minutes.

Serves 6

CALORIES 130; FAT 5g.; SATURATED FAT 1g.; PROTEIN 6g.; CARBOHYDRATE 17g.; FIBER 4g.; CHOLESTEROL 0mg.; SODIUM 425mg.

Vegetables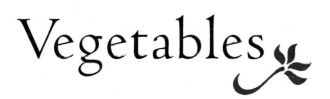

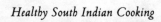

~:ACORN SQUASH MASALA PORIYAL:~

A seasoned stir-fry vegetable dish that can be served with lemon rice, yogurt rice, or as a side dish with any meal.

2 cups acorn squash
2 tablespoons corn oil
1/4 teaspoon asafoetida powder
4 to 6 curry leaves (optional)
1 whole dried red chili pepper
1 teaspoon black mustard seeds
1 teaspoon urad dal
1 medium onion, cut lengthwise
1 small tomato, chopped
1/2 teaspoon turmeric powder
1/2 teaspoon cayenne powder (more, if desired)
3/4 cup tomato sauce
1 teaspoon salt
1/4 cup unsweetened powdered coconut

1. Acorn squash has a tough skin. Cut the squash in half and cook the halves in a microwave for 1 to 2 minutes so that it is easy to cut the squash. Remove the pulp and skin. Cut squash into small chunks.

2. Place oil in skillet over medium heat. When oil is hot, but not smoking, add asafoedtida powder, curry leaves, and red pepper.

3. Add mustard seeds and urad dal and cover. Fry until mustard seeds pop and urad dal is golden brown.

4. Add onion and tomato and stir-fry for 1 minute.

5. Add turmeric powder and cayenne powder. Stir well.

6. Add tomato sauce and salt. Mix well. When the mixture begins to bubble, add the acorn squash and stir well.

7. Cover and cook over medium heat until the squash becomes somewhat soft. Add a small amount of water (about 1 tablespoon) periodically to facilitate the cooking process.

8. Add coconut powder and stir well.

Serves 6

CALORIES 102; FAT 6g.; SATURATED FAT 2g.; PROTEIN 1g.; CARBOHYDRATE 12g.; FIBER 2g.; CHOLESTEROL 0mg.; SODIUM 555mg.

~:BEANS KOOTU:~

Green beans cooked with creamy yellow split peas, cumin, and ginger, Beans Kootu is delicious served with plain rice, yogurt rice, or as a side dish with any meal.

1/4 cup yellow split peas
1/2 teaspoon turmeric powder
2 tablespoons corn oil
2 to 4 curry leaves
1 teaspoon black mustard seeds
1 teaspoon urad dal
1/3 cup chopped onion
1 tablespoon minced ginger
1 green chili, chopped
2 cups chopped green beans
1 teaspoon cumin powder
1 teaspoon salt

1. Boil 3 cups of water in a saucepan over medium heat. Add split peas and 1/4 teaspoon turmeric powder. Cook, uncovered, for about 30 minutes until split peas become creamy. If water evaporates during cooking process, add 1/2 cup more water to the saucepan. Mash the cooked split peas with masher while they are hot. Set aside.

2. Heat oil in a saucepan over medium heat. When oil is hot, but not smoking, add curry leaves, mustard seeds, urad dal. Wait for the mustard seeds to pop and urad dal to turn golden.

3. Immediately add onion, ginger, and green chili. Stir well and add remaining 1/4 teaspoon turmeric powder.

4. Add green beans to the saucepan. Stir and add cumin powder and salt. Blend the ingredients well in the saucepan.

5. Add creamy split pea mixture together with just enough water to cover the beans and cook, covered, over medium-low heat (approximately 10

minutes) until beans are tender, but not overcooked.

Serves 4

CALORIES 135; FAT 7g.; SATURATED FAT 1g.; PROTEIN 6g.; CARBOHYDRATE 17g.; FIBER 6g.; CHOLESTEROL 0mg.; SODIUM 547mg.

～Beans Poriyal～

Green beans with split peas, ginger, and coconut, Beans Poriyal makes a tasty side dish for any meal.

1/4 cup yellow split peas
3/4 teaspoon turmeric powder
2 tablespoons canola or corn oil
4 to 6 curry leaves (optional)
1 teaspoon black mustard seeds
2 teaspoons urad dal
1 pound green beans, diced (stems removed), about 3 cups
1 teaspoon minced fresh ginger
1 green chili pepper, finely chopped (optional)
1 teaspoon salt
1/2 teaspoon chutney powder
1/4 cup fresh or unsweetened powdered coconut

1. Boil 2 cups of water. Add split peas and 1/4 teaspoon turmeric powder. Cook split peas over medium heat, uncovered, for about 20 minutes. Drain and set aside.

2. Heat oil in a large skillet over medium heat with curry leaves. When oil is hot, but not smoking, stir in mustard seeds and urad dal. Cover and heat until mustard seeds burst (listen for popping sound) and urad dal is golden.

3. Add beans and stir well. Add ginger and green chili. Cook over medium heat for about a minute.

4. Add salt and remaining 1/2 teaspoon of turmeric powder. Add chutney powder. Mix well.

5. Cover beans and cook over low heat without water for 5 to 7 minutes. Note: a sprinkle or two of water may, however, be added on top of the green beans to facilitate the cooking process.

6. When beans are tender but still crisp, add cooked split peas and coconut. Stir well. Serve immediately or remove from heat and keep covered until serving time. Be careful not to overcook beans.

Serves 6

CALORIES 125; FAT 7g.; SATURATED FAT 2g.; PROTEIN 5g.; CARBOHYDRATE 15g.; FIBER 7g.; CHOLESTEROL 0mg.; SODIUM 440mg.

Variation: To make **Beans and Cabbage Poriyal**, use 1 1/2 cups diced green beans and 1 1/2 cups coarsely shredded cabbage. Follow the above recipe through Step5. In Step 6, when beans are tender but still crisp, add shredded cabbage. Stir-fry for about 3 minutes until cabbage is slightly cooked. Add cooked split peas and coconut. Stir well.

⌁BELL PEPPER MASALA⌁

Bell pepper with onions, tomatoes and ginger, Bell Pepper Masala is a delicious accompaniment to any meal.

2 tablespoons canola or corn oil
1/4 teaspoon asafoetida powder
1 teaspoon black mustard seeds
1 teaspoon urad dal
1 cup onion, chopped lengthwise
1/2 cup chopped tomato
1/2 tablespoons chopped ginger root
1/2 teaspoon turmeric powder
1/2 teaspoon cayenne powder
1/2 teaspoon salt
3 cups bell peppers, chopped lengthwise (1 1/2-inch to 2-inch pieces)
1/4 cup plain low-fat yogurt

1. Heat oil in a cast-iron skillet over medium heat. When oil is hot, but not smoking, add asafoetida, mustard seeds and urad dal. Fry, covered, until mustard seeds burst (listen for popping sound) and urad dal is golden brown.

2. Add onion, tomato, and ginger. Stir-fry for 1 minute over medium heat.

3. Add turmeric powder, cayenne powder, and salt. Mix well to obtain a thick paste-like consistency.

4. Add bell peppers and blend well with sauce. Cover and reduce heat to low. Continue cooking until bell peppers are just tender, stirring occasionally. Be careful not to overcook!

5. Transfer cooked vegetables from the skillet to a bowl. Allow to cool for a few minutes. Stir in yogurt and mix well.

Serves 4

CALORIES 118; FAT 7g.; SATURATED FAT 1g.; PROTEIN 2g.; CARBOHYDRATE 14g.; FIBER 6g.; CHOLESTEROL trace; SODIUM 285mg.

‿:BELL PEPPER AND TOMATO PACHADI:‿

A delicious combination of vegetables cooked with dal in tamarind paste, this dish is delicious served with rice, chappati, and poori.

1/4 cup yellow split peas
1/2 teaspoon turmeric powder
2 tablespoons canola or corn oil
1 whole dried red chili pepper
4 to 6 curry leaves
1/4 teaspoon asafoetida powder
1 teaspoon black mustard seeds
1 teaspoon urad dal
1/4 cup chopped onion
3/4 cup chopped tomato
2 cups green bell peppers, cut into small pieces
1/2 teaspoon cayenne powder
1/2 teaspoon cumin powder
1 teaspoon salt
1/4 teaspoon tamarind paste
1/4 cup tomato sauce
1/4 cup chopped fresh coriander

1. Boil about 2 cups of water. Add yellow split peas with 1/4 teaspoon turmeric powder and cook for about 20 minutes over medium heat, uncovered, until split peas are semi-soft. Set aside.

2. Heat oil in a saucepan over medium heat. When oil is hot, but not smoking, add red chili pepper, curry leaves, asafoetida, mustard seeds, and urad dal. Cover and fry over medium heat until mustard seeds pop and urad dal is golden brown.

3. Add onion and tomato. Add remaining 1/4 teaspoon turmeric powder and stir for a few minutes.

4. Add green peppers, split peas, cayenne powder, cumin powder, salt, and

tamarind paste.

5. Add tomato sauce and about 1/4 cup of water. When the mixture begins to boil, add coriander. Stir well.

6. Cover and cook over medium heat until green pepper is tender.

Serves 6

CALORIES 113; FAT 5g.; SATURATED FAT trace; PROTEIN 5g.; CARBOHYDRATE 16g.; FIBER 5g.; CHOLESTEROL 0mg.; SODIUM 615mg.

Variation:
Try **Masoor dal** or **Moong dal** instead of yellow split peas in Step 1 of the above recipe for a delightful variation.

∽ Black-eyed Peas Masala Poriyal ∽

A hearty stir-fry dish with coconut, Black-eyed Peas Masala Poriyal is excellent served with chappati or poori or as accompaniment to a rice dish, especially yogurt rice.

> 2 tablespoons corn oil
> 3 to 4 tiny pieces cinnamon stick
> 1 teaspoon black mustard seeds
> 2 teaspoons urad dal
> 1/4 cup chopped tomato
> 1/2 cup chopped onion
> 1/4 teaspoon turmeric powder
> 3/4 cup tomato sauce
> 1/2 teaspoon cayenne powder
> 1 teaspoon salt (more if desired)
> 1 package (16 ounces) frozen black-eyed peas
> 2 tablespoons powdered unsweetened coconut

1. Heat corn oil in a medium-size skillet over medium heat. When oil is hot, but not smoking, add cinnamon sticks, mustard seeds, and urad dal. Cover and fry until mustard seeds burst (listen for popping sound) and urad dal is golden brown (about 30 seconds).

2. Add the tomato and onion. Stir-fry for 1 to 2 minutes. Add turmeric powder and stir.

3. Add tomato sauce, cayenne powder, and salt. Mix well.

4. Add frozen black-eyed peas and blend well into ingredients in skillet. Cook, covered, over medium-low heat, adding 1 cup of warm water and stirring often.

5. When peas are just tender (10 to 12 minutes) add powdered coconut. Mix well.

Serves 6

CALORIES 182; FAT 6g.; SATURATED FAT 1g.; PROTEIN 8g.; CARBOHYDRATE 26g.; FIBER 6g.; CHOLESTEROL 0mg.; SODIUM 547mg.

Variation:

Frozen butter beans (16 ounces) may be substituted for black-eyed peas.

☙ BROCCOLI PODIMAS ☙

A satisfying broccoli dish made with split peas and spices coarsely ground
and steamed, Broccoli Podimas can be served as a side dish with any meal.

1/2 cup yellow split peas
2 dried red chili peppers (more, if desired)
1/2 teaspoon fennel seeds
1 teaspoon cumin seeds
3 tablespoons corn oil
4 to 5 curry leaves (optional)
1 teaspoon black mustard seeds
2 teaspoons urad dal
1 cup chopped onion
1/2 teaspoon chutney powder
1 teaspoon salt (more, if desired)
4 cups finely chopped broccoli (including stems)
1/4 cup unsweetened powdered coconut

1. Soak split peas in enough water to cover for 30 minutes. Drain peas
and coarsely grind in blender with red pepper, fennel, and cumin. It is
best to grind the split peas in small batches. Add only enough water to
facilitate the grinding process. Ground split peas should have the texture
of coarse cornmeal.

2. Pour coarsely ground mixture in a microwave dish and cook, uncovered, on high in a microwave oven for 3 minutes. The mixture after cooking in microwave will feel somewhat hard. Set aside and cool for 5
minutes.

3. Heat corn oil with curry leaves in a cast-iron skillet over medium heat.
When oil is hot, but not smoking, stir in mustard seeds and urad dal.
Cover and fry until mustard seeds burst (listen for popping sound) and
urad dal is golden.

4. Add onion to skillet and cook for 30 seconds.

5. Add all of the split pea mixture to ingredients in skillet. Blend well. Fry over medium-low heat until the split peas become golden brown and grainy in texture (3 to 5 minutes). Be certain to stir frequently. If split peas begin to stick to bottom of skillet, add a small amount of corn oil as needed to facilitate the process.

6. Stir in chutney powder and salt. Add broccoli and blend well with split pea mixture. Cover and cook over low heat until broccoli becomes tender (approximately another 7 minutes). Be certain to stir frequently. Remove from heat.

7. Sprinkle powdered coconut over broccoli and stir well. Cover to keep warm until serving.

Serves 6

CALORIES 162; FAT 8g.; SATURATED FAT 2g.; PROTEIN 8g.; CARBOHYDRATE 20g.; FIBER 8g.; CHOLESTEROL 0mg.; SODIUM 383

Variations:

Green Beans Podimas: Instead of broccoli, substitute 3 cups of diced green beans.

Carrot Podimas: Use 4 cups of shredded carrots in place of broccoli.

Cabbage Podimas: Use 3 cups of coarsely shredded cabbage in place of broccoli.

Follow the recipe as above.

ꙮ Broccoli with Coconut Poriyal ꙮ

An easy-to-prepare broccoli stir-fry that makes an excellent side dish at any meal.

1 tablespoon canola or corn oil
1 teaspoon black mustard seeds
1 teaspoon urad dal
3/4 cup chopped onion
4 cups coarsely chopped broccoli (including stems)
1 green chili pepper, finely chopped
1 teaspoon salt
1/2 teaspoon chutney powder
1/2 cup freshly ground or powdered unsweetened coconut

1. Heat oil in a large skillet or wok over medium heat. When oil is hot but not smoking, stir in mustard seeds and urad dal. Cover and heat until mustard seeds burst (listen for popping sound) and urad dal is golden.

2. Add onion and stir for 30 seconds.

3. Add broccoli, green chili pepper, salt, and chutney powder to skillet and stir well. Cook, covered, for 5 to 7 minutes.

4. When the broccoli is tender but still crisp, add the coconut and stir well.

Serves 4 to 6

CALORIES 107; FAT 8g.; SATURATED FAT 3g.; PROTEIN 2g.; CARBOHYDRATE 7g.; FIBER 3g.; CHOLESTEROL 0mg.; SODIUM 231mg.

~:BRUSSELS SPROUTS AND CHICKPEA PORIYAL:~

A hearty and fiber-rich stir-fry dish, Brussels Sprouts and Chickpea Poriyal can be served as a side dish with any meal.

About 4 cups fresh brussels sprouts
1 tablespoon corn oil
1 teaspoon black mustard seeds
1 teaspoon urad dal
1 medium onion, chopped
1/2 teaspoon salt
1/2 teaspoon chutney powder or 1 green chili pepper, chopped
1 can (15 ounces) chickpeas, rinsed and drained
1/2 cup freshly ground or powdered unsweetened coconut

1. Coarsely chop brussels sprouts.

2. Heat oil in a large skillet or wok over medium heat. When oil is hot, but not smoking, stir in mustard seeds and urad dal. Cover and fry until mustard seeds burst (listen for popping sound) and urad dal is golden.

3. Add onion and stir for 30 seconds.

4. Add brussels sprouts, salt, and chutney powder to skillet and stir well. Cook, covered, for 2 minutes over medium heat. Be careful not to over-cook brussels sprouts.

5. Add chickpeas and coconut. Mix well and cook for an additional minute.

Serves 6

CALORIES 336; FAT 9g.; SATURATED FAT 3g.; PROTEIN 16g.; CARBOHYDRATE 51g.; FIBER 16g.; CHOLESTEROL 0mg.; SODIUM 211mg.

ᜪBRUSSELS SPROUTS MASALA PORIYALᜪ

Brussels sprouts, cooked using tomatoes and seasonings and blended with coconut, makes a favorite accompaniment to any meal.

2 tablespoons corn oil
2 to 3 small sticks cinnamon
1/2 bay leaf, crumbled
1 teaspoon black mustard seeds
1 teaspoon urad dal
1/2 cup chopped onion
1 cup chopped tomato
1/8 teaspoon turmeric powder
1/4 teaspoon cayenne powder (more, if desired)
1/2 teaspoon salt
1/2 cup tomato sauce
2 cups quartered brussels sprouts
1 teaspoon unsweetened powdered coconut

1. Place oil in a saucepan over medium heat. When oil is hot, but not smoking, add cinnamon sticks and bay leaf. Immediately add mustard seeds and urad dal. Wait until mustard seeds pop and urad dal turns golden.

2. Add onion and tomato. Add turmeric powder and cook until onions are tender.

3. Add cayenne powder and salt and cook for a minute. Add tomato sauce. Stir well.

4. Add brussels sprouts and blend sprouts well into seasonings. Add 1/2 cup of warm water and cook over medium-low heat, covered, until brussels sprouts are tender.

5. Add coconut powder and mix well.

Serves 4

CALORIES 125; FAT 8g.; SATURATED FAT 1g.; PROTEIN 3g.; CARBOHYDRATE
14g.; FIBER 5g.; CHOLESTEROL 0mg.; SODIUM 469mg.

✌CABBAGE WITH COCONUT PORIYAL﹀

An easy-to-make stir-fry cabbage dish with coconut, Cabbage Poriyal can be served as a side dish with any meal or as an accompaniment to plain rice and sambhar.

2 tablespoons corn oil
4 to 6 curry leaves (optional)
1 teaspoon black mustard seeds
2 teaspoons urad dal
4 cups shredded cabbage
1 teaspoon minced fresh ginger
1/2 green chili pepper, chopped
1/2 teaspoon salt (more, if desired)
1 tablespoon freshly ground or unsweetened powdered coconut

1. Place oil in a wok or skillet over medium heat. When oil is hot, but not smoking, stir in curry leaves, mustard seeds, and urad dal. Cover and fry until mustard seeds burst (listen for popping sound) and urad dal is golden.

2. Add cabbage, ginger, and green chili pepper. Stir well into seasonings and add salt. Cover and cook over low heat until cabbage is tender (about 3 minutes) but still crisp.

3. Add the coconut and stir well.

Serves 4

CALORIES 98; FAT 8g.; SATURATED FAT 1g.; PROTEIN 2g.; CARBOHYDRATE 6g.; FIBER 3g.; CHOLESTEROL 0mg.; SODIUM 281mg.

❦CABBAGE AND PEAS PORIYAL❧

An easy-to-prepare stir-fry that makes a tasty and unique side dish for any meal.

1 1/2 tablespoons canola or corn oil
1 teaspoon mustard seeds
2 teaspoon urad dal
4 to 6 curry leaves (optional)
2 cups coarsely cut cabbage
1/2 teaspoon turmeric powder
1 cup frozen peas
1 teaspoon salt
1/2 teaspoon chutney powder
1/2 cup freshly ground or unsweetened powdered coconut

1. In a saucepan, heat oil over medium heat until hot, but not smoking. Add mustard seeds, urad dal, and curry leaves. Fry, covered, until mustard seeds burst (listen for popping sounds) and urad dal is golden.

2. Add cabbage and turmeric powder. Mix well. Continue cooking, uncovered, over medium heat for 1 to 2 minutes, stirring frequently.

3. Add peas, salt, and chutney powder. Stir well.

4. Cook, covered, over medium heat for 2 minutes.

5. When cabbage and peas are cooked, stir in coconut. Do not overcook vegetables.

Serves 4

CALORIES 129; FAT 9g.; SATURATED FAT 3g.; PROTEIN 3g.; CARBOHYDRATE 11g.; FIBER 4g.; CHOLESTEROL 0mg.; SODIUM 584mg.

↭ CABBAGE AND POTATO KOOTU ↫

Kootu is a thick, lightly seasoned vegetable dish cooked with ginger in a creamy dal base. Serve as a side dish with rice.

1/2 cup toor dal
1/2 teaspoon turmeric powder
2 tablespoons corn oil
2 to 3 curry leaves (optional)
1 teaspoon black mustard seeds
1 teaspoon urad dal
1/2 cup chopped onion
1 green chili pepper, minced (more, if desired)
1 tablespoon minced fresh ginger root
1/2 cup Idaho potato, shredded the same size as cabbage
2 cups coarsely shredded cabbage (cut as for coleslaw)
1 teaspoon cumin powder
1 teaspoon salt

1. Boil 4 cups of water in a tall saucepan. Add toor dal together with 1/4 teaspoon turmeric powder. Reduce heat to medium and cook dal, uncovered, until it becomes creamy (approximately 30 minutes). If most of the water evaporates before dal becomes creamy add an additional cup of water and continue to cook. It helps to mash cooked dal in saucepan with a potato masher. Set aside.

2. Heat oil in a saucepan over medium heat. Add curry leaves.

3. When oil is hot, but not smoking, add mustard seeds and urad dal. Cover and cook until mustard seeds burst (listen for popping sound) and urad dal is golden.

4. Add onion, chili, and ginger. Stir well.

5. Add potato and stir-fry a few minutes and then add the cabbage. Stir-fry approximately 1 minute.

6. Add remaining 1/4 teaspoon turmeric powder, cumin powder, and salt. Stir well.

7. Immediately add cooked creamy toor dal with about 1 cup of water. Cover and cook over medium heat for 8 to 10 minutes, stirring frequently so that potatoes do not stick to the bottom of the pan.

8. Cook until the vegetables are tender.

Serves 6

CALORIES 138; FAT 5g.; SATURATED FAT 1g.; PROTEIN 6g.; CARBOHYDRATE 19g.; FIBER 4g.; CHOLESTEROL 0mg.; SODIUM 365mg.

Variation:
To make **Cabbage Kootu,** just use 3 cups of shredded cabbage and omit the potatoes in the above recipe.

⌒:Cabbage with Scrambled Eggs:⌒

An easy, unique, stir-fry dish with cabbage and eggs that can be served as side dish with any meal.

2 tablespoons corn oil
4 to 6 curry leaves (optional)
1 teaspoon black mustard seeds
1 teaspoon urad dal
4 cups coarsely shredded cabbage
1 green chili pepper, chopped (optional)
1/2 teaspoon turmeric powder
1 teaspoon salt
1 teaspoon chutney powder
2 eggs
3/4 cup onion, cut lengthwise

1. In a skillet, heat oil over medium heat until hot, but not smoking. Add curry leaves, mustard seeds, and urad dal. Fry, covered, until mustard seeds burst (listen for popping sound) and urad dal is golden (about 30 seconds).

2. Add cabbage, green chili, and turmeric powder. Mix well. Continue cooking, covered, over low heat for 1 to 2 minutes, stirring frequently.

3. Add salt and chutney powder. Stir well. Do not overcook cabbage.

4. Whip eggs and pour over cabbage. Scramble until the eggs are cooked with cabbage. Add the onion to cabbage and stir well.

Serves 6

CALORIES 91; FAT 6g.; SATURATED FAT 1g.; PROTEIN 3g.; CARBOHYDRATE 6g.; FIBER 2g.; CHOLESTEROL 62mg.; SODIUM 384mg.

⌒Carrot Pachadi⌒

Carrots in yogurt salad, this dish can be served as a salad with rice, poori, and chappati.

> 2 cups peeled and shredded carrots
> 1/2 green chili pepper, chopped
> 2 cups plain yogurt
> 1 teaspoon corn oil
> 1/2 teaspoon asafoetida powder
> 1 teaspoon black mustard seeds
> 1 teaspoon urad dal
> 1/2 teaspoon salt (more, if desired)

1. Mix carrots and green chili.

2. Add yogurt to carrot mixture and stir well.

3. Place corn oil in a small saucepan (such as a butter warmer) and heat over medium heat.

4. When oil is hot, but not smoking, add asafoetida powder, mustard seeds, and urad dal. Cover and fry until mustard seeds pop and urad dal is golden brown.

5. Add the fried spices to the yogurt and mix well. Add salt and mix well.

Serves 4

CALORIES 108; FAT 1g.; SATURATED FAT trace; PROTEIN 8g.; CARBOHYDRATE 17g.; FIBER 2g.; CHOLESTEROL 2mg.; SODIUM 376mg.

⚜ *Healthy South Indian Cooking*

⌣ CARROT PORIYAL ⌣

A delightful stir-fry of baby carrots with coconut, Carrot Poriyal can be served as a side dish with any meal.

2 cups fresh baby carrots
1 tablespoon corn oil
4 to 6 curry leaves
1 dried red chili pepper
1 teaspoon black mustard seeds
2 teaspoon urad dal
1/4 teaspoon chutney powder
1/2 teaspoon salt
1 teaspoon coconut powder

1. Steam or microwave baby carrots in a small amount of water for about 5 minutes.

2. Place corn oil in a skillet over medium heat. When oil is hot, but not smoking, add curry leaves, red pepper, mustard seeds, and urad dal. Fry a few seconds until mustard seeds pop and urad dal turns golden.

3. Add carrots to the skillet and stir well into seasonings. Add chutney powder and salt. Mix well.

4. Cook, covered, over medium-low heat until carrots are cooked according to your taste.

5. Mix coconut powder with carrots.

Serves 4

CALORIES 91; FAT 4g.; SATURATED FAT 1g.; PROTEIN 2g.; CARBOHYDRATE 12g.; FIBER 3g.; CHOLESTEROL 0mg.; SODIUM 309mg.

↶CAULIFLOWER AND PASTA SALAD↷

An innovative and refreshing dish, Cauliflower and Pasta Salad can be served as a light snack or as an accompaniment to any grilled or baked meat dish.

1 cup small pasta shells (any flavor)
2 tablespoons corn oil
1 teaspoon black mustard seeds
1 teaspoon urad dal
1/2 onion, chopped
1 to 2 green chili peppers, chopped
3 cups cauliflower florets
1 teaspoon salt
1/2 teaspoon chutney powder (more, if desired)
1/4 cup chopped fresh coriander
1/2 cup roasted cashew halves (optional)

1. Boil 3 cups of water. When water is at boiling point, add pasta. Cook pasta until tender. Drain water and set cooked pasta aside.

2. In a skillet or wok, heat corn oil over medium heat. When oil is hot, but not smoking, add mustard seeds and urad dal. Cover and fry over medium heat until mustard seeds pop and urad dal is golden brown.

3. Add onion and green chilies. Stir-fry for a minute. Onion should remain crisp. Then add cauliflower and cook for about 2 minutes.

4. Add cooked pasta shells and stir.

5. Add salt and chutney powder and mix well. Cook, covered, for an additional minute or two.

Healthy South Indian Cooking

6. Garnish with coriander and cashew halves.

Serves 6

CALORIES 193; FAT 10g.; SATURATED FAT 2g.; PROTEIN 6g.; CARBOHYDRATE 21g.; FIBER 3g.; CHOLESTEROL 0mg.; SODIUM 374mg.

~:Cauliflower Kootu:~

Delightful, seasoned cauliflower cooked with ginger in creamy base dal, this kootu may be served over plain rice or yogurt rice, or as a side dish with any meal.

1/2 cup toor dal
1/2 teaspoon turmeric powder
2 tablespoons corn oil
1/4 teaspoon asafoetida powder
4 to 6 curry leaves
1 teaspoon black mustard seeds
1 teaspoon urad dal
1/4 cup chopped onions
1 tablespoon finely minced fresh ginger
1 teaspoon finely chopped green chili pepper
3 cups cauliflower, cut in 1-inch to 1 1/2-inch chunks (including short stems)
1/2 teaspoon cumin powder
1/2 teaspoon salt
1 tablespoon unsweetened powdered coconut

1. Bring 4 cups of water to a boil in a saucepan. Add toor dal and 1/4 teaspoon turmeric powder. Reduce heat to medium and cook, uncovered, for about 30 minutes until dal becomes creamy. If water seems to evaporate during the cooking process, add another cup of water and cook until dal becomes creamy.

2. Heat corn oil in a saucepan over medium heat. When oil is hot, but not smoking, add asafoetida and curry leaves.

3. Add mustard seeds and urad dal. Cover and cook until mustard seeds burst and urad dal turns golden.

4. Add onions, ginger, chili, and remaining 1/4 teaspoon turmeric powder.

5. Add cauliflower. Blend well with the seasonings in the saucepan.

Healthy South Indian Cooking

6. Add creamy toor dal, cumin powder, and salt. Add about 3/4 cup warm water to the dal. Stir cauliflower well with the dal mixture for a minute or two.

7. Cover and cook over low heat until cauliflower is just tender (2 to 4 minutes). Add coconut powder. Stir and cook for an additional minute. Do not overcook cauliflower.

Serves 4

CALORIES 200; FAT 8g.; SATURATED FAT 1g.; PROTEIN 5g.; CARBOHYDRATE 25g.; FIBER 7g.; CHOLESTEROL 0mg.; SODIUM 295mg.

⌁CAULIFLOWER MASALA PORIYAL⌁

This cauliflower stir-fry with onions, tomatoes, and spices makes a colorful and tasty side dish.

2 tablespoons corn oil
2 to 3 small pieces cinnamon stick
2 teaspoons black mustard seeds
2 teaspoons urad dal
1 small onion, chopped
1 small tomato, cut in small chunks
1/2 teaspoon turmeric powder
1/2 teaspoon cayenne powder (more, if desired)
1/2 cup tomato sauce
1 teaspoon salt
3 cups cauliflower, cut in 1-inch to 1 1/2-inch chunks (including short stems)
2 teaspoons unsweetened powdered coconut (optional)

1. Heat corn oil in a skillet or wok over medium heat. When oil is hot, but not smoking, add cinnamon stick, mustard seeds, and urad dal. Fry, covered, until mustard seeds burst (listen for popping sound) and urad dal is golden brown.

2. Add onion and tomato. Stir-fry for 1 minute over medium heat.

3. Add turmeric powder and cayenne powder. Stir well over medium heat for a minute. Add tomato sauce and salt. Mix well to obtain a thick paste-like consistency.

4. Add cauliflower chunks and blend carefully with sauce. Cover and cook over medium heat for 2 minutes.

5. Stir in coconut powder. Continue cooking until cauliflower is just tender, stirring occasionally. Be careful not to overcook! Note: If there is too much sauce in skillet, cook, uncovered, over low heat for few more minutes.

Serves 4

CALORIES 126; FAT 8g.; SATURATED FAT 1g.; PROTEIN 3g.; CARBOHYDRATE 14g.; FIBER 5g.; CHOLESTEROL 0mg.; SODIUM 749mg.

Variation:
- Grind 2 small slices of ginger with 2 cloves of garlic in blender. Add just enough water to make a paste. Before adding cauliflower in Step 4, add garlic and ginger paste to the cooking mixture. Then add cauliflower. Cook over medium heat, following the above recipe.

- To make **Cauliflower and Potato Masala Poriyal,** use 1 1/2 cups of peeled and cubed potatoes (1 inch cubes). Partially cook potatoes in a small saucepan with enough water to cover potatoes. Add 1/4 teaspoon turmeric powder and salt to the potatoes. When potatoes are partially cooked, drain and place in a small bowl. Set aside. Follow the above recipe for Cauliflower Masala Poriyal. In Step 4, add partially cooked potatoes with cauliflower chunks and proceed with the recipe.

⌁Cauliflower Poriyal⌁

A light, easy-to-prepare stir-fry that enhances any lunch or dinner.

2 tablespoons corn oil
1 dried red chili pepper
4 to 6 curry leaves
1 teaspoon black mustard seeds
1 teaspoon urad dal
3 cups cauliflower, cut in 1-inch chunks (including short stems)
1/2 teaspoon salt
1 teaspoon cumin powder

1. Place corn oil in a skillet over medium heat. When oil is hot, but not smoking, add red chili pepper, curry leaves, mustard seeds, and urad dal. Wait until mustard seeds pop and urad dal turns golden.

2. Immediately add cauliflower to the skillet and mix well with the seasonings.

3. Add salt and cumin powder to cauliflower and stir well.

4. Add about 2 tablespoons water to cauliflower and cook, covered, over medium-low heat until cauliflower is tender (about 5 minutes). Do not overcook cauliflower.

Serves 2

CALORIES 191; FAT 15g.; SATURATED FAT 2g.; PROTEIN 5g.; CARBOHYDRATE 13g.; FIBER 5g.; CHOLESTEROL 0mg.; SODIUM 583mg.

ᴄ·CHANA DAL SOONDAL·~

A unique high-fiber dish of chana dal and fresh coconut, Chana Dal Soondal is delicious served as a snack, or as a side dish. In South India, soondal is frequently offered as a prasad (offering) during religious ceremonies at home and in temples.

1/2 cup chana dal
1/4 teaspoon turmeric powder
1 teaspoon corn oil
2 to 4 curry leaves
1 whole dried red chili pepper
1 teaspoon mustard seeds
1 teaspoon urad dal
1/2 teaspoon salt
1/4 teaspoon asafoetida powder
1/2 teaspoon minced fresh ginger root
1/2 cup freshly ground or unsweetened powdered coconut

1. Soak chana dal in 1 cup of water for 30 minutes. Drain water and set aside.

2. Boil 1 cup of water in a saucepan. Add chana dal and turmeric powder. Cook dal, uncovered, until it becomes soft (about 15 minutes). Drain water and set aside.

3. Place corn oil in a skillet and heat over medium heat. When oil is hot, but not smoking, add curry leaves, red pepper, mustard seeds, and urad dal. Wait until mustard seeds pop and urad dal turns golden.

4. Add chana dal and blend well with seasonings in the skillet over low heat.

5. Add salt, asafoetida powder, and ginger. Mix well with chana dal. Add coconut and mix well.
Serves 4

CALORIES 172; FAT 6g.; SATURATED FAT 3g.; PROTEIN 8g.; CARBOHYDRATE

๛Chickpea Soondal๛

A delightful combination of chickpeas cooked with ginger and coconut, Chickpea Soondal is often served as a snack during teatime or as a side dish. Like Chana Dal Soondal (page 223), this dish is also served during religious ceremonies.

1 can (15 ounces) chickpeas (garbanzo beans)
1 tablespoon canola or corn oil
1 dried red chili pepper
1 teaspoon black mustard seeds
1 teaspoon urad dal
1/2 teaspoon turmeric powder
1/2 teaspoon salt
1/2 teaspoon chutney powder
1 teaspoon minced fresh ginger root
1/4 cup freshly ground or powdered unsweetened coconut

1. Drain chickpeas, rinse, and set aside.

2. Heat oil in medium-size skillet or wok over medium heat. When oil is hot, but not smoking, stir in red chili pepper, black mustard seeds, and urad dal. Cover and fry until mustard seeds burst (listen for popping sound) and urad dal is golden.

3. Immediately add chickpeas, turmeric powder, salt, and chutney powder and mix well. Add ginger and cook for additional minute or two.

4. Add coconut and stir.

Serves 2 to 4

CALORIES 237; FAT 8g.; SATURATED FAT 2g.; PROTEIN 8g.; CARBOHYDRATE 34g.; FIBER 7g.; CHOLESTEROL 0mg.; SODIUM 781mg.

◇Chickpea and Bell Pepper Poriyal◇

Vegetables seasoned and cooked in tomato sauce, this dish can be served with rice or bread.

1 can (15 ounces) chickpeas
2 teaspoons corn oil
5 to 6 very small pieces cinnamon stick
1 teaspoon black mustard seeds
2 teaspoons urad dal
1/2 cup chopped onion
1/2 cup chopped tomato
1/4 teaspoon turmeric powder
1/2 teaspoon cayenne powder (more, if desired)
1 cup tomato sauce (more, if needed)
1/2 teaspoon salt (more, if desired)
3 cups chopped green bell peppers
1 to 2 teaspoons unsweetened powdered coconut

1. Drain and rinse chickpeas.

2. Place oil in a cast-iron skillet (or any saucepan) over medium heat until oil is hot, but not smoking.

3. Add pieces of cinnamon stick, mustard seeds, and urad dal to the oil. Cover and cook until mustard seeds pop and urad dal is golden brown.

4. Add onion and tomato and stir-fry for 1 to 2 minutes over medium heat. Add turmeric powder and stir.

5. Add cayenne powder and mix well. Add 1 cup tomato sauce and salt to skillet. Allow the mixture to boil.

6. Add chickpeas and green peppers. Add more tomato sauce, if needed, to cover chickpeas. Mix well.

7. Cover skillet and cook vegetables over medium heat for about 5 minutes. A small amount of water (1 to 2 tablespoons) may be added to skillet to facilitate the cooking process. Be careful not to overcook vegetables.

8. Stir in coconut powder and serve.

Serves 6

CALORIES 144; FAT 3g.; SATURATED FAT trace; PROTEIN 5g.; CARBOHYDRATE 27g.; FIBER 6g.; CHOLESTEROL 0mg.; SODIUM 641mg.

Variation:
For a delicious variation, you can omit bell pepper and 1/2 cup tomato sauce to create **Chickpea Masala Poriyal.**

↷CORN PORIYAL↶

A lightly seasoned corn dish, this poriyal can be served as a snack or as a side dish with any meal.

1 tablespoon corn oil
4 to 6 curry leaves
1 dried red chili pepper
1 teaspoon black mustard seeds
2 teaspoons urad dal
3 cups frozen corn
1/4 teaspoon chutney powder
1/2 teaspoon salt
1 teaspoon unsweetened powdered coconut powder

1. Place corn oil in a skillet over medium heat. When oil is hot, but not smoking, add curry leaves, red pepper, mustard seeds, and urad dal. Fry for a few seconds until mustard seeds pop and urad dal turns golden.

2. Add frozen corn, chutney powder, and salt. Blend corn well with the seasonings.

3. Add coconut powder. Mix well.

Serves 6

CALORIES 103; FAT 3g.; SATURATED FAT trace; PROTEIN 3g.; CARBOHYDRATE 18g.; FIBER 3g.; CHOLESTEROL 0mg.; SODIUM 181mg.

⌇CUCUMBER PACHADI⌇

A refreshing dish of cucumber in seasoned yogurt that can be served with baked or grilled chicken or any flavored rice.

2 cups fat-free plain yogurt
2 cups peeled and shredded cucumber
1/2 teaspoon salt
1 green chili, chopped
1 teaspoon corn oil
1/4 teaspoon asafoetida powder
1 teaspoon black mustard seeds
1 teaspoon urad dal

1. Empty the yogurt into a bowl and beat it well until it is smooth.

2. Add cucumber, salt, and green chili to the yogurt. Mix well.

3. Place corn oil in a small saucepan and heat over medium heat. When oil is hot, but not smoking, add asafoetida powder, mustard seeds, and urad dal. Cover and fry until mustard seeds pop and urad dal is golden brown. Pour the spices over the yogurt and mix well.

Serves 4

CALORIES 94; FAT 2g; SATURATED FAT trace; PROTEIN 8g.; CARBOHYDRATE 12g.; FIBER 1g.; CHOLESTEROL 2mg.; SODIUM 356mg.

Variation:
To make **Potato Pachadi**, instead of using cucumbers, use 2 cups boiled potatoes. Peel and slice boiled potatoes. Add to plain yogurt. Add the other ingredients as above and mix.

～CUCUMBER AND TOMATO YOGURT SALAD～

Refreshing and easy-to-make, this salad with yogurt is very colorful and pleasing to the palate. It is an excellent accompaniment to any meal.

1 1/2 cups fresh pickling cucumber, peeled and diced
3/4 cup diced tomato
3/4 cup diced red onion
1 green chili pepper, finely diced (optional)
1 teaspoon black pepper and cumin powder
1/2 teaspoon salt
1 1/2 cups fat-free plain yogurt
1/4 cup chopped fresh coriander

1 Place the vegetables in a serving bowl.

2. Blend black pepper and cumin powder and salt into yogurt.

3. Pour yogurt mixture over diced vegetables and stir to coat vegetables. Taste and add additional seasonings if desired.

4. Refrigerate at least 1 hour. Garnish with coriander before serving.

Note: You may use regular cucumbers instead of fresh pickling cucumbers if you desire. Fresh pickling cucumbers are used in this recipe for extra crunchiness.

Serves 4

CALORIES 101; FAT 1g.; SATURATED FAT trace; PROTEIN 8g.; CARBOHYDRATE 18g.; FIBER 6g.; CHOLESTEROL 2mg.; SODIUM 346mg.

⌁Eggplant Masala⌁

Delightful, aromatic eggplant cooked with tomatoes, onion, and garlic, Eggplant Masala complements many rice and vegetable dishes. As a delicious appetizer, it can be served over cocktail breads and crackers.

3 tablespoons corn oil
1/4 teaspoon asafoetida powder
4 to 5 curry leaves (optional)
1 teaspoon black mustard seeds
1 teaspoon urad dal
1/2 cup onion, cut in small lengthwise pieces
1/2 cup coarsely chopped tomato
3 cloves garlic, quartered
1/2 teaspoon turmeric powder
3 cups eggplant, cut in small oblong pieces
1 cup tomato sauce
1/2 teaspoon salt
1/4 teaspoon cayenne powder
1 teaspoon cumin powder
2 teaspoons unsweetened powdered coconut

1. Heat oil in a cast-iron skillet over medium heat with asafoetida powder and curry leaves. When oil is hot, but not smoking, stir in mustard seeds and urad dal. Cover and fry until mustard seeds burst (listen for popping sound) and urad dal is golden.

2. Add onion, tomato, and garlic. Add turmeric powder. Stir-fry for 2 minutes.

3. Add eggplant to the ingredients in skillet and stir well. Add tomato sauce. Blend well.

4. Add salt, cayenne, and cumin powder. Add 4 tablespoons of water and stir well. Continue to cook, covered, over medium-low heat for 12 to 15 minutes or until eggplant becomes tender and sauce is thick. Stir often.

5. Add coconut powder. Stir briefly for a few minutes.

Serves 4

CALORIES 158; FAT 12g.; SATURATED FAT 2g.; PROTEIN 3g.; CARBOHYDRATE 13g.; FIBER 4g.; CHOLESTEROL 0mg.; SODIUM 644mg.

Variation: To make a wonderful **Eggplant Rice (Vangibhath)**, add 2 cups cooked plain white or basmati rice to the Eggplant Masala. Stir over medium-low heat and blend well. Stir in 1/4 cup roasted peanuts and continue to stir well. You may add 1/2 teaspoon more salt if desired.

⌁ Eggplant and Potato Masala ⋙

Eggplant and potato cooked in a seasoned tomato sauce, this dish is especially delicious served with any flavored rice.

> 2 medium Idaho potatoes
> 6 baby eggplants (or) 1/2 large eggplant
> 5 tablespoons canola or corn oil
> 2 to 3 small pieces cinnamon stick
> 1 teaspoon cumin seeds
> 1/2 cup onion, cut into lengthwise pieces
> 1 cup diced tomato
> 3/4 teaspoon turmeric powder
> 1/2 teaspoon cayenne powder
> 1 teaspoon salt
> 1/4 teaspoon garam masala powder
> 1 cup tomato sauce
> 1 to 2 tablespoons freshly ground or unsweetened powdered coconut

1. Wash the potatoes. (Do not peel). Cut lengthwise into small pieces to make about 2 cups.

2. Cut eggplant lengthwise into small pieces to make about 2 cups.

3. Place oil in a heavy skillet over medium heat. When oil is hot but not smoking, add cinnamon stick and cumin seeds. Cover and fry until seeds are golden brown.

4. Add onion and tomato. Stir-fry for a few minutes.

5. Add potatoes and turmeric powder. Mix well and cook over medium heat, stirring often, for 3 to 5 minutes until potatoes are slightly cooked. Add eggplant and mix well.

6. Add cayenne powder, salt, and garam masala powder. Stir in tomato sauce and mix well. You may add about 1/4 cup of water to facilitate the cooking process.

7. Cover and cook over low heat until vegetables are tender.

8. Add coconut powder and mix well.

Serves 4 to 6

CALORIES 212; FAT 14g.; SATURATED FAT 1g.; PROTEIN 3g.; CARBOHYDRATE 21g.; FIBER 4g.; CHOLESTEROL 0mg.; SODIUM 732mg.

⁓Eggplant Kootu⁓

Mildly seasoned eggplant cooked with creamy dal, this Chettinad delight goes particularly well with plain or yogurt rice.

1/2 cup toor dal
1/2 teaspoon turmeric powder
2 tablespoons corn oil
4 to 6 curry leaves
1 dried red chili pepper
1 teaspoon black mustard seeds
1 teaspoon urad dal
1/2 teaspoon cumin seeds
1/2 cup chopped onion
2 cups chopped eggplant (with skin)
1 teaspoon salt
1 teaspoon cumin powder

1. Boil 4 cups of water in a saucepan over medium heat. Add toor dal and 1/4 teaspoon turmeric powder. Reduce heat to medium and cook, uncovered, for about 30 minutes until dal becomes creamy. If water evaporates during the cooking process, add another cup of water and cook until dal becomes creamy.

2. Place oil in a saucepan over medium heat. When oil is hot, but not smoking, add curry leaves, chili pepper, mustard seeds, urad dal, and cumin seeds. Fry until mustard seeds pop and urad dal turns golden.

3. Add onion and eggplant together with remaining 1/4 teaspoon turmeric powder. Stir well into seasonings in saucepan.

4. Add creamy toor dal plus 2 cups of warm water to the eggplant in saucepan. Add salt and cumin powder. Stir well.

5. Cook, covered, over medium heat until eggplant becomes tender, about 5 to 7 minutes.

Serves 4

CALORIES 197; FAT 8g.; SATURATED FAT 1g.; PROTEIN 8g.; CARBOHYDRATE 26g.; FIBER 6g.; CHOLESTEROL 0mg.; SODIUM 542mg.

ᴖGREEN PEAS PORIYALᴖ

A green pea stir-fry that is a versatile side dish.

> *1 package (10 to 16) ounces frozen green peas*
> *2 teaspoons corn oil*
> *2 to 3 curry leaves (optional)*
> *1 teaspoon black mustard seeds*
> *1 teaspoon urad dal*
> *1/2 green chili pepper, chopped (or) 1 dried red chili pepper*
> *1/2 teaspoon salt (more, if desired)*
> *1 teaspoon chutney powder (optional)*
> *1 tablespoon freshly ground or powdered unsweetened coconut*

1. Cook peas according to package directions. Set aside.

2. In a skillet, heat corn oil over medium heat. When oil is hot, but not smoking, add curry leaves, mustard seeds, and urad dal. Cook, covered, until mustard seeds pop and urad dal is golden brown.

3. Add peas and chili. Stir-fry for a minute.

4. Add salt and chutney powder and stir gently, being careful not to mash the peas.

5. Add the coconut powder and stir gently.

Serves 2 to 4

CALORIES 112; FAT 4g.; SATURATED FAT 1g.; PROTEIN 6g.; CARBOHYDRATE 15g.; FIBER 5g.; CHOLESTEROL 0mg.; SODIUM 463mg.

ᴗ:Kerala Aviyal:ᴗ

Mixed vegetables cooked with coconut and spices named from its origin in the South Indian state of Kerala, this highlight of South Indian cuisine is served as a side dish with plain rice accompanied by either sambhar or rasam.

2 cups Idaho potatoes, washed, peeled, and cut lengthwise 1 1/2 x 1/2 inches
1/2 cup carrots, peeled and cut same size as potatoes
1/2 cup green beans, cut in half same length as potatoes
1 cup Fordhook (large) lima beans
1/2 teaspoon turmeric powder
1 teaspoon salt (more, if desired)
1 green bell pepper
1/4 cup fresh or unsweetened powdered coconut
2 teaspoons cumin
1 1/2 tablespoons minced fresh ginger root
3 green chili peppers (more, if desired)
3/4 cup buttermilk
1/4 cup fat-free yogurt
1 tablespoon coconut oil
4 to 6 curry leaves

1. In a large saucepan place potatoes, carrots, green beans, and lima beans with enough water to cover vegetables. Stir in turmeric powder and salt.

2. Cook vegetables, covered, over medium heat until tender, about 10 minutes. Add more water if needed. Be careful not to overcook the vegetables. Set aside saucepan with vegetables.

3. Cut bell pepper lengthwise into strips the same size as the potatoes and set aside.

4. Place coconut, cumin, ginger, and chilies in blender with buttermilk. Grind to a coarse consistency and pour over vegetables in saucepan.

5. Stir gently. Add bell pepper and cook over low heat until ingredients are cooked through. Remove saucepan from heat.

6. Add yogurt and stir gently.

7. Heat coconut oil in a butter warmer. When oil is hot, but not smoking, add curry leaves and pour over the vegetables, then gently stir.

Serves 4

CALORIES 216; FAT 6g.; SATURATED FAT 5g.; PROTEIN 8g.; CARBOHYDRATE 35g.; FIBER 6g.; CHOLESTEROL 1mg.; SODIUM 606mg.

ᴌɪᴍᴀ Bᴇᴀɴs Mᴀsᴀʟᴀ

Lima beans cooked with seasonings in tomato sauce, this dish is delicious served with any flavored rice dish, in particular yogurt rice. It also may be enjoyed as a sandwich filling for pita bread.

1 package (16 ounces) frozen baby lima beans (about 2 cups)
1/2 teaspoon turmeric powder
1 teaspoon salt
2 tablespoons corn oil
2 to 3 very small pieces cinnamon stick
1 teaspoon black mustard seeds
2 teaspoons urad dal
1/2 cup chopped onion
1 cup chopped tomato
1/2 teaspoon cayenne powder
1 cup tomato sauce
2 tablespoons unsweetened powdered coconut

1. Cook lima beans in a saucepan with 1 cup of water, 1/4 teaspoon turmeric powder, and 1/2 teaspoon salt until tender (approximately 3 minutes). Set aside but do not drain.

2. Place oil in a skillet over medium heat. When oil is hot, but not smoking, add pieces of cinnamon stick, mustard seeds, and urad dal. Cover and cook over medium heat until mustard seeds pop and urad dal is golden brown.

3. Add onion and tomato and stir for a few minutes. Add remaining 1/4 teaspoon turmeric powder and stir well over medium heat.

4. Add cayenne powder and remaining 1/2 teaspoon salt and stir well. Add tomato sauce.

5. When mixture begins to boil, add undrained cooked lima beans and stir well.

6. Cover and cook over medium heat until lima beans are tender.

7. Add coconut powder and stir well.

Serves 6

CALORIES 178; FAT 6g.; SATURATED FAT 1g.; PROTEIN 7g.; CARBOHYDRATE 27g.; FIBER 5g.; CHOLESTEROL 0mg.; SODIUM 645mg.

∿ LIMA BEANS PORIYAL ∿

An easy-to-prepare lima beans stir-fry, Lima Beans Poriyal can be served as a side dish for lunch or dinner.

1 package (10 to 16 ounces) frozen baby or Fordhook (large) lima beans
1 teaspoon salt
1 teaspoon turmeric powder
2 tablespoons corn or canola oil
4 to 6 curry leaves (optional)
1 whole dried red chili pepper
1 teaspoon black mustard seeds
1 teaspoon urad dal
1 small onion, chopped
1 teaspoon chutney powder
1 tablespoon unsweetened powdered coconut

1. Bring 1 cup of water to boil. Add frozen lima beans with 1/2 teaspoon salt and 1/2 teaspoon turmeric powder. Reduce heat and cook gently until tender, 10 to 12 minutes. You may also cook lima beans in microwave according to package directions.

2. Place corn oil in a cast-iron or any skillet over medium heat. When oil is hot, but not smoking, stir in curry leaves, red chili pepper, mustard seeds, and urad dal. Cover and fry until mustard seeds pop and urad dal is golden brown.

3. Add onion and stir-fry for a minute. Add drained lima beans and remaining 1/2 teaspoon turmeric powder and mix well. Blend over medium heat.

4. Add remaining 1/2 teaspoon salt and chutney powder and stir. Add coconut powder and blend the seasonings well with lima beans.
Serves 4 to 6

CALORIES 139; FAT 6g.; SATURATED FAT 1g.; PROTEIN 5g.; CARBOHYDRATE 17g.; FIBER 3g.; CHOLESTEROL 0mg.; SODIUM 457mg.

∽ MADRAS POTATO PORIYAL ∽

An exquisitely seasoned dish, this culinary classic from Tamil Nadu is a wonderful accompaniment to any meal.

3 cups peeled and cubed Idaho potatoes
1/2 teaspoon turmeric powder
2 tablespoons corn oil
2 to 3 small pieces cinnamon stick
1 bay leaf, crumbled
1 teaspoon black mustard seeds
1 teaspoon urad dal
3/4 cup onion, cut lengthwise
1/2 cup chopped tomato
1/4 teaspoon cayenne powder
1/2 teaspoon cumin powder
1/2 cup tomato sauce
1/2 teaspoon salt (more, if desired)
1/4 cup chopped fresh coriander

1. Parcook cubed potatoes, uncovered, with 1 1/2 cups water and 1/4 teaspoon turmeric powder in a saucepan over medium heat. When potatoes are half cooked, remove from heat and set aside. Do not drain any remaining water.

2. Place corn oil in a cast-iron skillet and heat over medium heat until oil is hot but not smoking. Add cinnamon sticks, bay leaf, mustard seeds, and urad dal. Fry until mustard seeds pop and urad dal turns golden.

3. Add onion and tomato and sauté for a few minutes, stirring frequently.

4. Add remaining 1/4 teaspoon turmeric powder, cayenne powder, cumin powder, and tomato sauce. Stir well.

5. Add potatoes and gently stir into mixture in skillet.

6. Add salt and cook, covered, over medium heat until potatoes absorb tomato sauce and become thoroughly cooked. Add 1 to 2 tablespoons of water if the potatoes need to cook more and the mixture becomes too thick.

7. Add coriander and stir gently.

Serves 4

CALORIES 196; FAT 8g.; SATURATED FAT 1g.; PROTEIN 4g.; CARBOHYDRATE 30g.; FIBER 5g.; CHOLESTEROL 0mg.; SODIUM 467mg.

✥Madras Vegetable Medley✥

An innovative and colorful stir-fry of beets, cauliflower, and lima beans, Madras Vegetable Medley is easy to make and is a delightful accompaniment to any meal.

1 package (16 ounces) frozen lima beans (2 cups)
2 tablespoons corn oil
4 to 6 curry leaves
2 to 4 small cinnamon sticks
1 teaspoon black mustard seeds
2 teaspoons urad dal
1 cup peeled and thinly sliced beets
1/2 teaspoon salt (more, if desired)
1/2 teaspoon chutney powder
1 cup cauliflower florets
2 tablespoons freshly grated or unsweetened powdered coconut

1. Cook frozen lima beans according to package directions (10 minutes).

2. Place corn oil in a wok or cast-iron skillet over medium heat. When oil is hot, but not smoking, add curry leaves, cinnamon sticks, mustard seeds, and urad dal. Cover and fry until mustard seeds pop and urad dal is golden.

3. Add beets and lima beans together with salt and chutney powder. Blend well and cook, covered, over medium heat for a few minutes.

4. Add cauliflower and continue cooking, covered, for a few minutes until vegetables are tender.

5. Add coconut and stir well.
Serves 6

CALORIES 145; FAT 6g.; SATURATED FAT 1g.; PROTEIN 6g.; CARBOHYDRATE 19g.; FIBER 4g.; CHOLESTEROL 0mg.; SODIUM 230mg.

✄   *Healthy South Indian Cooking*

◡:Mixed Vegetable Kurma:◡

This highly aromatic coconut-based sauce is made with mixed vegetables such as potatoes, dried green peas, beets, carrots, and tomatoes. Vegetable kurma can be served with poori, chappati, idli, dosai, over plain rice or as a side dish to any meal.

1/4 cup dried green peas
1/2 cup unsweetened powdered or freshly ground coconut
2 green chilies
10 raw almonds
1 tablespoon khus khus (white poppy seeds)
2 teaspoons cumin seeds
1/2 teaspoon fennel seeds
1 tablespoon sliced fresh ginger root
1 tablespoon roasted chickpeas (chana dalia)
2 tablespoons corn oil
4 to 6 curry leaves
1 bay leaf, crumbled
2 to 3 small pieces cinnamon stick
1/4 cup chopped onion
1/2 cup chopped tomato
1/4 teaspoon turmeric powder
1 cup peeled potatoes, cut into small cubes
1/4 cup peeled and thinly sliced beets
1/4 cup peeled and sliced carrots (same size as beets)
1 teaspoon curry powder
1 clove
1/4 teaspoon cardamom
1 teaspoon salt
1/2 cup chopped fresh coriander
1/4 cup buttermilk

1. Soak dried green peas for 2 hours and then cook them with enough water to cover for about 20 minutes. Set aside.

2. Blend coconut, green chilies, almonds, khus khus, 1 teaspoon cumin,

fennel seeds, ginger, and roasted chickpeas in 2 cups of warm water and grind to a smooth thick paste. Set aside.

3. Place corn oil in a wide-bottomed saucepan over medium heat. When oil is hot, but not smoking, add curry leaves, bay leaf, cinnamon stick, and remaining I teaspoon cumin seeds. Stir-fry to a golden brown.

4. Add onion and tomato to the saucepan and stir-fry for a few minutes. Add turmeric powder and mix well.

5. Add the cut vegetables to the saucepan. Add curry powder. Stir the seasonings with the vegetables for a minute.

6. Add the ground spice kurma sauce from the blender to the vegetables in saucepan. Add the cooked peas. Add 2 cups of warm water and mix thoroughly.

7. Add clove, cardamom, and salt. Blend well with vegetable sauce in saucepan. Add coriander.

8. When the mixture begins to boil, reduce heat to medium-low. Stir often and cook the vegetables, covered, until potatoes are cooked.

9. Turn off the heat. Add buttermilk to the vegetable kurma and blend gently.

Serves 6

CALORIES 184; FAT 10g.; SATURATED FAT 3g.; PROTEIN 6g.; CARBOHYDRATE 23g.; FIBER 8g.; CHOLESTEROL trace; SODIUM 394mg.

Variation:
To enhance the flavor of vegetable kurma, you may add I tablespoon of canola oil or corn oil and I tablespoon of melted butter (ghee) in Step 3 if you desire.

～MIXED VEGETABLE PORIYAL～

This colorful stir-fry dish is made with potatoes, beets, brussels sprouts, and lima beans lightly seasoned and cooked in tomato sauce. It can be served as a side dish with any meal or used to make vegetable wraps.

3 tablespoons corn oil
2 to 3 very small pieces cinnamon stick
1 bay leaf, crumbled
1 teaspoon black mustard seeds
2 teaspoons urad dal
1/2 cup chopped onion
1/2 cup finely chopped tomatoes
1/4 teaspoon turmeric powder
1 cup peeled Idaho potatoes, cut into 1-inch cubes
1 package (16 ounces) frozen baby lima beans (2 cups)
1 cup tomato sauce
1/4 cup peeled and thinly sliced beets
1/4 cup brussels sprouts, quartered
1/2 teaspoon cayenne powder
1 teaspoon cumin powder
1 teaspoon salt
2 tablespoons powdered unsweetened coconut

1. Heat corn oil in a cast-iron skillet over medium heat. When oil is hot, but not smoking, add cinnamon sticks, bay leaf, mustard seeds, and urad dal. Cover and heat until mustard seeds burst (listen for popping sound) and urad dal is golden.

2. Add onion and tomatoes. Stir and cook briefly. Add turmeric powder and mix well.

3. Add potatoes and lima beans and stir well with above seasonings for few minutes. Stir in tomato sauce.

4. Add beets and brussels sprouts. Stir well.

5. Add cayenne powder, cumin powder, and salt. Blend the seasonings well with the vegetables and cook, covered, over medium heat.

6. Add about 1 cup of warm water so that the vegetables cook without sticking to the bottom of the skillet.

7. Blend carefully. Be certain not to overcook or mash the vegetables.

8. Add coconut powder. Stir briefly and immediately remove from heat.

Note: Leftovers can be refrigerated and may be used to make vegetable wraps with any type of tortillas or pita bread. Serve them for lunch.

Serves 6

CALORIES 201; FAT 9g.; SATURATED FAT 2g.; PROTEIN 6g.; CARBOHYDRATE 27g.; FIBER 5g.; CHOLESTEROL 0mg.; SODIUM 641mg.

~:Mushroom and Pepper Poriyal:~

An innovative and enticing stir-fry dish that can be served with yogurt rice or as a side dish with any meal.

3 mild poblano (banana) peppers
1 1/2 cups (8 ounces) coarsely chopped fresh mushrooms
1 tablespoon corn oil
1 teaspoon black mustard seeds
1 teaspoon urad dal
1/2 cup chopped onion
1/2 cup chopped tomato
1/4 teaspoon turmeric powder
1/2 cup tomato sauce
1/4 teaspoon cayenne powder
1/2 teaspoon cumin powder
1/2 teaspoon salt

1. Chop the peppers into the same size as the chopped mushrooms. Set aside.

2. Place corn oil in a wok or iron skillet over medium heat. When oil is hot, but not smoking, add mustard seeds and urad dal.

3. When mustard seeds pop and urad dal turns golden, add onion and tomato. Add turmeric powder and stir-fry for a few minutes.

4. Add tomato sauce, cayenne powder, cumin powder, and salt. Cook for a few minutes.

5. When the mixture thickens, add mushrooms and peppers. Stir well.

6. As the sauce continues to thicken, stir-fry vegetables well and remove from heat.

Serves 4

CALORIES 97; FAT 4g.; SATURATED FAT trace.; PROTEIN 3g.; CARBOHYDRATE 14g.; FIBER 3g.; CHOLESTEROL 0mg.; SODIUM 459mg.

～Mushroom and Onion Fry～

An innovative and easy-to-prepare stir-fry dish that complements any meal.

2 cups cut fresh mushrooms (caps and stems)
2 tablespoons corn oil
1 teaspoon cumin seeds
1 cup onion, cut lengthwise
1 tablespoon minced garlic
1/4 teaspoon black pepper and cumin powder (more, if desired)
1/2 teaspoon salt

1. Wash mushrooms thoroughly. Cut into chunks of uniform size (halves or quarters).

2. Heat oil in a skillet over medium heat. When oil is hot, but not smoking, add cumin seeds. Fry until seeds are golden brown.

3. Add onion and garlic and mix well with ingredients in skillet.

4. Add mushrooms and toss with onions. Cook, uncovered, for few minutes over medium high heat until mushrooms are cooked.

5. Add black pepper and cumin powder and salt. Blend well into the ingredients in skillet.

Serves 4.

CALORIES 89; FAT 7g.; SATURATED FAT 1g.; PROTEIN 1g.; CARBOHYDRATE 6g.; FIBER 1g.; CHOLESTEROL 0mg.; SODIUM 270mg.

⌐:Mushroom Masala:~

Lightly seasoned mushrooms cooked in tomato sauce, Mushroom Masala can be served as an accompaniment with many other dishes.

1 teaspoon corn oil
1 small stick cinnamon
1 crumbled bay leaf
1/2 teaspoon cumin seeds
1/2 cup chopped onion
1/4 cup chopped tomato
1/4 cup tomato sauce
1/4 teaspoon cayenne powder
1/2 teaspoon cumin powder
1/2 teaspoon salt
2 cups (8 ounces) fresh mushrooms, quartered
1/4 cup chopped fresh coriander

1. Place corn oil in a wok or in an iron skillet over medium heat. When oil is hot, but not smoking, add cinnamon, bay leaf, and cumin.

2. Immediately add the onion and tomato.

3. Stir-fry for a few minutes, and then add tomato sauce, cayenne powder, cumin powder, and salt. When the mixture thickens, add the chopped mushrooms and stir well.

4. Cook mushrooms, uncovered, on low heat for 3 minutes. Garnish with coriander. Stir and serve.

Serves 4

CALORIES 57; FAT 2g.; SATURATED FAT trace; PROTEIN 2g.; CARBOHYDRATE 11g.; FIBER 4g.; CHOLESTEROL 0mg.; SODIUM 459mg.

ᴏᴋʀᴀ Mᴀsᴀʟᴀ

Okra lightly seasoned and cooked with tomato, Okra Masala goes well
with any flavored or plain rice dish.

2 tablespoons corn oil
1/4 teaspoon asafoetida powder
1 teaspoon black mustard seeds
2 teaspoons urad dal
1/2 cup chopped onion
1/2 cup chopped tomato
1/2 teaspoon turmeric powder
1/2 teaspoon cayenne powder (more, if desired)
1/2 teaspoon cumin powder
1/2 cup tomato sauce
1 teaspoon salt
2 cups fresh okra, sliced, or 2 cups frozen cut okra
1 tablespoon unsweetened powdered coconut

1. Place oil in skillet over medium heat. When oil is hot, but not smoking,
add asafoetida, mustard seeds, and urad dal. When mustard seeds pop and
urad dal turns golden, add onion and tomato. Stir-fry for a minute.

2. Add turmeric powder, cayenne powder, cumin powder, tomato sauce,
and salt. Cook the seasonings with onion mixture for a minute or two.

3. Add okra and stir for a minute or two.

4. Cover and cook over low heat until okra is tender.

5. Add powdered coconut and cook for an additional minute.

Serves 4

CALORIES 129; FAT 8g.; SATURATED FAT 1g.; PROTEIN 3g.; CARBOHYDRATE
13g.; FIBER 5g.; CHOLESTEROL 0mg.; SODIUM 729mg.

ᵜ FRIED OKRA ᵜ

Lightly seasoned and pan-fried, this authentic okra specialty enhances any vegetarian meal.

3 cups fresh okra
1/2 teaspoon turmeric powder
1 teaspoon cayenne powder
1 teaspoon cumin powder
1 teaspoon salt
4 tablespoons corn oil
1/2 teaspoon asafoetida powder
4 to 6 curry leaves
1 teaspoon mustard seeds
1 teaspoon urad dal
1/2 cup onion, cut lengthwise
1/2 cup chopped tomato

1. Wash, remove ends, and cut okra lengthwise. Combine okra with turmeric, cayenne, cumin and salt in a bowl. Mix to coat well.

2. Heat corn oil in a skillet. When oil is hot, but not smoking, add asafoetida powder, curry leaves, mustard seeds, and urad dal.

3. When mustard seeds pop and urad dal turns golden, add onion and tomato. Stir fry for a minute and add coated okra.

4. Cook, covered, over medium heat, stirring often until okra becomes soft (5 to 6 minutes).

Serves 4.

CALORIES 170; FAT 14g.; SATURATED FAT 2g.; PROTEIN 2g.; CARBOHYDRATE 10g.; FIBER 4g.; CHOLESTEROL 0mg.; SODIUM 543mg.

ᴥ

⌁Onion and Tomato Salad⌁

This yogurt salad is a delightful accompaniment to any meal, eastern or western.

1 cup onion, cut lengthwise
1 cup chopped tomato
1/2 green chili, chopped
1 cup plain fat-free yogurt
1/4 teaspoon salt

1. Mix onion, tomato, and green chili.

2. Add enough yogurt to blend well with the vegetables.

3. Add salt and mix well.

Note: It is not necessary to have precise measurements for the onion and tomato. Quantities of each can be blended to one's taste with the yogurt.

Serves 2

CALORIES 107; FAT 1g.; SATURATED FAT trace; PROTEIN 8g.; CARBOHYDRATE 18g.; FIBER 2g.; CHOLESTEROL 2mg.; SODIUM 368mg.

⌁Paruppu Masiyal⌁

A Tamil Nadu favorite, Paruppu Masiyal is often served with ghee (clarified butter) over plain rice as a first course in a meal. Even when served over just plain rice without ghee, this creamy base dal is a delightful dish.

1/4 cup toor dal
1/4 teaspoon turmeric powder
2 cloves garlic, crushed
1/4 teaspoon salt
3/4 teaspoon cumin powder
2 to 4 curry leaves, chopped

1. Boil 3 cups of water in a tall saucepan. Add toor and turmeric powder. Reduce heat to medium and cook, uncovered, for about 30 minutes until dal becomes creamy. If water evaporates during the cooking process, you may add another 1/2 cup of water and cook until dal becomes creamy. You may use a masher to achieve the correct consistency of the dal.

2. Transfer dal to a bowl with 1/2 cup water and mix well.

3. Add garlic, salt, cumin powder, and curry leaves to creamy dal. Mix well.

Serves 4

CALORIES 54; FAT trace; SATURATED FAT trace; PROTEIN 3g.; CARBOHYDRATE 10g.; FIBER 2g.; CHOLESTEROL 0mg.; SODIUM 136mg.

ᴄᴘOTATO CURRY FOR POORIᴄᴏ

Potatoes cooked with onions, tomatoes, and ginger, this dish is delicious served with poori or chappati.

4 cups Idaho potatoes, quartered
1 1/2 teaspoons salt
1 teaspoon turmeric powder
2 tablespoons corn oil
1 bay leaf
2 to 3 small pieces cinnamon stick
1 teaspoon black mustard seeds
1 teaspoon urad dal
1 1/2 cups onion, cut lengthwise
1/2 cup chopped tomato
2 green chili peppers, finely chopped
1 tablespoon chopped fresh ginger root
1 teaspoon curry powder
1 teaspoon lemon juice (optional)
1/4 cup fresh coriander leaves

1. Cook potatoes, covered, in boiling water with 1/2 teaspoon salt and 1/2 teaspoon turmeric for about 1/2 hour or until tender. Water should just cover potatoes. Peel and mash potatoes. (Do not add milk). Set aside and keep warm. (Potatoes may also be cooked in a pressure cooker.)

2. Heat oil in skillet over medium heat. When oil is hot, but not smoking, crumble bay leaf and stick cinnamon into oil. Stir in mustard seeds and urad dal. Cover and fry until mustard seeds burst (listen for popping sound) and urad dal is golden.

3. Immediately add onion, tomato, chili, and ginger. Cook, stirring, about 1 minute.

4. Stir in remaining 1/2 teaspoon turmeric powder. Add mashed potatoes. Stir in curry powder. Stir in about 3/4 cup of water, remaining 1 tea-

spoon salt, and lemon juice. Add coriander and mix well. Cook over low to medium heat for 2 to 4 minutes.

5. Taste and add additional seasonings if desired.

Note: Potato curry may also be made thicker by eliminating water (Step 4) and may be used thus as a sandwich filling or with pita bread.

Serves 6

CALORIES 149; FAT 5g.; SATURATED FAT 1g.; PROTEIN 3g.; CARBOHYDRATE 25g.; FIBER 5g.; CHOLESTEROL 0mg.; SODIUM 546mg.

⌁Potato Kurma⌁

Cooked in a delectable coconut-based sauce, Potato Kurma can be served over plain rice, Bell Pepper Tomato Rice, Vegetable Pulaoo Rice, and Tomato Rice, or with poori and any other Indian breads.

1/2 cup unsweetened powdered or freshly ground coconut
3 green chili peppers (more, if desired)
10 raw almonds
1 tablespoon khus khus (white poppy seeds) (optional)
2 teaspoons cumin seeds
1 teaspoon fennel seeds
2 thick slices fresh ginger root
1 tablespoon roasted chana
2 tablespoons corn oil
4 to 6 curry leaves
1 bay leaf, crumbled
3 to 4 small pieces cinnamon stick
1 cup onion, chopped coarsely lengthwise
1/2 cup chopped tomatoes
4 cups peeled and cubed Idaho potatoes
1/2 teaspoon turmeric powder
1 teaspoon curry powder
1 teaspoon salt (more, if desired)
1/2 cup chopped fresh coriander

1. Blend coconut, green chilies, almonds, khus khus, 1 teaspoon cumin seeds, 1/2 teaspoon fennel, ginger, and roasted chana in blender and grind with 2 cups hot water. Grind ingredients into a smooth paste.

2. Place corn oil in a wide-bottomed saucepan over medium heat. When corn oil is hot but not smoking, add curry leaves, bay leaf, cinnamon stick, remaining 1 teaspoon cumin, and 1/2 teaspoon fennel. Stir and fry to a golden brown.

3. Add onion and 1/4 cup chopped tomatoes to saucepan and stir-fry for

a few minutes.

4. Add potatoes to the mixture. Add turmeric powder and stir well for a minute. Add curry powder. Blend the seasonings well with potatoes for couple of minutes.

5. Add the ground spices from the blender to the potato mixture. Add salt and 2 cups of warm water and mix thoroughly.

6. When mixture begins to boil, reduce the heat to low. Add the remaining 1/4 cup tomato and the coriander. Cover and cook potatoes until tender.

Serves 6

CALORIES 101; FAT trace; SATURATED FAT trace; PROTEIN 3g.; CARBOHYDRATE 23g.; FIBER 4g.; CHOLESTEROL 0mg.; SODIUM 365mg.

Variation:
To enhance the flavor of potato kurma, add 1 tablespoon of canola or corn oil and 1 tablespoon of melted butter (ghee) in Step 2.

CALORIES 137; FAT 5g.; SATURATED FAT 3g.; PROTEIN 3g.; CARBOHYDRATE 23g.; FIBER 4g.; CHOLESTEROL 11mg.; SODIUM 385mg.

⌁Potato Moong Dal Pachadi⌁

Potatoes and tomatoes cooked in moong dal and simmered with fresh coriander, this pachadi is delicious served over plain rice, or as an accompaniment to most Indian vegetables, rice dishes, and breads.

1/2 cup moong dal
1/2 teaspoon turmeric powder
2 tablespoons corn oil
4 to 6 curry leaves
1 dried red chili pepper
1/4 teaspoon asafoetida
1 teaspoon black mustard seeds
1 teaspoon urad dal
1 cup peeled and chopped potato
1/2 cup chopped tomato
1/2 teaspoon cayenne powder
1/2 teaspoon salt
1/4 cup chopped fresh coriander

1. Boil 2 cups of water. Reduce heat to medium and add moong dal with 1/4 teaspoon turmeric powder. Cook, uncovered, for 20 minutes until moong dal become soft. Do not drain. Set aside.

2. Place oil in a small saucepan over medium heat. When oil is hot, but not smoking, add curry leaves, red pepper, asafoetida, mustard seeds, and urad dal. Fry, covered, over medium heat until mustard seeds pop and urad dal turns golden brown.

3. Immediately add potato and tomato. Stir well with the seasonings.

4. Add remaining 1/4 teaspoon turmeric powder, the cayenne powder, and salt. Mix well with vegetables in saucepan.

5. Add cooked moong dal with 2 cups of warm water to the above mixture and stir well. When the mixture begins to bubble, add coriander and let it simmer. Slow cook until potatoes are cooked.

Serves 4

CALORIES 207; FAT 7g.; SATURATED FAT 1g.; PROTEIN 8g.; CARBOHYDRATE 29g.; FIBER 6g.; CHOLESTEROL 0mg.; SODIUM 280mg.

⌣:POTATO AND OKRA MANDI:⌣

A uniquely flavored combination of potatoes and okra, cooked in tamarind sauce, this dish is especially delicious served with yogurt rice.

1/2 cup frozen black-eyed peas
2 tablespoons corn oil
1/4 teaspoon asafoetida powder
2 to 4 curry leaves
1 teaspoon black mustard seeds
1 teaspoon urad dal
1/4 cup chopped onions
4 garlic cloves, halved
1/2 green chili pepper, chopped
1 cup peeled and cubed potato (1/4 inch cubes)
1/2 cup frozen cut okra
1/4 teaspoon turmeric powder
1/2 teaspoon tamarind paste
1/4 teaspoon cayenne powder
1/2 teaspoon cumin powder
1/2 teaspoon salt (more, if desired)
1/4 cup tomato sauce

1. Place frozen black-eyed peas and 1/2 cup of water in a small microwave dish. Cook on high heat for 7 minutes. Set aside.

2. Place corn oil in a saucepan over medium heat. When oil is hot, but not smoking, add asafoetida, curry leaves, mustard seeds, and urad dal. Cover and fry until mustard seeds pop and urad dal is golden brown.

3. Add onions, garlic, and chili pepper and cook for 1 to 2 minutes, stirring frequently.

4. Add potatoes, okra, and black-eyed peas and mix well. Add turmeric powder and blend well over medium heat.

5. Add tamarind paste and 3 cups of warm water to the vegetables in the saucepan. Blend the vegetables well with tamarind paste.

6. Add cayenne powder, cumin powder, and salt and mix well.

7. Add tomato sauce and let the vegetables cook, covered, over medium-low heat, stirring often, until vegetables are tender.

Serves 4

CALORIES 148; FAT 4g.; SATURATED FAT 1g.; PROTEIN 4g.; CARBOHYDRATE 18g.; FIBER 3g.; CHOLESTEROL 0mg.; SODIUM 419mg.

∽Potato Masala∿

A seasoned stir-fry dish, Potato Masala makes a delicious filling for samosa, bonda, and masala dosai. It may also be served with poori or chappati, or as a side dish with any type of rice.

2 medium to large Idaho potatoes with skins, cut in halves
1/2 teaspoon turmeric powder
1 teaspoon salt
2 tablespoons corn oil
1/4 teaspoon asafoetida
3 to 4 curry leaves (optional)
1 teaspoon black mustard seeds
1 1/2 teaspoon urad dal
1 cup chopped onion
1/2 cup chopped tomato
1 green chili, chopped
1 tablespoon minced fresh ginger root
1/4 teaspoon cayenne powder (more, if desired)
1/4 cup minced fresh coriander

1. Cook potatoes with sufficient water to cover in a covered kettle over medium heat with 1/4 teaspoon turmeric and 1/2 teaspoon salt for approximately 20 minutes or until potatoes become soft. Drain water from cooked potatoes. Peel and coarsely chop potatoes; set aside.

2. In a cast-iron skillet, heat corn oil over medium heat. When oil is hot, but not smoking, add asafoetida and curry leaves. Immediately add mustard seeds and urad dal. Fry, covered, until mustard seeds burst (listen for popping sound) and urad dal is golden.

3. Add onion, tomato, green chili, and ginger. Stir-fry for 1 minute. Add the remaining 1/4 teaspoon of turmeric powder, 1/2 teaspoon of salt, and cayenne powder. Stir well.

4. Add potatoes and stir gently as you blend them with ingredients in skillet. Cover and cook over medium heat for 2 to 3 minutes, so flavors will blend well. Taste for seasonings and add more salt, if desired. Add coriander and mix well.

Serves 4 to 6

CALORIES 122; FAT 6g.; SATURATED FAT 1g.; PROTEIN 3g.; CARBOHYDRATE 16g.; FIBER 2g.; CHOLESTEROL 0mg.; SODIUM 437mg.

‌POTATOES ROASTED WITH GARLIC AND TOMATOES‌

Pan-fried with garlic and tomatoes, these potatoes are an excellent accompaniment to any flavored rice and vegetable dishes.

2 Idaho potatoes
1/2 teaspoon turmeric powder
1/2 teaspoon salt (more, if desired)
3/4 teaspoon cayenne powder
4 tablespoons corn oil
1/2 teaspoon asafoetida powder
4 to 5 curry leaves (optional)
1 teaspoon black mustard seeds
2 teaspoons urad dal
1 tomato, chopped
2 garlic cloves, chopped
2 tablespoons unsweetened powdered coconut

1. Thoroughly wash raw potatoes. Cut each potato in half with skin on. Then cut the potatoes into quarters and next cut quarters into slices approximately 1/4-inch wide.

2. Place potato pieces in a large bowl. Sprinkle with turmeric powder, salt, and cayenne powder. Toss potato pieces in bowl to cover evenly with spices.

3. Pour corn oil into a cast-iron skillet over medium heat. When oil is hot, but not smoking, add asafoetida and curry leaves. Immediately add the mustard seeds and urad dal. Stir briefly and cover. Fry until mustard seeds burst (listen for popping sound) and the urad dal is golden.

4. Add the seasoned potato pieces to skillet. Cook, covered, over low-medium heat for few minutes. Add tomato and garlic to the potatoes and cook over medium-low heat. Be certain to stir the potatoes every few minutes to prevent sticking. Cover and cook until potatoes are tender.

5. Uncover skillet when potatoes are tender and continue to fry over low heat until potatoes become crisp. Stir frequently. Add powdered coconut and stir gently.

Serves 4

CALORIES 249; FAT 16g.; SATURATED FAT 3g.; PROTEIN 4g.; CARBOHYDRATE 25g.; FIBER 3g.; CHOLESTEROL 0mg.; SODIUM 278mg.

ᴗ: SEASONED ROASTED POTATOES :ᴗ

Lightly seasoned and pan-fried, these potatoes are particularly delicious
served with any flavored rice dish.

2 cups peeled and cubed Idaho potatoes (1-inch cubes)
1/4 teaspoon turmeric powder
1/2 teaspoon salt
1/2 teaspoon cayenne powder (more, if desired)
1/2 teaspoon cumin powder
3 tablespoons corn oil
4 to 5 curry leaves
1/4 teaspoon asafoetida powder

1. Place potatoes in a small saucepan. Add water just to cover potatoes
and bring to a boil. Do not cover saucepan. After the water begins to
boil, reduce heat.

2. Add turmeric powder and salt to the potatoes.

3. Parboil (half cook) potatoes. Be careful not to overcook the potatoes.

4. When potatoes are parcooked, drain potatoes and place in a small bowl.

5. Sprinkle cayenne powder and cumin powder over potatoes and shake
bowl to cover potatoes evenly.

6. Place corn oil in a cast-iron skillet over medium heat. When oil is hot,
but not smoking, add curry leaves and asafoetida powder.

7. Place potatoes in skillet. Cook over very low heat until golden brown.
Turn frequently.
Serves 4

CALORIES 141; FAT 10g.; SATURATED FAT 1g.; PROTEIN 1g.; CARBOHYDRATE
11g.; FIBER 1g.; CHOLESTEROL 0mg.; SODIUM 271mg.

∽Spinach Kootu∽

Spinach blended with creamy split peas, garlic, and cumin, Spinach Kootu is delicious served over plain rice. Its mild, delicate taste will enhance any meal.

1/2 cup yellow split-peas or moong dal
1/4 teaspoon turmeric powder
2 tablespoons corn oil
1 dried whole red chili pepper
1 teaspoon black mustard seeds
1 teaspoon urad dal
1/4 cup chopped onion
4 cloves garlic, finely chopped
1 package (10 ounces) frozen chopped spinach
1 teaspoon cumin powder
1 teaspoon salt
1 green chili pepper, chopped (optional)

1. Bring 4 cups of water to a boil. Add yellow split peas and turmeric powder. Reduce heat to medium high and cook, uncovered, for about 30 minutes until split peas become creamy. If water seems to have evaporated during the cooking process, add another cup of water and cook until split peas becomes creamy. Set aside.

2. Heat oil in a saucepan over medium heat. When oil is hot, but not smoking, stir in red chili pepper, mustard seeds, and urad dal. Fry, covered, until mustard seeds burst (listen for popping sound) and urad dal is golden.

3. Add onion and garlic. Stir-fry for approximately 1 minute.

4. Add frozen spinach to saucepan. Add cooked split pea mixture and 1 cup of water.

5. Add cumin powder, salt, and green chili pepper, if desired, to spinach mixture. Blend well with ingredients in saucepan.

6. Cover and cook over low heat for another 5 to 7 minutes, until spinach is done and all ingredients are thoroughly blended.

Note: To make Spinach Kootu with a creamier consistency increase yellow split peas in the above recipe to 3/4 cup and cook with an additional 1 cup of water.

Serves 6

CALORIES 113; FAT 5g.; SATURATED FAT 1g.; PROTEIN 7g.; CARBOHYDRATE 16g.; FIBER 7g.; CHOLESTEROL 0mg.; SODIUM 403mg.

Variation: For a hearty enhancement, you may add 1/2 cup frozen baby lima beans (uncooked) to the spinach in Step 4 to create **Spinach and Lima Beans Kootu.** You may also add an additional 1/2 cup water and 1/2 teaspoon cumin powder if desired.

∿ SPINACH PORIYAL ∿

Spinach stir-fried with split peas and coconut, Spinach Poriyal is excellent served with rice or chappati. You may also use it to stuff mushrooms or as a unique topping for crackers.

1/2 cup dry yellow split peas
1/4 teaspoon turmeric powder
2 tablespoons corn oil
1 whole dried red chili pepper
1 teaspoon black mustard seeds
1 teaspoon urad dal
1 cup chopped onion
1 package (10 ounces) frozen chopped spinach
1 teaspoon salt
2 tablespoons ground fresh or unsweetened powdered coconut (optional)

1. Boil about 2 cups of water. Add yellow split peas with turmeric powder and cook, uncovered, for about 20 minutes over medium heat, until split peas are semi-soft. If water evaporates before peas become tender, add an additional 1/4 cup of water. When split peas are tender, set aside.

2. Heat corn oil with red whole pepper in a cast-iron or any skillet over medium heat. When oil is hot, but not smoking, stir in mustard seeds and urad dal. Fry until mustard seeds burst (listen for popping sound) and urad dal is golden.

3. Add onion and stir for 1 minute.

4. Add frozen spinach and 1/2 cup water. Blend well with mixture in skillet. Add salt. Cover and cook over medium heat approximately 5 minutes until spinach is tender, stirring occasionally.

5. Add drained split peas to spinach mixture. Blend thoroughly.

6. Sprinkle with coconut. Stir briefly and serve.

Serves 4

CALORIES 179; FAT 8g.; SATURATED FAT 2g.; PROTEIN 10g.; CARBOHYDRATE 25g.; FIBER 11g.; CHOLESTEROL 0mg.; SODIUM 604mg.

Variation:
For **Spinach Poriyal with Moong Dal** substitute 1/2 cup moong dal for yellow split peas. Reduce water in Step 1 to 1 1/2 cups as moong dal will cook very quickly (10 minutes).

~:Sugar Snap Peas Poriyal:~

An innovative easy-to-prepare stir-fry, Sugar Snap Peas Poriyal goes well with most dishes.

2 cups sugar snap pea pods
1 tablespoon corn oil
1 teaspoon black mustard seeds
2 teaspoons urad dal
1/2 teaspoon chutney powder
1/2 teaspoon salt
3/4 cup onion, cut lengthwise
2 tablespoons freshly ground or unsweetened powdered coconut

1. Remove ends of pea pods and peel off strings. Wash thoroughly.

2. Pour corn oil in a saucepan and heat over medium heat. When oil is hot, but not smoking, add mustard seeds and urad dal. Heat, covered, until mustard seeds pop and urad dal is golden brown.

3. Reduce heat to low and add snap pea pods.

4. Add chutney powder and salt and stir well. Cover and cook over low heat until just tender (about 3 minutes).

5. Add onion and coconut. Onion should remain crisp.

6. Stir well and serve with rice or bread.

Serves 4

CALORIES 75; FAT 5g.; SATURATED FAT 1g.; PROTEIN 2g.; CARBOHYDRATE 7g.; FIBER 2g.; CHOLESTEROL 0mg.; SODIUM 269mg.

Variation:

Cooked moong dal will enhance the taste of the above recipe:
Cook 1/4 cup of moong dal in 1 cup of water with 1/4 teaspoon turmeric powder for about 10 minutes until dal becomes tender. Add cooked moong dal to the recipe in Step 5.

⌇Tomato Moong Dal Pachadi⌇

Tomatoes and coriander simmered with moong dal, this versatile pachadi goes well with plain rice, yogurt rice, or any Indian bread.

1/4 cup moong dal
1/2 teaspoon turmeric powder
2 tablespoons corn oil
2 to 4 curry leaves
1 dried red chili pepper
1/4 teaspoon asafoetida
1 teaspoon black mustard seeds
1 teaspoon urad dal
1 cup chopped tomato
1/4 teaspoon cayenne powder or 1/2 green chili, chopped
1/2 teaspoon salt
1/4 cup chopped fresh coriander

1. Boil 2 cups of water. Reduce heat to medium and add moong dal with 1/4 teaspoon turmeric powder. Cook, uncovered, for about 20 minutes until moong dal becomes soft. Set aside.

2. In a small saucepan heat oil over medium heat. When oil is hot, but not smoking, add curry leaves, red pepper, asafoetida, mustard seeds, and urad dal. Fry, covered, over medium heat until mustard seeds pop and urad dal turns golden brown.

3. Immediately add tomato. Stir well with the seasonings.

4. Add remaining 1/4 teaspoon turmeric powder, cayenne powder, and salt. Mix well with vegetables in saucepan.

Healthy South Indian Cooking

5. Add cooked moong dal with 2 cups of warm water to the above mixture and let it simmer over low heat for about 2 minutes.

6. Add coriander and let simmer for a few additional minutes.

Serves 4

CALORIES 133; FAT 7g.; SATURATED FAT 1g.; PROTEIN 4g.; CARBOHYDRATE 13g.; FIBER 3g.; CHOLESTEROL 0mg.; SODIUM 273mg.

⌣ TOMATO PACHADI ⌣

Seasoned yogurt salad with onion and tomatoes, this pachadi is a refreshing accompaniment to any other dish.

1 teaspoon corn oil
1 whole dried red chili pepper
1/4 teaspoon asafoetida powder
1 teaspoon black mustard seeds
1 teaspoon urad dal
1 cup chopped onion
1 cup chopped tomato
1/2 teaspoon cayenne powder
2 cups plain fat-free yogurt
1 teaspoon salt
2 tablespoons chopped fresh coriander leaves

1. Place corn oil in saucepan over medium heat. When oil is hot, but not smoking, add red peppers, asafoetida, mustard seeds, and urad dal. Cook, covered, until mustard seeds pop and urad dal is golden.

2. Add chopped onion and tomato. Stir-fry for a few minutes.

3. Add cayenne powder and cook for few minutes.

4. Transfer ingredients from saucepan to a mixing bowl and blend in yogurt.

5. Add salt and stir. Garnish with coriander leaves.

Serves 4

CALORIES 105; FAT 2g.; SATURATED FAT trace; PROTEIN 8g.; CARBOHYDRATE 16g.; FIBER 1g.; CHOLESTEROL 2mg.; SODIUM 626mg.

ᴠYOGURT SALADᴠ

A creamy salad featuring red onions and tomatoes, yogurt salad is particularly delicious served with vegetable pulaoo or chicken biriyani rice.

1 cup red onion, cut in lengthwise pieces
1 green chili pepper, chopped
1/2 cup chopped tomato
1 1/2 cups low-fat or fat-free plain yogurt
1/2 teaspoon salt (or to taste)
1 teaspoon fresh chopped coriander

1. Combine onion, chili, and tomato with yogurt. Add salt to taste. Chill at least 1 hour before serving.

2. Garnish with coriander.

Serves 2 to 4

CALORIES 103; FAT trace; SATURATED FAT trace; PROTEIN 8g.; CARBOHYDRATE 17g.; FIBER 2g.; CHOLESTEROL 2mg.; SODIUM 455mg.

⌁Zucchini Kootu⌁

Zucchini cooked with ginger, cumin, and creamy lentils, this kootu is delicious served with plain rice or yogurt rice. As with other kootus, Zucchini Kootu is a mild and flavorful accompaniment to any meal.

1/2 cup toor dal
1/2 teaspoon turmeric powder
2 tablespoons corn oil
1/4 teaspoon asafoetida powder
4 to 6 curry leaves (optional)
1 teaspoon black mustard seeds
1 teaspoon urad dal
1/4 cup chopped onion
1 green chili pepper, chopped
3 cups peeled and cubed zucchini
1 teaspoon minced fresh ginger root
1 teaspoon cumin powder
1 teaspoon salt
1 tablespoon powdered coconut

1. Bring 4 cups of water to a boil. Add toor dal and 1/4 teaspoon turmeric powder. Reduce heat to medium high. Cook, uncovered, for about 30 minutes until dal becomes creamy. If water seems to evaporate during the cooking process, add another cup of water and cook until dal becomes creamy.

2. Heat corn oil in a saucepan over medium heat. When oil is hot, but not smoking, add asafoetida and curry leaves.

3. Add mustard seeds and urad dal. Cover and cook until mustard seeds burst and urad dal turns golden.

4. Add onion, chili pepper, and remaining 1/4 teaspoon turmeric powder.

5. Add zucchini and ginger. Blend well with onions and green chili pepper.

6. Add creamy toor dal, cumin powder, and salt. Add 3/4 cup of warm water to the dal. Stir zucchini well with seasonings for 1 to 2 minutes.

7. Cover and simmer until zucchini is tender (about 5 minutes.) Add coconut powder. Stir and cook for an additional minute.

Serves 4

CALORIES 198; FAT 8g.; SATURATED FAT 1g.; PROTEIN 9g.; CARBOHYDRATE 25g.; FIBER 7g.; CHOLESTEROL 0mg.; SODIUM 543mg.

Variations:
To make **Chow-Chow Kootu**, you may use chayote known as chow-chow, a kind of squash instead of zucchini. 2 chayote, peeled and chopped, will yield approximately 3 cups.

You may also use yellow split peas or moong dal instead of toor dal to make this kootu for a different but equally good flavor.

Nonvegetarian Dishes

~:CHICKEN BIRIYANI RICE:~

Biriyani is a highly aromatic and elaborate basmati rice dish that can be either vegetarian or nonvegetarian. Chicken Biriyani Rice is a delicious accompaniment to Chicken Kurma, Egg Masala, and any of the yogurt salads.

1 recipe Garlic and Pepper Chicken (page 295)
3 tablespoons butter
2 to 3 small cinnamon sticks
1 bay leaf, crumbled
3 to 4 curry leaves (optional)
2 cups basmati rice, rinsed and drained
1/4 teaspoon turmeric powder
4 to 6 whole cloves
1 teaspoon cardamom powder
1 tablespoon minced fresh ginger
1/4 teaspoon garam masala powder
2 to 3 threads saffron
1 teaspoon salt (more, if desired)
1/4 cup chopped fresh coriander
1/2 cup onion, cut in lengthwise pieces
1/2 cup roasted cashew pieces

1. Prepare chicken and set aside.

2. Preheat oven to 350 degrees.

3. Melt butter in a large nonstick, wide-bottomed saucepan over medium heat. Add cinnamon sticks, bay leaf, and curry leaves. Add rinsed basmati rice. Stir-fry for 4 to 5 minutes, until rice becomes slightly toasted.

4. Add turmeric powder, whole cloves, 1/2 teaspoon cardamom powder, ginger, and 4 cups of hot water.

5. Reduce heat to low. Immediately add garam masala powder, saffron threads, salt, and coriander. Stir well. Heat, uncovered, until mixture

reaches the boiling point.

6. Cover saucepan and continue cooking over low heat until all liquid evaporates and rice is tender.

7. When rice is cooked, set aside to cool for a few minutes.

8. Add prepared chicken from skillet to rice and fluff the rice gently.

9. Add onion and stir into rice. Taste to see if the seasonings are good.

10. To complete the biriyani rice, transfer the above rice with chicken into a rectangular baking dish. Sprinkle top with cashew pieces. Cover the dish with aluminum foil. Place in oven for about 30 minutes to heat through and to maximize the aromatic flavor of rice.

Serves 6

CALORIES 349; FAT 13g.; SATURATED FAT 5g.; PROTEIN 8g.; CARBOHYDRATE 52g.; FIBER 3g.; CHOLESTEROL 16mg.; SODIUM 471mg.

ᔕCHETTINAD CHICKEN CHOPSᔓ

Boneless, skinless chicken thighs simmered in a seasoned tomato sauce and lightly fried, chicken chops are a distinctly satisfying accompaniment to any rice and vegetable dish.

1 pound (or 6 pieces) boneless, skinless chicken thighs
1 tablespoon corn oil
1/3 cup finely chopped onion
1/4 cup chopped tomato
1 tablespoon finely minced garlic
1/4 teaspoon turmeric powder
1 teaspoon vindaloo curry paste (see note below)
2 teaspoons cumin powder
1/2 teaspoon salt
1/4 cup tomato sauce

Egg Batter:
2 eggs
1/2 teaspoon salt
1/2 teaspoon turmeric powder
1 cup oil for frying

1. Cut each thigh in half. Wash chicken, drain, and set aside.

2. Place oil in a cast-iron skillet over medium heat. When oil is hot, but not smoking, add onion, tomato, and garlic and sauté for a few minutes until the vegetables become tender.

3. Add chicken pieces and brown.

4. Add turmeric powder and stir well.

5. Add vindaloo curry paste, cumin powder, and salt.

6. Add tomato sauce and 1/4 cup warm water. Continue to cook chicken

in sauce over medium heat, covered, being careful to spoon sauce over chicken as it cooks.

7. When chicken is tender, remove chicken from sauce and place on platter.

8. The sauce remaining in skillet can be transferred to a small serving bowl and served over rice or pasta. Garnish with fresh coriander for extra flavor.

9. Set a platter, lined with paper towels, beside the stove to hold fried chicken chops.

10. Make the batter: Beat eggs with salt and turmeric powder. Dip chicken pieces in egg batter. Heat oil in a skillet or wok and fry a few pieces at a time. When pieces are fried thoroughly (about 1 minute each side), set aside on a platter. Serve warm.

Note: If you have no vindaloo curry paste, use 1/2 teaspoon cayenne powder and 1/2 cup tomato sauce instead. Blend well.

Serves 4

CALORIES 340; FAT 22g.; SATURATED FAT 3g.; PROTEIN 30g.; CARBOHYDRATE 5g.; FIBER 1g.; CHOLESTEROL 160mg.; SODIUM 771mg.

~:CHETTINAD CHICKEN KULAMBU:~

Slow-cooked in an aromatic sauce seasoned with garlic and ginger, Chicken Kulambu is delicious served over plain rice or accompanied by chappati. This South Indian specialty is comparable to the well-known Vindaloo Chicken dish.

3 tablespoons corn or canola oil
2 to 3 small pieces cinnamon stick
1 bay leaf, crumbled
1/4 teaspoon fennel seeds
1/2 teaspoon whole cumin seeds
1/2 teaspoon urad dal
1/2 cup chopped onion
1/4 cup chopped tomato
3 cloves garlic, quartered
1 tablespoon minced fresh ginger
1/4 teaspoon turmeric powder
2 pounds (boneless, skinless) chicken breasts or thighs
2 teaspoons curry powder
1 teaspoon cayenne powder
1 teaspoon vindaloo curry paste (more, if desired)
1 cup tomato sauce
1/2 teaspoon black pepper and cumin powder
1 teaspoon salt
1/4 cup chopped fresh coriander

1. Heat oil in a wide saucepan over medium heat.

2. When oil is hot, but not smoking, add cinnamon stick, bay leaf, fennel seeds, cumin, and urad dal. Fry until urad dal turns golden.

3. Add onion, tomato, garlic, and ginger and sauté for a few minutes. Add turmeric powder.

4. Cut chicken into small (stew-size pieces). Add chicken pieces to

saucepan and continue to sauté for several minutes until chicken turns opaque.

5. Add curry powder, cayenne powder, vindaloo curry paste, and tomato sauce with approximately 2 cups of water. Stir in black pepper and cumin powder. Add salt and continue cooking over medium-low heat for several minutes.

6. Add coriander. Reduce heat to low. Cook, covered, stirring often until chicken is tender (approximately 20 minutes). If the sauce becomes too thick, you may add an additional small amount of both water and tomato sauce as desired.

Serves 4

CALORIES 305; FAT 17g.; SATURATED FAT 2g.; PROTEIN 28g.; CARBOHYDRATE 13g.; FIBER 4g.; CHOLESTEROL 108mg.; SODIUM 1060mg.

Variations:
▪ You may also use bone-in chicken thighs or breasts to make chicken kulambu.

▪ You may substitute cornish hen for chicken and follow the above recipe to make **Cornish Hen Kulambu.** Cut the cornish hen into 4 to 6 small pieces and proceed with the recipe.

⌣: Chettinad Chicken Kurma :⌣

Tender pieces of chicken in an exquisite coconut-based sauce, Kurma can
be served over plain rice, biriyani rice, or basmati rice with peas, or can
accompany any Indian bread.

2 pounds skinned chicken (about 6 pieces such as thighs or breasts)
3/4 cup unsweetened powdered or freshly ground coconut
4 small slices fresh ginger root
2 cloves garlic
2 green chili peppers, or 2 to 4 dried red chili peppers (more, if desired)
1/4 cup roasted chickpeas (chana dalia)
12 raw almonds
3 teaspoons cumin seeds
2 tablespoons khus khus (white poppy seeds)
1 teaspoon fennel seeds
4 to 6 small pieces cinnamon stick
1 tablespoon butter
2 tablespoons corn oil or canola oil
1 1/2 bay leaves, crumbled
8 to 10 curry leaves
3/4 cup onion, cut lengthwise
1/2 cup chopped tomato
1/2 teaspoon turmeric powder
2 teaspoon salt
1 teaspoon curry powder
3/4 teaspoon cardamom powder
1/3 cup minced fresh coriander

1. Cut chicken thighs and breasts into small pieces. Wash the chicken
pieces, drain, and set aside.

2. In an electric blender, grind together coconut, ginger, garlic, chilies,
roasted chickpeas, almonds, 1 1/2 teaspoon cumin seeds, the khus khus,
1/2 teaspoon fennel seeds, and 2 to 3 small pieces of cinnamon stick.
Use 3 cups of hot water to facilitate the grinding process. (Water must

be hot for coconut to blend properly.) Process on high for at least 5 minutes until mixture has a creamy, liquid consistency. Set kurma sauce aside.

3. Heat butter and oil in a large saucepan over medium heat. When the oil is hot, but not smoking, add bay leaves, curry leaves, and remaining 2 to 3 pieces cinnamon stick, remaining 1 1/2 teaspoons cumin seeds, and 1/2 teaspoon fennel seeds. Fry until seeds are golden.

4. Immediately add onion and tomato and cook for a few minutes. Add turmeric powder and mix well.

5. Add the chicken pieces to saucepan. Stir well and cook, uncovered, over medium-high heat for 3 to 5 minutes, until chicken becomes opaque and slightly brown.

6. Pour kurma sauce over chicken mixture in saucepan. Add salt, curry powder, and 1 cup warm water. Mix well. Add cardamom powder. Cook, covered, over low heat, until chicken becomes tender (approximately 20 minutes), stirring occasionally.

7. Add coriander and continue cooking over low heat for a few minutes.

Note: If you find kurma sauce to be too spicy, add 1/4 cup tomato sauce and stir well at low heat. You may also use boneless chicken thighs to make chicken kurma in order to reduce the cooking time.

Serves 4

CALORIES 620; FAT 31g.; SATURATED FAT 13g.; PROTEIN 62g.; CARBOHYDRATE 27g.; FIBER 9g.; CHOLESTEROL 139mg.; SODIUM 1272mg.

∿ CHETTINAD CHICKEN PORIYAL ∿

Tender pieces of chicken simmered in a ginger and garlic sauce, Chettinad Chicken Poriyal can be served with plain rice, lemon rice, or any other flavored rice.

2 pounds chicken (about 6 pieces: thighs, halved breasts)
4 tablespoons corn oil
2 to 4 very small cinnamon sticks
1 bay leaf, crumbled
1/4 teaspoon whole black peppercorns (about 6 peppercorns)
1/4 teaspoon fennel seeds
1/2 teaspoon cumin seeds
1 cup chopped onion
1/4 cup chopped tomato
6 cloves garlic, chopped
1 heaping tablespoon minced fresh ginger
1/2 teaspoon turmeric powder
1 1/2 teaspoons curry powder
3/4 teaspoon cayenne powder
1 teaspoon salt
3/4 teaspoon black pepper and cumin powder
1 cup tomato sauce

1. Wash chicken thoroughly and remove skin. Chicken parts may be cooked whole or cut into smaller pieces (thighs or breasts). Set aside.

2. In a wide-bottomed iron skillet, place corn oil and heat over medium heat. When oil is hot, but not smoking, add cinnamon sticks, bay leaf, and peppercorns. Cover and heat until peppercorns pop.

3. Add fennel and cumin seeds. Fry until cumin seeds become brown.

4. Add onion, tomato, garlic, and ginger.

5. Add turmeric powder and curry powder and stir well. Stir the seasonings and cook until onions are tender.

6. Add chicken pieces. Brown well and cook on high heat until chicken become opaque (partially cooked). Reduce heat.

7. Add cayenne powder, salt, and black pepper and cumin powder. Stir well.

8. Add tomato sauce and blend into ingredients in skillet.

9. During the cooking process, check often and stir frequently to prevent the chicken from sticking to skillet. Add 1 cup of water at 1/4 cup intervals to enable the thorough cooking of the chicken without it sticking to the skillet.

10. Cook, covered, over medium-low heat until chicken becomes tender and has absorbed the flavors of the sauce (30 to 45 minutes).

Serves 4

CALORIES 438; FAT 18g.; SATURATED FAT 3g.; PROTEIN 55g.; CARBOHYDRATE 15g.; FIBER 5g.; CHOLESTEROL 132mg.; SODIUM 1063mg.

Variations:
You may also use boneless chicken thighs and breasts and follow the above recipe. If chicken thighs and breasts are cut into small pieces cooking time will be less in Step 10.

✌ GARLIC AND PEPPER CHICKEN ~

Chicken stir-fried with garlic and ginger, this dish goes particularly well with Tomato Rice and Green Beans Poriyal. It can also be used as a filling for pita bread.

2 pounds boneless, skinless chicken thighs (see note below)
3 tablespoons canola or corn oil
4 to 5 small pieces cinnamon stick
1 bay leaf, crumbled
2 dried red chili peppers (more, if desired)
1 teaspoon cumin seeds
1/2 teaspoon fennel seeds
1 teaspoon urad dal
1/2 cup chopped onion
10 garlic cloves, cut in half
1/2 teaspoon turmeric powder
1 tablespoon minced fresh ginger
1 1/2 teaspoons ground black pepper and cumin powder
1 1/2 teaspoons salt
1 teaspoon curry powder (more, if desired)
3/4 teaspoon cayenne powder
1/4 cup chopped fresh coriander
1 onion, chopped lengthwise (optional)

1. Cut chicken into medium-size pieces. Rinse, drain, and set aside.

2. Heat oil in a cast-iron skillet over medium heat. When oil is hot, but not smoking, add cinnamon sticks, bay leaf, and red chili peppers.

3. Add cumin, fennel seeds, and urad dal.

4. Add onion and garlic. Sauté for few minutes. Stir in turmeric powder.

5. Add chicken and ginger to skillet. Cook, covered, over low heat until the chicken is partially cooked.

6. Add black pepper and cumin powder, salt, curry powder, and cayenne powder together with coriander. Stir well to coat the chicken with spices. Add 1/4 to 1/2 cup of warm water, adding 1/4 cup of water at a time. Stir and cook chicken, covered, over medium heat for 12 to 15 minutes.

7. To enhance flavor or to increase tenderness of chicken, add onions over the chicken and continue cooking. Simmer until the onions are cooked to preferred degree of doneness.

Note: Boneless skinless chicken breasts may be used in place of chicken thighs, but more water (1/2 to 1 cup) will have to be added in Step 7 to maintain moistness. Adjust other seasonings according to taste.

Serves 4 to 6

CALORIES 343; FAT 16g.; SATURATED 3g.; PROTEIN 38g.; CARBOHYDRATE 10g.; FIBER 3g.; CHOLESTEROL 145mg.; SODIUM 801mg.

⌒CHETTINAD EGG KULAMBU⌒

Boiled eggs cooked with spices in a tamarind sauce, Egg Kulambu can be served over plain rice or as an accompaniment to idli, dosai, and chappati.

4 large eggs
3 tablespoons corn oil
2 to 3 small pieces cinnamon stick
1/2 bay leaf, crumbled
4 to 6 curry leaves
1/4 teaspoon fenugreek
1/4 teaspoon cumin seeds
1/4 teaspoon fennel seeds
1/2 teaspoon urad dal
1/2 cup chopped onion
1/4 cup chopped tomato
6 to 8 cloves garlic, peeled and chopped
1/2 green chili, chopped
1/4 teaspoon turmeric powder
1 teaspoon curry powder
1/2 teaspoon cayenne powder
1/2 teaspoon tamarind paste
1 teaspoon black pepper and cumin powder
1 teaspoon salt
1 cup tomato sauce
1/4 cup finely chopped fresh coriander

1. Hard boil the eggs. Peel and set eggs aside.

2. Heat corn oil in a saucepan over medium heat. When oil is hot, but not smoking, add cinnamon stick, bay leaf, curry leaves, fenugreek, cumin, fennel seeds, and urad dal. Stir gently until urad dal is golden brown.

3. Immediately add onion, tomato, garlic, and chili to saucepan. Stir and add turmeric powder.

4. When onion is tender, add curry powder, cayenne powder, tamarind paste, and black pepper and cumin powder. Add salt, tomato sauce, and 1 cup of water. Mix well and allow the mixture to boil for about 2 minutes. Add coriander.

5. When the mixture starts to boil, reduce the heat and allow to simmer over low heat for about 2 minutes.

6. Score boiled eggs with cross marks on each end (i.e. cut the eggs slightly on each end) and add the eggs to the simmering sauce so that they will absorb the flavor of the sauce.

7. Spoon the sauce over the eggs. Remove from heat. Cover and let the eggs soak in the sauce until served.

Note: You may add an additional 1/2 cup of tomato sauce for a milder taste.

Serves 4

CALORIES 306; FAT 20g.; SATURATED FAT 4g.; PROTEIN 11g.; CARBOHYDRATE 25g.; FIBER 8g.; CHOLESTEROL 249mg.; SODIUM 1290mg.

⌣ Egg Masala I ⌣

Boiled eggs simmered in a rich sauce, Egg Masala may accompany any lunch or dinner entree.

4 eggs
1 teaspoon corn oil
1/4 teaspoon cumin seeds
1/2 teaspoon urad dal
1/2 cup chopped onion
1/2 cup chopped tomatoes
2 cloves garlic, coarsely chopped
1/4 cup finely chopped fresh coriander
1/4 teaspoon turmeric powder
1/4 teaspoon cayenne powder
1/4 teaspoon cumin powder
1/2 teaspoon black pepper and cumin powder
1/4 teaspoon tamarind paste
1/2 teaspoon salt
1/4 cup tomato sauce

1. Hard boil the eggs. Peel the eggs and set aside.

2. Heat the corn oil in a small cast-iron skillet over medium heat. When oil is hot, but not smoking, add the cumin and urad dal. Cover and stir until urad dal is golden brown.

3. Immediately add the onion, tomatoes, garlic, and coriander to skillet. Add turmeric powder and stir briefly.

4. When onion is tender, add cayenne powder, cumin powder, and black pepper and cumin powder. Add tamarind paste, salt, and tomato sauce. Stir well to blend all the ingredients.

5. Cook, uncovered, over medium heat for 3 to 4 minutes. Lower the heat.

6. Cut eggs in half lengthwise. Add eggs to the sauce. Spoon sauce over the eggs. Blend eggs gently into mixture. Cover and allow eggs to stay in the sauce for several minutes before serving.

Serves 4

CALORIES 101; FAT 6g.; SATURATED FAT 2g.; PROTEIN 6g.; CARBOHYDRATE 5g.; FIBER 1g.; CHOLESTEROL 187mg.; SODIUM 418mg.

~:Egg Masala II:~

A unique version of boiled eggs simmered in an oil-free sauce, Egg Masala is a welcome accompaniment to any meal.

4 large eggs
1 teaspoon minced fresh ginger
2 cloves garlic
1 teaspoon unsweetened coconut powder
1/2 cup chopped onion
1/2 cup chopped tomatoes
1/4 teaspoon cayenne powder
1/2 teaspoon black pepper and cumin powder
1/4 teaspoon garam masala powder
1/2 teaspoon salt
1/4 cup tomato sauce
1/4 cup minced fresh coriander

1. Hard boil the eggs. Peel and set aside.

2. Place ginger, garlic, and coconut powder with 1/4 cup of water in a blender and grind to a smooth paste.

3. Sauté onion in a small skillet without oil for 2 to 3 minutes over medium heat. Add tomatoes and cook until tomatoes are soft.

4. Add ground paste to skillet and blend with other ingredients.

5. Stir in cayenne powder, black pepper and cumin powder, garam masala powder, and salt. Cook for a few minutes.

6. Add tomato sauce and blend with ingredients in skillet.

7. Stir in coriander. Add boiled eggs to sauce. Eggs may be served whole or cut in half. The sauce should be scooped over the eggs.

Serves 4

CALORIES 166; FAT 10g.; SATURATED FAT 3g.; PROTEIN 13g.; CARBOHYDRATE 6g.; FIBER 1g.; CHOLESTEROL 399mg.; SODIUM 480mg.

↙SEASONED SCRAMBLED EGGS↝

Scrambled eggs South Indian style are a seasoned variation of a familiar dish that can be served with breakfast, lunch and dinner.

4 large eggs
1/4 teaspoon turmeric
1/2 teaspoon salt
2 tablespoons corn oil
1 teaspoon black mustard seeds
1 teaspoon urad dal
1/2 cup finely chopped onions
1/2 finely chopped green chili
2 tablespoons dry roasted cashew halves (optional)

1. Beat the eggs with turmeric and salt. Set aside.

2. Place corn oil in a skillet over medium heat. When oil is hot, but not smoking, add mustard seeds and urad dal. Cover and fry until mustard seeds pop and urad dal turns golden.

3. Immediately add onions and chili. Cook for a minute.

4. Add the beaten eggs to the skillet. Fry until well done. You may add cashew halves after the eggs are cooked. Toss and serve.

Serves 4

CALORIES 145; FAT 12g.; SATURATED FAT 2g.; PROTEIN 6g.; CARBOHYDRATE 4g.; FIBER 1g.; CHOLESTEROL 187mg.; SODIUM 323mg.

~: MEEN KULAMBU :~

Cooked in a thick, aromatic tamarind sauce, Fish kulambu is particularly tasty when prepared several hours prior to serving because the fish will absorb the flavor of the sauce over a period of time. Serve Meen Kulambu over white rice or as an accompaniment to idli, dosai, or chappati.

The best fish to buy for this recipe are halibut, haddock, whitefish, pomfret (an Indian favorite) also known as pompano, and sierra (also known as king fish). Have the fish cut into steaks or small fillets, as you desire.

3 tablespoons corn oil
4 to 6 curry leaves (optional)
1/2 teaspoon fenugreek seeds
1/2 teaspoon fennel seeds
1/2 teaspoon cumin seeds
1/2 teaspoon urad dal
1 cup chopped onion
1/4 cup garlic cloves, quartered
1 green chili pepper, cut lengthwise
1/4 cup chopped tomato
1/2 teaspoon turmeric powder
1/4 teaspoon cayenne powder
2 teaspoons curry powder
1 teaspoon black pepper and cumin powder
1 teaspoon salt
1 cup tomato sauce
1/2 teaspoon tamarind paste
1 pound firm-fleshed fish, cut into pieces 1-inch thick
1/2 cup chopped fresh coriander

1. Place oil in a large saucepan over medium heat. When oil is hot, but not smoking, add curry leaves, fenugreek, fennel, cumin seeds, and urad dal. Cover and fry until urad dal is golden.

2. Add onion, garlic, chili pepper, and tomato. Stir-fry for about 1

❦ *Healthy South Indian Cooking*

minute.

3. Blend in turmeric powder and cook for another minute.

4. Add cayenne powder, curry powder, black pepper and cumin powder, and salt. Stir and cook for another minute.

5. Add tomato sauce and tamarind paste. Blend well into mixture. Add about 2 cups of water. Stir well and allow mixture to simmer, uncovered, for few minutes over medium-low heat.

6. When mixture begins to boil, add fish steaks and spoon sauce carefully over fish. Add coriander. Continue cooking over low heat, covered, for 5 to 7 minutes until fish is opaque and flaky.

7. Sauce should be stirred several times during the cooking process and more water added, if necessary. Use the handles of the saucepan to swirl the sauce, rather than risk breaking the fish steaks with a spoon.

8. When fish is done, remove saucepan from heat. Cover and let it remain at room temperature until serving. If fish is not served immediately, reheat only briefly before serving.

Serves 4

CALORIES 282; FAT 13g.; SATURATED FAT 2g.; PROTEIN 26g.; CARBOHYDRATE 15g.; FIBER 3g.; CHOLESTEROL 36mg.; SODIUM 971mg.

☙ MEEN VARUVAL ☙

Meen Varuval, a traditional Chettinad specialty, is fish that is first marinated, then fried. Possible fish to buy for this recipe are halibut, haddock, whitefish, pomfret (an Indian favorite) also known as pompano, and sierra, also known as king fish or salmon. This dish can be served as an accompaniment to any meal that includes plain white rice.

4 fish steaks, 1/2-inch thick (about 1 pound)
1 tablespoon chopped fresh ginger
1 tablespoon chopped garlic
1 tablespoon fresh lemon juice
1/4 teaspoon turmeric powder
1/2 teaspoon salt
1/2 teaspoon cayenne powder
1 cup corn oil for frying

1. Wash fish steaks in water. Dry with paper towels and set aside.

2. Grind ginger and garlic with lemon juice and 4 tablespoons water to a smooth paste.

3. Add turmeric powder, salt, and cayenne to the above paste and blend thoroughly.

4. Coat both sides of fish steaks with paste and marinate for at least 4 hours, covered and refrigerated, on a glass platter.

5. Heat corn oil in iron skillet over medium heat until hot, but not smoking.

6. Fry each fish steak on both sides until golden brown.

7. Set a platter, lined with paper towels, beside stove to hold fried fish. Serve immediately.

Note: Instead of fish steaks, you may also use fish fillets to make fried fish.

Serves 4

CALORIES 340; FAT 28g.; SATURATED FAT 4g.; PROTEIN 20g.; CARBOHYDRATE 1g.; FIBER trace; CHOLESTEROL 49mg.; SODIUM 328mg.

⌁Chettinad Lamb Kulambu⌁

Lamb Kulambu is another Chettinad specialty that is delicious served over plain rice or with idli and dosai.

> 1 pound lamb round bone chops (or) leg of lamb or goat meat
> 2 tablespoons corn oil
> 1/2 bay leaf, crumbled
> 2 to 4 small sticks cinnamon
> 2 to 4 curry leaves (optional)
> 1/4 teaspoon fenugreek seeds
> 1 teaspoon cumin seeds
> 1/4 teaspoon fennel seeds
> 1 teaspoon urad dal
> 1/2 cup chopped onion
> 4 cloves garlic, chopped
> 1 tablespoon fresh minced ginger
> 1/2 cup chopped tomato
> 1/2 teaspoon turmeric powder
> 2 teaspoons curry powder
> 1/2 teaspoon cayenne powder
> 1/2 teaspoon black pepper and cumin powder
> 1/2 cup tomato sauce
> 1 teaspoon salt
> 1/4 cup chopped fresh coriander

1. Cut lamb or goat into small pieces as if for stew. Remove fat. Rinse the meat under cold water several times. Drain and set aside.

2. Heat oil in a saucepan or pressure cooker over medium heat. When oil is hot, but not smoking, crumble bay leaf, cinnamon stick, and curry leaves into oil.

3. Add fenugreek, cumin, fennel seeds, and urad dal. Stir-fry until urad dal turns golden.

Healthy South Indian Cooking

4. Immediately add onion, garlic, ginger, and tomato. Add turmeric powder and cook until onions are tender.

5. Increase heat to medium high. Add lamb and stir for 3 to 5 minutes until lamb is coated with turmeric mixture and begins to turn pink.

6. Add curry powder, cayenne powder, black pepper and cumin powder.

7. Stir and mix the powders well into meat. Add tomato sauce and salt. Cook and stir for another 2 minutes. Add 2 cups of water.

8. When mixture begins to boil, add coriander and reduce heat to medium-low.

9. If cooking in saucepan, cover and cook about 45 minutes, stirring often, until meat is tender. Additional water can be added, about 1/4 cup at a time, if the sauce becomes too thick or if the meat is not yet tender. If cooking in pressure cooker, cover and cook for 10 to 15 minutes, until meat is tender and the kulambu sauce has thickened.

Serves 4

CALORIES 261; FAT 14g.; SATURATED FAT 3g.; PROTEIN 25g.; CARBOHYDRATE 11g.; FIBER 4g.; CHOLESTEROL 74mg.; SODIUM 799mg.

Variation: For **Lamb Poriyal:** Transfer the cooked lamb with sauce to a cast-iron skillet, stir-fry the mixture over medium-high heat until the sauce thickens and is absorbed by the meat.

~:SHRIMP IN EGGPLANT SAUCE:~

Shrimp in Eggplant Sauce, served over plain rice or yogurt rice, has a unique and enticing combination of flavors.

2 tablespoons corn oil
2 to 4 curry leaves (optional)
1 teaspoon cumin seeds
1/2 teaspoon fenugreek seeds
1 teaspoon urad dal
1/2 cup chopped onion
1/2 cup chopped tomato
2 cups eggplant, cut into small chunks
1/4 teaspoon turmeric powder
1/2 teaspoon cayenne powder (more, if desired)
1 teaspoon cumin powder
1 cup tomato sauce
1/2 teaspoon tamarind paste
1 teaspoon salt
1/2 pound raw or pre-boiled medium shrimp
(approximately 20), shells removed

1. Heat 2 tablespoons of corn oil in a saucepan over medium heat. When oil is hot, but not smoking, add curry leaves, cumin seeds, fenugreek, and urad dal.

2. Immediately add onion and tomato and cook for a few minutes. Add eggplant to saucepan and allow to simmer in the seasonings for a few minutes.

3. Mix in turmeric powder, cayenne powder, and cumin powder. Add tomato sauce, tamarind paste, salt, and 1 1/2 cups of warm water. Let eggplant slow cook over low heat, covered, until eggplant is soft and the sauce has thickened.

4. When the eggplant is cooked and the above mixture begins to thicken, add the shrimp. Cook for about 5 minutes. If the sauce is too thick, add an additional 1/2 cup to 1 cup of warm water and let it simmer for a few additional minutes.

Serves 6

CALORIES 103; FAT 5g.; SATURATED FAT 1g.; PROTEIN 8g.; CARBOHYDRATE 8g.; FIBER 2g.; CHOLESTEROL 58mg.; SODIUM 672mg.

⌁ Shrimp Masala ⌁

Shrimp pan-fried with ginger, garlic, and other seasonings, Shrimp Masala can accompany many flavored rice dishes and chappati or poori.

1 tablespoon corn oil
2 to 3 small pieces cinnamon stick
1 teaspoon cumin seeds
1/4 teaspoon fennel seeds
1 teaspoon urad dal
3/4 cup chopped onion
1/4 cup chopped tomato
4 to 5 cloves garlic, chopped
1 tablespoon minced fresh ginger
1 pound fresh shrimp, peeled and washed
1/2 teaspoon turmeric powder
1/2 teaspoon curry powder
1/4 cup tomato sauce
1/2 teaspoon cayenne powder
1 teaspoon salt
1 teaspoon black pepper and cumin powder
1/4 cup chopped fresh coriander

1. Place oil in an iron skillet over medium heat. When oil is hot, but not smoking, add cinnamon stick, cumin, fennel, and urad dal. Fry until spices are golden brown.

2. Add onion, tomato, garlic, and ginger. Stir-fry for a few minutes.

3. Add shrimp and cook with the seasonings for a minute. Stir in turmeric powder and curry powder. Cook until shrimp turn pink.

4. Add tomato sauce, cayenne powder, salt, and black pepper and cumin powder. Blend well and simmer for a few minutes.

5. Add coriander and stir-fry, uncovered, for an additional few minutes. (Shrimp is delicious when allowed to absorb the flavor of the seasoned sauce while stir-frying over medium heat).

Serves 4

CALORIES 159; FAT 5g.; SATURATED FAT 1g.; PROTEIN 20g.; CARBOHYDRATE 9g.; FIBER 3g.; CHOLESTEROL 175mg.; SODIUM 834mg.

∿ SHRIMP PASTA ∿

Shrimp Pasta is an innovative dish combining Indian and Western flavors.

1 cup pasta shells (preferably whole wheat)
1 tablespoon olive oil
1/2 teaspoon cumin seeds
1 cup chopped onion
2 to 3 garlic cloves, minced (more, if desired)
1 pound raw shrimp, shelled and deveined
1/4 cup Cajun (or spicy) bread crumbs
1/4 cup chopped tomato
1/2 cup chopped fresh coriander
1/2 teaspoon salt (more, if desired)
1/4 teaspoon ground black pepper

1. Boil pasta until just tender. Drain and set aside.

2. Place olive oil into a wok or large skillet. Heat over medium heat until oil is hot, but not smoking.

3. Add cumin to oil. Brown for a few seconds. Add onion and garlic and stir-fry for a few minutes.

4. Add shrimp to skillet and fry until shrimp turns pink. Be careful not to overcook shrimp.

5. Add cooked pasta shells and bread crumbs. Stir well.

6. Blend in tomato and coriander to pasta.

7. Add salt and black pepper. Stir-fry for an additional minute and serve.

Serves 6

CALORIES 169; FAT 3g.; SATURATED FAT 1g.; PROTEIN 16g.; CARBOHYDRATE 19g.; FIBER 2g.; CHOLESTEROL 117mg.; SODIUM 447mg.

⌁ GROUND TURKEY WITH SPLIT PEAS AND COCONUT ⌁

This is a particularly easy-to-make stir-fry using split peas or chana dal and coconut. You may, in fact, use any ground meat to make this delicious dish. For example, in the Chettinand region, Mutton Podimas are made by using ground lamb or goat meat.

1/2 cup dry yellow split peas or chana dal
1 teaspoons turmeric powder
2 tablespoons corn oil
1 bay leaf
2 to 4 small cinnamon sticks
1 teaspoon cumin seeds
1/2 teaspoon fennel seeds
1 cup chopped onion
2 to 4 cloves garlic, finely chopped
1 green chili pepper (more, if desired)
1 pound ground turkey
2 teaspoons curry powder
1/2 teaspoon cayenne powder
1/2 teaspoon cumin powder
1 teaspoon salt
1/4 cup shredded fresh or unsweetened powdered coconut

1. Boil 2 cups of water in a saucepan. Add split peas with 1/4 teaspoon turmeric powder. Reduce heat to medium and cook, uncovered, about 15 minutes until split peas are tender and water is absorbed. (Add an additional 1/2 cup of water, if water is absorbed before split peas are tender.) Drain any remaining water and set aside.

2. Heat oil in a large skillet over medium heat. When oil is hot, but not smoking, crumble bay leaf and cinnamon sticks into oil. Add cumin and fennel seeds.

3. Immediately add onion, garlic, chili, and the remaining 3/4 teaspoon

turmeric powder. Cook, stirring, for about a minute, until onions are tender. Add ground turkey and pan-fry for about 3 minutes until browned, stirring and breaking up meat as it cooks.

4. Stir in curry powder, cayenne, and cumin powder. Cover and cook 2 minutes. Stir in salt, cover, and cook another 5 minutes.

5. Stir in split peas; cover and cook another 2 minutes. Add coconut and stir well. Taste and add additional seasonings if desired.

Serves 4

CALORIES 361; FAT 19g.; SATURATED FAT 5g.; PROTEIN 29g.; CARBOHYDRATE 28g.; FIBER 11g.; CHOLESTEROL 90mg.; SODIUM 663mg.

Beverages & Desserts

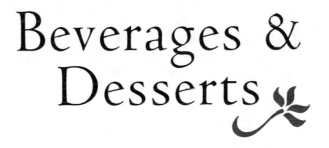

ᴄ:Buttermilk Drink:~

A refreshing beverage that cools your body, this drink is made from reduced-fat cultured buttermilk. It is an excellent source of vitamins A and D and calcium. In South India, people sometimes drink buttermilk instead of coffee and soft drinks. The buttermilk drink can be kept in the refrigerator for a long time. Always stir before serving. Buttermilk is also delicious served with ice, like iced-tea.

2 cups reduced-fat cultured buttermilk
4 cups cold water
1/4 teaspoon asafoetida powder (optional)
1 teaspoon cumin powder
1/4 teaspoon salt
2 to 4 chopped curry leaves (optional) or
1/4 cup minced fresh coriander

1. Mix buttermilk with water in a tall pitcher.

2. Add asafoetida, cumin powder, and salt. Stir well.

3. Add curry leaves or coriander and stir well.

4. Refrigerate and serve.

Serves 6

CALORIES 34; FAT 1g.; SATURATED FAT trace; PROTEIN 3g.; CARBOHYDRATE 4g.; FIBER trace; CHOLESTEROL 3mg.; SODIUM 180mg.

❖Madras Coffee❖

Traditional Madras Coffee, also known as Mysore Coffee, is made with coffee beans that are carefully selected, blended, and roasted. The coffee is brewed in a special vessel called a decoction container.

For a great tasting and easy-to-make version of Madras Coffee, you may use any premium instant coffee powder. Madras Coffee may also be prepared from any brewed coffee, provided it is brewed in a concentrated, espresso style.

1/2 cup 2% milk
1/2 cup water
1 teaspoon instant coffee powder
1 teaspoon sugar

1. In a cup mix milk and water. Transfer the mixture into a small saucepan. Let the mixture come to a full boil.

2. As the milk rises to the top (comes to a boil), remove from stove.

3. In another cup mix coffee powder and sugar. Pour the milk over coffee and sugar.

4. Transfer the contents from one cup to another a few times until a froth develops.

5. Pour the coffee into a cup and serve.

Serves I

CALORIES 81; FAT 2g.; SATURATED FAT 1g.; PROTEIN 4g.; CARBOHYDRATE 11g.; FIBER 0g.; CHOLESTEROL 9mg.; SODIUM 65mg.

✌INDIAN TEA I✌

Cardamom-flavored hot tea with milk—a perfect drink to relax with!

3/4 cup water
1/4 cup 2% milk
1 to 2 strong tea bags or 1 to 2 teaspoons loose black tea
1/4 teaspoon crushed cardamom or cardamom powder

1. Mix water and milk in a cup. Pour the mixture into a small saucepan and bring to a boil.

2. Immerse the teabag or loose tea in the boiling milk. Add the cardamom to milk mixture.

3. When the mixture rises to the top (begins to boil), remove from stove.

4. Either remove the tea bag or strain the tea and cardamom. Pour the tea into a cup. Add sugar to taste. Stir and serve.

Serves 1

CALORIES 37; FAT 1g.; SATURATED FAT 1g.; PROTEIN 2g.; CARBOHYDRATE 4g.;
FIBER trace; CHOLESTEROL 5g.; SODIUM 39mg.

∽Indian Tea II∽

You may also want to try the following variation of cardamom-flavored brewed tea.

2 cups water
1/2 teaspoon crushed cardamom or cardamom powder
1 to 2 strong tea bags or 1 to 2 teaspoons loose black tea
1/4 cup 2% milk

1. Boil water in a small saucepan. Add cardamom to the boiling water.

2. Immerse the tea bag or add loose tea to the rolling boiling water. Remove from heat and cover. Let tea stand in hot water for few minutes. Strain tea and cardamom. Transfer the tea essence to a teapot with lid.

3. Boil milk in a small saucepan or in microwave.

4. Pour tea and milk into a cup according to your taste. Add sugar to taste. Stir and serve.

Serves 2

CALORIES 19; FAT 1g.; SATURATED FAT trace; PROTEIN 1g.; CARBOHYDRATE 2g.; FIBER trace; CHOLESTEROL 2mg.; SODIUM 24mg.

༻ CARROT HALVA ༺

Carrots cooked in milk with sugar, cardamom, and saffron make a tempting treat!

10 *raw cashew halves*
1 *tablespoon melted butter*
1 *cup whole milk*
2 *cups grated carrots*
1/2 *cup sugar*
1/2 *teaspoon cardamom powder*
4 to 6 *threads saffron*

1. Fry cashew halves in butter. Set aside.

2. In a heavy bottomed saucepan, boil milk over medium heat.

3. When the milk comes to a boil, reduce heat to medium. Add grated carrots and sugar. Cook carrots over medium-low heat stirring often.

4. Add powdered cardamom, saffron, and roasted cashews. Mix well and stir until the mixture thickens.

5. Pour it in a glass plate or bowl and let cool before serving.

Serves 8 (1/4 cup per serving)

CALORIES 143; FAT 8g.; SATURATED FAT 4g.; PROTEIN 2g.; CARBOHYDRATE 18g.; FIBER 1g.; CHOLESTEROL 20mg.; SODIUM 85mg.

ᜁKESARIᜁ

A popular sweet dish made with cream of wheat, sugar, raisins, and cardamom powder, Kesari is served during breakfast or for tea.

3 tablespoons butter
1/4 cup raw cashews
1/2 cup regular cream of wheat
1 cup 2% milk
1 cup sugar
10 raisins
1/4 teaspoon cardamom powder
Pinch of kesari powder (or yellow food coloring)
Pinch of crystalline camphor (optional)

1. In a small nonstick skillet, melt 1 tablespoon butter. Fry cashews in butter until golden brown. Set cashews aside. Reserve the butter.

2. Add cream of wheat to the same butter and cook for a few minutes.

3. Add 1 cup of warm water and the milk. Stir into the mixture gently. Stir often.

4. Add sugar, raisins, cardamom, kesari powder, and camphor to cream of wheat and blend well over medium heat. Add the remaining 2 tablespoons butter and stir well until cream of wheat is cooked.

5. Add fried cashews to cream of wheat.

Serves 4

CALORIES 441; FAT 14g.; SATURATED FAT 7g.; PROTEIN 6g.; CARBOHYDRATE 75g.; FIBER 2g.; CHOLESTEROL 28mg.; SODIUM 122mg.

ᴑ:Moong Dal Payasam:ᴖ

Payasam is a sweet-flavored milk drink that serves as a dessert in South India. This particular payasam is also used in religious ceremonies in South India, and is enjoyed by devotees after prayers.

1/4 cup yellow moong dal
1/4 cup cashews
1 tablespoon butter or ghee (melted butter)
2 cups 2% milk
1/4 teaspoon cardamom powder
1/2 cup packed dark brown sugar
2 to 4 threads saffron

1. Bring 3 cups of water to boil. Add moong dal. Cook for 15 to 20 minutes, uncovered, until moong dal becomes soft. At the final stage of cooking, remove moong dal from heat and mash it with masher to a creamy consistency. Add additional 2 cups of water, dilute the dal mixture. Set aside.

2. Fry cashews in butter until golden brown and set aside.

3. Heat milk to boiling point in a saucepan.

4. Mix creamy dal with milk in the saucepan and cook over medium heat for 3 to 5 minutes stirring frequently.

5. Add cardamom, sugar, cashews, and saffron. Cook an additional few minutes over medium to low heat.

Note: This payasam can be served hot or cold. If you prefer to serve it cold, refrigerate for 2 to 3 hours before serving. Serve payasam in a cup.

Serves 4

CALORIES 269; FAT 10g.; SATURATED FAT 4g.; PROTEIN 7g.; CARBOHYDRATE 40g.; FIBER 2g.; CHOLESTEROL 18mg.; SODIUM 347mg.

❤️PALA PAYASAM❤️

A flavored sweet milk drink featuring almonds, saffron, and fruits, served as a dessert.

1/2 cup skinned almonds
4 cups 2% milk
1 cup sugar (more, if desired)
1 teaspoon cardamom powder
1 teaspoon saffron
Pinch of kesari powder (or yellow food coloring)
1 can (10 ounces) mixed fruit cocktail

1. Grind almonds with milk.

2. Pour into a heavy bottomed saucepan and heat the mixture over medium-low heat until it begins to boil.

3. Add sugar, cardamom, saffron, and kesari powder to the mixture and stir frequently.

4. After the mixture boils, set it aside and let cool.

5. Pour the fruit cocktail can contents along with the syrup into the above cooled mixture. Stir gently. Leave payasam in refrigerator until it is time to serve.

Note: Pala Payasam may thicken after refrigeration. Before serving, if payasam seems too thick, you may add additional 1 cup of skim milk to dilute it. Stir and serve.

Serves 6 (1/2 cup per serving)

CALORIES 304; FAT 9g.; SATURATED FAT 3g.; PROTEIN 8g.; CARBOHYDRATE 49g.; FIBER 11g.; CHOLESTEROL 12mg.; SODIUM 85mg.

ᴄRICOTTA CHEESE DESSERTᴄ

An innovative and easy-to-prepare dessert made from ricotta cheese and almonds flavored with rose essence.

1 pound regular or low-fat ricotta cheese
1 teaspoon kewra (rose) essence
1 cup white sugar
1/4 cup almond halves

1. Preheat oven to 350 degrees. Blend ricotta cheese and kewra thoroughly in a mixing bowl.

2. Add sugar and stir well.

3. Spread cheese mixture in a greased shallow baking pan.

4. Bake for 20 to 30 minutes until golden brown.

5. Garnish with almond halves. Cool for 30 to 45 minutes.

6. Cut into slices and serve.

Serves 8

CALORIES 202; FAT 7g.; SATURATED FAT 3g.; PROTEIN 7g.; CARBOHYDRATE 29g.; FIBER trace; CHOLESTEROL 17mg.; SODIUM 72mg.

✥TAPIOCA PAYASAM✥

Tapioca cooked in milk and flavored with saffron and cardamom.

1/4 cup raw cashew halves
1 tablespoon butter
1/2 cup tapioca (not quick cooking)
3 cups 2% milk or whole milk, as desired
Pinch of kesari powder (or yellow food coloring)
1/4 teaspoon cardamom powder
4 to 6 threads saffron
2 very small pieces cystalline camphor (optional)
1/2 cup sugar (more, if desired)
1/4 cup raisins (optional)

1. Fry cashew halves in 1/2 tablespoon butter in a small skillet or butter warmer over medium heat until evenly cooked. Remove cashews from skillet and set aside.

2. Melt another 1/2 tablespoon butter in a tall saucepan. Add tapioca, and cook for a few minutes in butter, stirring constantly.

3. Add milk slowly in 1 cup increments, stirring all the while, over medium to low heat, until tapioca cooks. When tapioca is cooked it will increase in size and will become softer (approximately 15 minutes).

4. Add kesari powder, cardamom, saffron threads, crystalline camphor, and sugar. Stir well over low heat.

5. Add cashew halves and raisins, if desired.

6. Serve in custard cups or sherbert glasses. You may serve payasam at room temperature or as a cold dessert.

Note: If room temperature serving is preferred, remove Tapioca Payasam from heat and cover it. Leave at room temperature until time of serving.

Even at room temperature, it thickens. Add additional warm milk and sugar as desired before serving.

If you prefer to serve payasam cold, leave it in the refrigerator, where it will thicken. Before serving, place it in a microwave oven and warm for a minute or two. Stir well and add additional cold milk until payasam reaches the desired consistency. You may also add additional sugar as desired.

Serves 4

CALORIES 352; FAT 9g.; SATURATED FAT 4g.; PROTEIN 8g.; CARBOHYDRATE 62g.; FIBER 1g.; CHOLESTEROL 18mg.; SODIUM 112mg.

❧ VERMICELLI PAYASAM ❧

This exquisite dessert features vermicelli cooked in milk with saffron and cardamom.

1/4 cup raw cashew halves
1 tablespoon butter
1/2 cup shredded vermicelli sticks
2 cups 2% milk or whole milk, as desired
1/4 teaspoon cardamom powder
4 to 6 threads saffron
1/2 cup sugar (more, if desired)
1/4 cup raisins (optional)

1. Fry cashew halves in 1/2 tablespoon butter in a small skillet or butter warmer over medium heat until evenly cooked. Remove cashews from skillet and set aside.

2. Melt another 1/2 tablespoon butter in a small saucepan. Add vermicelli. Fry vermicelli for a few minutes in butter over low-medium heat, stirring constantly.

3. Add milk slowly in 1 cup increments, stirring all the while, over medium to low heat until vermicelli cooks. When vermicelli cooks it becomes softer (5 to 7 minutes).

4. Add cardamom, saffron threads, and sugar. Stir and cook over low heat.

5. Add cashew halves and raisins, if desired.

6. Serve in custard cups or sherbet glasses. You may serve vermicelli payasam at a room temperature or as a cold dessert.

Note: If room temperature serving is preferred, remove Vermicelli Payasam from heat and cover. Leave at room temperature until time of serving. Even at room temperature, it will thicken. Add additional warm milk and sugar as desired before serving.

If you prefer to serve payasam cold, place it in the refrigerator, where it will thicken. Before serving, place payasam in microwave and warm for a minute or two. Stir gently and add additional cold milk until payasam reaches the desired consistency. You may also add additional sugar as desired.

Serves 4

CALORIES 298; FAT 8g.; SATURATED FAT 3g.; PROTEIN 7g.; CARBOHYDRATE 52g.; FIBER 1g.; CHOLESTEROL 13mg.; SODIUM 81mg.

⌁HOMEMADE YOGURT⌁

Yogurt (sometimes called "curd") is often served over plain rice as a last course in a meal because it is soothing and aids in digestion. Homemade yogurt (thayir) can be made without a yogurt maker using the following recipe.

1 cup 2% milk
1 teaspoon cultured buttermilk or 1 teaspoon of fat-free plain yogurt

1. Place milk in a small saucepan. Heat over medium heat until milk just approaches the boiling point and begins to rise to top of saucepan. Remove from heat.

2. Transfer milk to a small dish and allow to cool slightly until just warm to touch (about 30 minutes).

3. Add 1 teaspoon cultured buttermilk or yogurt to milk. Stir well.

4. Cover the dish and set aside at room temperature for 6 to 8 hours until the yogurt is formed.

5. Store the homemade yogurt in the refrigerator until serving.

Note: For richer homemade yogurt, you may use whole milk instead of 2% milk.

Makes 1 cup

CALORIES 123; FAT 5g.; SATURATED FAT 3.; PROTEIN 8g.; CARBOHYDRATE 12g.; FIBER 0g.; CHOLESTEROL 18mg.; SODIUM 127mg.

Suggested Menus

SUGGESTED MENUS

The abundance of similar seasonings and spices in South Indian dishes makes them very complementary in taste to each other. Certain dishes, however, are particularly well suited to being served together and enhance the enjoyment of the other. Impressions gained from preparing recipes in this book and your own taste preferences will soon guide you in selecting appropriate combinations of dishes for a meal. Meanwhile, we can suggest the following groupings.

SUGGESTED VEGETARIAN MENUS FOR MAIN MEALS

Plain Rice

Consider the above groupings as suggestions only. You can choose other kinds of sambhars or vegetables as you desire.

Pappadums are excellent accompaniments to the above meals. You may also add any item from the dessert section if you desire.

SUGGESTED NONVEGETARIAN MENUS

BREAKFAST, TEA, OR SNACK MENUS

Uppuma (Cream of Wheat or Cracked Wheat or Soji)93, 81, 95
Potato Sambhar or any Chutney 183, 103-119

Idiyappam 86
Kosamalli or Potato Moong Dal Pachadi 109, 261

Dosai. 82
Pearl Onion and Tomato Sambhar or
Onion and Potato Kose. 181, 114

Poori 91
Potato Curry for Poori 257

Chappati 80
Potato Kurma 259

Idli. 88
Any Sambhar or Chutney 151-187, 103-119

Adai. 78
Kosamalli. 109

Urad Dal Vadai 97
Any Chutney 103-119

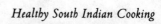

FUSION:
COMBINING SOUTH INDIAN AND WESTERN FOODS

Incorporating individual South Indian dishes into a typically Western meal can result in a delicious blending of tastes. The culinary term for the blending of dishes from different cuisines is "Fusion," very much a characteristic of the current world of food preparation with its increasingly cosmopolitan orientation. Many individual South Indian dishes "fuse" beautifully with Western favorites. The rich complexity of flavors and seasonings inherent in South Indian dishes blends especially well with simple mainstays of the Western menu, such as grilled chicken and fish. You only have to use your imagination to come up with your own creative and delicious combinations. We offer a few suggestions below:

A. With Grilled, Roasted, or Baked Chicken
Any One Flavored Rice Dish:
> Bell Pepper Tomato Rice with Cashews
> Coconut Rice
> Lemon Rice
> Spinach Rice
> Tamarind Rice
> Tomato Rice with Cashews

One or More Vegetable Dishes:
> Broccoli with Coconut Poriyal or Broccoli Podimas
> Cabbage and Peas Poriyal
> Cauliflower Poriyal
> Carrot Poriyal
> Eggplant Masala or Eggplant and Potato Masala
> Beans Poriyal
> Green Peas Poriyal
> Lima Beans Masala or Lima Beans Poriyal
> Sugar Snap Pea Pods Poriyal
> Potato Masala or Potatoes Roasted with Garlic and Tomatoes
> Spinach Poriyal
> Acorn Squash Masala Poriyal
> Tomato Pachadi
> Yogurt Salad

B. With Roasted Turkey
Any One flavored Rice Dish:
Bell Pepper Tomato Rice with Cashews
Cauliflower Rice
Savory Mushroom Rice
Vegetable Pulaoo Rice
One or More Vegetable dishes:
Beans Poriyal
Green Peas Poriyal
Potatoes Roasted with Garlic and Tomatoes
Acorn Squash Masala Poriyal

C. With Grilled Fish or Shrimp
Any One Flavored Rice Dish:
Coconut Rice
Lemon Rice
Black Pepper Rice with Cashews
Tamarind Rice
One or More Vegetable Dishes:
Cabbage with Coconut Poriyal
Potato Masala
Yogurt Salad

D. Vegetable Wraps and Sandwiches:
You can make any vegetable poriyal or masala dish from our vegetable section, such as Spinach Poriyal, Potato Masala, or Cabbage and Peas Poriyal, and use the vegetable as a filling for a vegetable wrap. Pita bread, wheat or flour tortillas can be used as a wrap. One can make delicious vegetarian sandwiches using any of the vegetable poriyal or masala recipes. One can also make **Chutney Sandwiches**, as a unique variation of the tea-time cucumber sandwich, using any of the South Indian chutneys as a spread.

E. Nonvegetarian Wraps:
Tuna Masala, Chettinad Chicken Poriyal (boneless), or Ground Turkey with Split Peas and Coconut, can be served as a delicious

sandwich filling with pita bread, wheat or flour tortillas, or regular sliced whole grain bread.

F. Vegetable Pastas:

Make a vegetable from the vegetable section, such as Mixed Vegetable Poriyal, Mixed Vegetable Kurma, or Broccoli Poriyal, and serve over angel hair pasta or over any type of pasta you prefer.

G. Nonvegetarian Pastas:

Boneless Chettinad Chicken Kurma or Chettinad Chicken Poriyal can be served over your choice of pasta for a hearty meal.

H. Novel Appetizers and Snack Ideas:

Tuna Masala over cocktail rye or French bread
Eggplant Chutney over French bread or crackers
Tomato or Coriander chutney with tortilla chips
Any chutney with French fried potatoes
Any chutney, sambhar or kulambu with tortillas, toasted bread, buttermilk pancakes

Although the above ideas of food combinations are unusual from a purely South Indian culinary perspective, you may find them truly enjoyable. Now, you can use your own creativity!

Index

ᴧᴗABOUT THE AUTHORSᴗᴧ

Alamelu Vairavan attended the University of Wisconsin-Milwaukee, while raising a family, and graduated with a B.S. degree from the School of Allied Health. Since graduation, Alamelu has been working in the long-term care field. She has also served as a clinical instructor for the University of Wisconsin-Milwaukee. In addition she has been a nursing home consultant in Health Information Management for various healthcare facilities. She received her Wisconsin Nursing Home Administrator's license in 1992. Currently, she is the Director of Health Information Management at The Waters of SevenOaks, Glendale, Wisconsin, where she also serves as a community relations specialist.

For relaxation, Alamelu enjoys teaching cooking classes and giving presentations on South India to various community groups. In particular, she enjoys interactions with senior citizens for whom she has a special affinity. She has appeared on several television shows including *Home Matters* on the Discovery Channel and *Regina's Vegetarian Table* on PBS.

Patricia Marquardt is a tenured Associate Professor of Foreign Languages at Marquette University in Milwaukee. Her academic degrees, all in the area of Latin and Ancient Greek, include a B.A. from Ripon College, an M.A. from the University of Chicago, and a Ph.D. from the University of Wisconsin-Madison. A native of Milwaukee, Patricia teaches in the Classical Languages program at Marquette University. She has published numerous scholarly articles in the areas of Classical Mythology, Homer, and Archaic Greek Poetry. Her research has taken her on trips worldwide, including Italy, Greece, Egypt, and Great Britain. Her greatest personal satisfaction, however, has come from her continuing engagement with Indian culture.

Susan Sharer Dunn is a Registered Dietician. She graduated with a degree in Dietetics from Mount Mary College in Milwaukee, Wisconsin. After attaining her Registration, she has worked as a Dietary Director in a long-term care facility in Glendale, Wisconsin. She also consulted in extended care, presented workshops to healthcare professionals, led weight loss programs, and has written a variety of articles for newspapers and trade publications. She has been an active member of gourmet clubs and has taught gourmet cooking at the University of Wisconsin extension. She and her husband Jeff now reside in Sedona, Arizona.

Also available from Hippocrene...

INDIAN-INTEREST TITLES

Treasury of Indian Love:
Poems & Proverbs from the Indian Sub-Continent
In the Languages of India and English
Edited by Christopher Shackle & Nicholas Awde
   This remarkable anthology includes over 100 unique and inspiring poems and proverbs of love from the languages of India, with side-by-side English translation. From ancient, classical texts to folksongs from all over India, these works explore all aspects of love—sensuality, matrimony, anger, jealously and faithfulness. The works are taken from 37 different Indian languages, including Sanskrit, Assamese, Bengali, Gujarati, Hindi, Kannada, Kashmiri, Malayalam, Marathi, Punjabi, Rajasthani, Tamil, and Urdu.
128 PAGES ▪ 5 X 7 ▪ ISBN 0-7818-0670-4 ▪ $11.95HC ▪ (768)

Folk Tales from Simla
Alice Elizabeth Dracott
   From Simla, once the summer capital of India under British rule, comes a charming collection of Himalayan folklore, known for its beauty, wit, and mysticism. These 56 stories, fire-side tales of the hill-folk of Northern India, will surely enchant readers of all ages. Eight illustrations by the author complete this delightful volume.
225 PAGES ▪ 5 1/2 X 8 1/2 ▪ 8 ILLUSTRATIONS ▪ ISBN 0-7818-0704-2 ▪ $14.95HC ▪ (794)

INDIAN LANGUAGE DICTIONARIES

Learn Bengali
160 PAGES ▪ ISBN 0-7818-0224-5 ▪ $7.95PB ▪ (190)

Hindi-English/English-Hindi Standard Dictionary
HARDCOVER: 30,000 ENTRIES ▪ 399 PAGES ▪ ISBN 0-7818-0387-X ▪ $37.50HC ▪ (280)
PAPERBACK: 30,000 ENTRIES ▪ 399 PAGES ▪ ISBN 0-7818-0470-1 ▪ $27.50PB ▪ (559)

English-Hindi Practical Dictionary
15,000 ENTRIES ▪ 399 PAGES ▪ ISBN 0-87052-978-1 ▪ $11.95PB ▪ (362)

Teach Yourself Hindi
209 PAGES ▪ ISBN 0-87052-831-9 ▪ $8.95PB ▪ (170)

Punjabi-English/English-Punjabi Dictionary
25,000 ENTRIES ▪ 424 PAGES ▪ ISBN 0-7818-0716-6 ▪ $24.95HC ▪ (144)

Concise Sanskrit-English Dictionary
18,000 ENTRIES ▪ 366 PAGES ▪ ISBN 0-7818-0203-2 ▪ $14.95PB ▪ (605)

INDIAN COOKBOOKS

Best of Goan Cooking
Gilda Mendonsa

From Goa—a region in Western India once colonized by the Portuguese—comes a cuisine in which the hot, sour and spicy flavors mingle in delicate perfection, a reflection of the combination of Arabian, Portuguese and Indian cultures that have inhabited the region. This book is a rare and authentic collection of over 130 of the finest Goan recipes and 12 pages of full color illustrations. Starting with exotic cocktails and appetizers to set the mood, the book moves on to savory fish, poultry and meats. Some unusual vegetarian preparations—Feijoada, breadfruit curry, sprouted lentil curry—make interesting accompaniments. Also, pickles and chutneys made with mangoes, shrimp, lemons and chilies add a touch of adventure. Delicious desserts complete the meal, while a special section highlights tea-time snacks like tarts, cakes, cookies, and halwas.

106 PAGES ▪ 7 X 9 1/4 ▪ 12 PAGES COLOR ILLUSTRATIONS ▪ ISBN 0-7818-0584-8 ▪ $8.95PB ▪ (682)

The Indian Spice Kitchen:
Essential Ingredients and Over 200 Authentic Recipes
Monisha Bharadwaj

This richly produced, wonderfully readable cookbook, written by the food consultant to the celebrated London restaurant, Bombay Brasserie, takes you on an unforgettable culinary journey along the spice routes of India with over 200 authentic recipes and stunning color photographs throughout. Simple step-by-step recipes, all adapted for the North American kitchen, allow the home chef to create delicious foods with precious saffron, aromatic tamarind, and delicately fragrant turmeric, mustard and chilies.

The recipes are arranged by featured ingredient in a full range of soups, breads, vegetarian and meat dishes, beverages and desserts. Among those included are "Lamb with Apricots," "Cauliflower in Coconut and Pepper Sauce," and "Nine Jewels Vegetable Curry." This cookbook includes historical and cultural information on each ingredient, facts on storing and preparation, medicinal and ritual uses, and cooking times and serving suggestions for all recipes.

240 PAGES ■ 8 X 10 1/4 ■ COLOR PHOTOGRAPHS THROUGHOUT ■ ISBN 0-7818-0801-4 ■ $17.50PB ■ (513)

OTHER COOKBOOKS OF INTEREST FROM HIPPOCRENE

Afghan Food & Cookery
Helen Saberi

This classic source for Afghan cookery is now available in an updated and expanded North American edition! This hearty cuisine includes a tempting variety of offerings: lamb, pasta, chickpeas, rice pilafs, flat breads, kebabs, spinach, okra, lentils, yogurt, pastries and delicious teas, all flavored with delicate spices, are staple ingredients. The author's informative introduction describes traditional Afghan holidays, festivals and celebrations; she also includes a section "The Afghan Kitchen," which provides essentials about cooking utensils, spices, ingredients and methods.

312 PAGES ■ 5 1/2 X 8 1/4 ■ ILLUSTRATIONS ■ $12.95PB ■ 0-7818-0807-3 ■ (510)

Imperial Mongolian Cooking :
Recipes from the Kingdoms of Genghis Khan
Marc Cramer

Imperial Mongolian Cooking is the first book to explore the ancient culinary traditions of Genghis Khan's empire, opening a window onto a fascinating culture and a diverse culinary tradition virtually unknown in the West.

These 120 easy-to-follow recipes encompass a range of dishes—from Appetizers, Soups and Salads to Main Courses (Poultry & Game, Lamb, Beef, Fish & Seafood), Beverages and Desserts. Among them are "Bean and Meatball Soup," "Spicy Steamed Chicken Dumplings," "Turkish Swordfish Kabobs," and "Uzbek Walnut Fritters." The recipes are taken from the four khanates (kingdoms) of the empire that include the following modern countries: Mongolia, Chinese-controlled Inner Mongolia, China, Bhutan, Tibet, Azerbaijan, Kyrgyzstan, Tajikistan, Turkmenistan, Uzbekistan, Kazakhstan, Georgia, Armenia, Russia, Poland, Ukraine, Hungary, Burma, Vietnam, Iran, Iraq, Afghanistan, Syria and Turkey. The author's insightful introduction, a glossary of spices and ingredients, and list of sample menus will assist the home chef in creating meals fit for an emperor!

211 PAGES ▪ 5 1/2 X 8 1/2 ▪ ISBN 0 7818-0827-8 ▪ $24.95HC ▪ (20)

The Art of Uzbek Cooking
Lynn Visson

A historical crossroads in Central Asia, Uzbekistan and its cuisine reflect the range of nationalities that form the country and continue to flourish there. This collection of 175 authentic Uzbek recipes includes chapters on Appetizers & Salads; Soups; Meat, Poultry & Fish; Plovs; Stuffed Pastries; Dumplings; Pasta & Pancakes; Vegetables; Breads; Desserts; Drinks; and even Suggested Menus.

278 PAGES ▪ 5 1/2 X 8 1/4 ▪ ILLUSTRATIONS ▪ $24.95HC ▪ 0-7818-0669-0 ▪ (767)

Egyptian Cooking
Samia Abdennour

Originally published in Egypt, this ever-popular guide to Egyptian cooking has now been revised for a North American audience. Egyptian cuisine has been influenced by several Mediterranean culinary traditions, including Turkish, Palestinian, Lebanese, Greek and Syrian. These nearly 400 recipes, all adapted for the North American kitchen, represent the best of authentic Egyptian home cooking.

From appetizers to desserts, some recipes included are `Arnabit musa a`a (Moussaka Cauliflower), Samak bi-l-tahina (Fish with tahina sauce), Kosa matbukha bi-l-zabadi (Zucchini stewed in yogurt), and Lahma mu'assaga (Savory Minced Beef). The chapters included are Mezze, Breakfast, Main Courses, Sweets and Desserts, Beverages, Kitchen Utensils, and Spices. This classic cookbook also includes a glossary of Arabic terms for ingredients, translated into English, and useful tips on shopping and using traditional cooking utensils.

199 PAGES ▪ 5 1/2 X 8 1/2 ▪ 0-7818-0643-7 ▪ $12.95PB ▪ (727)

Cuisines of Portuguese Encounters

Cherie Y. Hamilton

This fascinating collection of 225 authentic recipes is the first cookbook to encompass the entire Portuguese-speaking world and explain how Portugal and its former colonies influenced each other's culinary traditions. Included are dishes containing Asian, South American, African, and European spices, along with varied ingredients like piripiri pepper, coconut milk, cilantro, manioc root, bananas, dried fish, seafood and meats. The recipes range from appetizers like "Pastel com o Diabo Dentro" (Pastry with the Devil Inside from Cape Verde), to main courses such as "Frango à Africana" (Grilled Chicken African Style from Mozambique) and "Cuscuz de Camarão" (Shrimp Couscous from Brazil), to desserts like "Pudim de Côco" (Coconut Pudding from Timor). Menus for religious holidays and festive occasions, a glossary, a section on mail-order sources, a brief history of the cuisines, and a bilingual index will assist the home chef in creating meals that celebrate the rich, diverse, and delicious culinary legacy of this old empire.

378 PAGES ▪ 6 X 9 ▪ DRAWINGS ▪ ISBN 0-7818-0831-6 ▪ $24.95HC ▪ (91)

All prices subject to change without prior notice. To purchase Hippocrene Books contact your local bookstore, call (718) 454-2366, or write to: HIP-POCRENE BOOKS, 171 Madison Avenue, New York, NY 10016. Please enclose check or money order, adding $5.00 shipping (UPS) for the first book and $.50 for each additional book.